— *1368* —

1 3 6 8

China and the Making of the Modern World

ALI HUMAYUN AKHTAR

STANFORD UNIVERSITY PRESS
Stanford, California

STANFORD UNIVERSITY PRESS
Stanford, California

Library of Congress Cataloging-in-Publication Data
Names: Akhtar, Ali Humayun, author.
Title: 1368 : China and the making of the modern world / Ali Humayun Akhtar.
Description: Stanford, California : Stanford University Press, 2022. | Includes bibliographical
    references and index.
Identifiers: LCCN 2021050071 (print) | LCCN 2021050072 (ebook) | ISBN 9781503627475 (cloth) |
    ISBN 9781503631519 (epub)
Subjects: LCSH: China—History—Ming dynasty, 1368-1644. | China—History—Qing dynasty,
    1644-1912. | China—Commerce—History. | China—Foreign relations.
Classification: LCC DS753 .A35 2022 (print) | LCC DS753 (ebook) | DDC 951/.026—dc23/
    eng/20211013
LC record available at https://lccn.loc.gov/2021050071
LC ebook record available at https://lccn.loc.gov/2021050072

Cover art: A Seated Portrait of Ming Emperor Zhu Yuanzhang, reign 1368–1398 291.4 x 162.8 cm, silk. Public domain image via Wikimedia Commons.
Cover design: Rob Ehle

Typeset by Newgen North America in 11.5/14 Centaur MT Pro

CONTENTS

Photographs appear after page 46 and page 106.

For my parents,
Dr. Humayun Aftab Akhtar
and
Ms. Yosria M. Zaki El-Sabban,
and for my siblings

PREFACE

When did China lose its innovative edge to powers like the United Kingdom and the United States? What is China's future in the global manufacturing landscape that it now dominates? As China expands its economic place in the world, will the West pursue a new path to high-tech industrialization, or alternatively will it continue on the road of globalization and labor outsourcing adopted in the 1970s? Navigating these questions requires an understanding of how the twentieth-century world of globalization came into being. It requires understanding how western Europe first came to dominate an Asian economic landscape once oriented around China, Japan, and Southeast Asia. This book tells the story of China's first modern global age, placing special emphasis on encounters between Beijing and the West since the Age of Exploration. From the start of the Great Ming dynasty in 1368 to the end of the Qing in 1912, the making of modern China is also the story of the making of the modern world. In its origins, it is the story of how western European shipping came to bypass the once dominant Italian and Middle Eastern markets of the medieval world. By the end of the two Opium Wars (ca. 1839–1842, 1856–1860), western Europe's "Age of Discoveries" in search of the so-called Far East trade transformed a once global China into something very different. In the words of Napoleon, China had become a "sleeping lion" across the seas and oceans where Ming treasure ships once sailed.

In some ways, even before China's encounters with Europe's global shipping networks during the Age of Exploration, China was always a global power. Xian, home of the legendary Terracotta Army and one of the region's earliest mosques, was a key node along the ancient silk routes. But there was a global turn that took place with the arrival of European powers in the South China Sea, a turn that had its roots decades earlier. In the early 1400s, in the first years of the Ming's establishment, Beijing made its own turn to the open seas. On the eve of Portugal and Spain's arrival in Melaka and Manila, Beijing cultivated an unprecedented degree of political and cultural proximity with the maritime states of the South China Sea and Indian Ocean. Between 1405 and 1433, a century before Magellan charted the first trans-Pacific shipping routes from Acapulco to Manila, the Ming commissioned a series of diplomatic missions that set sail for all of the geographies where Spain and Portugal looked for profits after 1492: Japan, Thailand, the Malay peninsula, the Indian subcontinent, Iran, East Africa, and the Arabian gateways of the Mediterranean. Intent on projecting Beijing's naval and manufacturing power around the world, the Ming's convoy of treasure ships traversed the Indian Ocean and South China Sea with cargoes of commodities that eventually dominated western European trade portfolios: porcelain, precious metals, embroidered textiles, tea, and other rare items produced in China and neighboring states.

Led by Muslim admiral Zheng He of Yunnan, China's own age of exploration—a maritime diplomatic overture—accelerated the movement not only of Chinese material culture around the world but also Chinese political and social networks. This transfer occurred especially throughout Southeast Asia, where western European powers a century later would begin building the commercial portfolios and design expertise that would eventually drive European industrialization. In the interim centuries, from the 1500s through the 1800s, the lore of Chinese and Southeast Asian port cities took on new and unprecedented dimensions. In the earlier part of this history, following the arrival of Iberian vessels in Manila and Macau, Jesuit linguists trained as go-betweens for diplomacy in China and Japan. By the end of the sixteenth century, Portuguese and Spanish business networks fully bypassed Italian and Middle Eastern middlemen for access to the region, but they were on the verge of being eclipsed themselves by two newcomers: the Dutch and the British. With the support of the rising Dutch Republic and British monarchy, the Dutch and British East India Companies followed their Iberian neighbors to the South China Sea in the 1600s. They negotiated settlement agreements in selected Asian centers and outright conquered others, all while maintaining a degree of distance from China's own military might. Change was afoot, however, with the onset of technological advances in western Europe that included the development of industrial machinery and the steam engine.

And by the 1800s, as British mass production and weapons manufacturing reached an unprecedented degree of sophistication, the tables had turned. China was on the verge of eclipse.

The rise of the British Industrial Revolution and the end of the Opium Wars in the mid-1800s saw a once powerful China pass into the world's geopolitical periphery. Beijing's political and territorial losses on the mainland, together with Commodore Perry's arrival in Edo in 1853, signaled a seismic shift in China's political and cultural currency that had a tremendous impact on the region. Under the leadership of samurai-turned-politicians, Japan took the lead in embarking on an unprecedented high-tech industrial transformation that turned away from Chinese political models and coopted British and American advances. China's own transformation, built on Tokyo's Anglo-Japanese model, was a slower affair. With roots in the final decades of the Qing era, and following a series of halting advances that carried through the tumultuous twentieth century, the industrial transformation of China finally occurred after the economic reforms of the late 1970s and the transfer of technological know-how from Japan and the West to China's new manufacturing centers: Tianjin, Qingdao, Ningbo, Shenzhen, and others. Since the 2000s, on the heels of China's acceptance into the World Trade Organization with the then president of the United States' enthusiastic support, debates about China as a post-Soviet "superpower" have been in full bloom.

From the perspective of the story told in this book, in sum, China's rapid emergence as a high-tech commercial player is the second iteration of its place as an international manufacturing power since the onset of global maritime navigation. The international renown associated with tech hubs like Shenzhen and Shanghai today evokes Europe's earlier fascination with Chinese commodities manufactured in porcelain-producing Jingdezhen and tea-exporting Quanzhou. What makes this new iteration significant is how it continues to be overlooked by many economists, politicians, and historians. In the same way many economic historians place China on the periphery of a more British-centered picture of world history since the Age of Exploration, politicians frequently underestimate the extent that China's industrialization since the 1970s points to its emergence as a new economic and military superpower in Asia. What the long-duration history told in this book illustrates is that with the European Union's rising economic crises, China in many ways already is a superpower, and the tensions between international development institutions like the World Bank and the One Belt One Road initiative illustrate that emerging markets have yet to determine how exactly they navigate their own place in this shifting landscape. With the goal of understanding this changing geopolitical landscape and its long-duration origins, this book offers a new picture of China's global encounters since the Great Ming and the making of the modern world.

— *1368* —

CHAPTER 1

Five Hundred Years across the Indian Ocean and South China Sea

When did China, one of the leading manufacturing centers of the ancient world, lose its innovative edge to Europe, and to what extent did China's older legacy during the Great Ming (1368–1644) and Qing dynasties (1644–1912) pave the way for modern industrialization? As China reemerges as a manufacturing superpower, should Western countries maintain their trade policies in Asia's emerging markets in accordance with the economics of globalization, or alternatively should a now deindustrialized West embark on a new high-tech industrialization independent of a newly industrialized Asia? Answering these questions requires a long-duration understanding of global history, and more specifically, a picture of how an industrialized western Europe first came to dominate a once China-centered Asian economic world.

CHINA AND THE WEST: FIVE HUNDRED YEARS OF EXCHANGE

China's impact on the modern economy has its roots in the era of the Ming dynasty (1368–1644), when European maritime navigation first bypassed the Middle East in pursuit of the legendary Spice Islands (Maluku Islands, Indonesia) and the storied commodities of China: silk, silver, scent, porcelain, and the like. It was during the Ming era when Spanish and Portuguese seafaring expeditions first charted direct routes to the doorsteps of China, specifically Manila and Macau in the South China Sea. What the Iberians found was a world that was deeply enmeshed with China in terms of politics, commerce, and culture. Just a century before Magellan's trans-Pacific expedition from Acapulco to Manila (1519–1521), the Ming led China's own variety of an "age of exploration." The dynasty commissioned a series of diplomatic expeditions to ports across Northeast Asia, Southeast Asia, South Asia, East Africa, and the Middle East. The admiral that led the expeditions, Zheng He of Yunnan, was a Muslim of part Bukharan ancestry. The crewmate who documented the expeditions, Ma Huan, was also Muslim. Their backgrounds reflected the global dimensions of Ming-era Chinese political culture, which was in continuity with China's earlier Yuan (Mongol), Song, and Tang eras. Across all of these earlier centuries, inland cities like Xian and coastal cities like Quanzhou were centers of exchange that saw merchants from the Middle East and Central Asia come and go and, in many cases, settle permanently in Chinese cities.[1] Stories about Quanzhou circulated so widely in the Middle East in the medieval centuries that the city came to be known by an Arabic nickname: Zaytun (Italian: Zaiton). Against the backdrop of these earlier connections between China and its Middle Eastern trade partners, what Zheng He's expeditions represented was a new projection across the South China Sea and Indian Ocean of Beijing's global political and material culture. It was an image that the Ming sought to cultivate both locally and abroad—that is, across China's overland and maritime frontiers in the worlds of Southeast Asia's sultanates, Northeast Asia's shogunates, Central Asia's khanates, and an increasingly Ottoman-dominated Middle East.

What made the timing of Zheng He's expeditions impactful was the collapse in the previous century of Asia's most influential empires and the rise of a litany of new states in the 1400s. In the lead-up to the European Age of Exploration, the most strategically located maritime states were the various sultanates close to the Spice Islands: the Sultanates of Melaka on the Malay peninsula, Brunei on the coast of Borneo close to Manila, Pasai on the northern tip of Sumatra, Bantam on the island of Java, and the like. In a development that helped recenter China within the Asia-Pacific region, Zheng He's diplomatic expeditions subsumed the Sultanate of Melaka into a patron-client relationship that provided a variety of mutual benefits. For Melaka's part, the sultanate's connection with the Ming protected Melaka from invasion by Thailand's powerful Ayutthaya Kingdom (1350–1767) further north. Melaka, in turn, represented the Ming's gateway to Indian Ocean commodities and the Spice Islands.

In the 1500s, it was these sultanates that the Portuguese and Spaniards encountered upon their arrival in the South China Sea from either direction. What made them Europe's first gateway to China were the relationships the sultanates had already developed with the Ming in Beijing back in the 1400s. This connection was apparent during the Spanish conquest of the Philippines. When the governor of the Spanish Americas Miguel López de Legazpi arrived in the Philippines in the 1560s, he described a region with commodities and merchants that pointed to a local connection with both the sultan of Brunei and the emperors of China and Japan. De Legazpi and his crew found in Manila a group of Japanese merchants living in one of a variety of Japantowns that were scattered across Southeast Asia's ports. Private Japanese commerce in the fifteenth-century South China Sea, like the commerce of private Chinese merchants in local "junk" ships, represented one of the forerunners of what the Portuguese and later Dutch mastered in the seventeenth century: inter-Asian commerce, or more specifically, the purchase and sale of Asian commodities—especially Chinese commodities—across Asian ports.

It was in this Sinocentric world that the Iberian powers built their first global commodities portfolios in the 1500s. The endeavor was made possible, in part, through the skills of Iberian-sponsored polyglot Jesuits who played the role of diplomatic go-betweens in both Beijing and Nagasaki. China's markets were open for the first time to western European merchants, which meant that Middle Eastern and Italian merchants would no longer be the exclusive middlemen for Iberian access to the so-called Indies (Spanish: Indias)—that is, the lands beyond the Indian subcontinent in East and Southeast Asia. For the Iberians in the 1500s, the first profits came about not only through participation in the inter-Asian trade patterns, but also through the transport of Chinese and Japanese commodities back to Europe via Portuguese-held Goa and Spanish-held Manila and Acapulco. Iberian merchants, like their later Dutch and British competitors, purchased finished textiles from the Persian and Deccan coasts and brought them northward to Japanese ports, and on their return trips brought Japanese silver bullion southward to China and Southeast Asia for additional profits. Official and private Chinese trade provided access to high-priced Chinese manufactured items—tea, porcelain, silks, scent, and the like—that would, in turn, be sold for the highest profits in Europe.

One of the most remarkable phenomena that could observed in this history was the extent that the Iberians, like their Dutch and British successors, exercised utmost caution in their diplomatic relationships with Beijing in a manner that contrasted with their more aggressive military conquests throughout Southeast Asia. In the same way the Portuguese diplomatically secured their settlement in Macau while outright conquering Beijing's ally in Melaka, the Dutch likewise proceeded more carefully in their settlement in Taiwan (Fort Zeelandia) out of Beijing's sight just years after conquering the Sultanate of Banten. The Dutch similarly cultivated diplomatic relations with the rising Tokugawa shogunate with the utmost care, securing a trade agreement that lasted into the end of the shogunate in the late 1800s. What these patterns of diplomacy signaled was that even after a transfer of power in China from the Ming to the Qing dynasty (1644–1912), which coincided with the Japanese Tokugawa period (1603–1867), European powers understood Beijing to be as fearsome and formidable a player as ever.[2] By the 1800s, however, change was afoot, and it would come rapidly with the eruption of the Opium Wars.

The Opium Wars

The Opium Wars were originally an escalation of trade disagreements between China and the British, and the outcomes were staggering in terms of Beijing's territorial losses and diminished authority over ports previously under its purview. More specifically, the British East India Company in the early 1800s grew resistant to growing Chinese restrictions on the export of Chinese tea and import of British-manufactured opium. When the Chinese government destroyed a cargo of the narcotic, the British government stepped in, and the two governments began their first full-scale war. While the British operated sophisticated warships, China—legendary home of gunpowder technology—was still using shotguns, crossbows, and wooden boats in the 1800s that dated back to early Ming-era military strategies.[3] Back in the Ming era, Chinese military technology was cutting edge and was marveled at by visitors from the Ottoman Empire. By the end of the Qing, it lagged far enough behind European technology to help earn China the moniker "sleeping lion" in the writings of Napoleon. It was, perhaps, fitting that only a few decades after Napoleon's career, it was a legion of French military experts who participated in the modernization of Japan's army in the era of intra-European competition for influence in late nineteenth-century Japan and China.

In this long-duration history of modern China dating back to the Ming, the Opium Wars represented an unprecedented escalation of military conflict

between China and a European power. China in the 1800s was not the formidable military force it once was in the 1500s and 1600s, which meant that
the Chinese coast was more exposed than ever to new military players. The
increasingly industrialized powers of western Europe stepped into that void,
putting them in a position to be able to force new diplomatic and commercial
arrangements on Beijing in what came to be known as "gunboat diplomacy."
With the British Empire taking the lead, new trade agreements in the late
1800s allowed a variety of European-made commodities to be forced onto
Chinese and Japanese markets in a way that had never been seen before. In a
move that would have lasting consequences, individual Chinese and Japanese
reformers took advantage of the multiplicity of European powers in competition with one another. Individual Qing- and Tokugawa-era reformers
of the late 1800s secured European political and technological know-how
in return for a kind of patron-client relationship that was, from the start,
never intended to be permanent in the eyes of these Chinese and Japanese
reformers. The end of the century saw the start of reforms in China's military and urban infrastructure, but a full-scale political and socioeconomic
transformation would occur much sooner in Japan.

Japanese administrators in the late 1800s observed developments in China
with particular alarm. In the Opium Wars' aftermath, as Beijing lost control
of Chinese ports, the last samurai and shoguns of Japan accelerated a process
already in motion: the industrialization of the shogunate on the eve of its
transformation into one of the twentieth century's most powerful military
empires. In Japan's favor was its centuries-old diplomatic and commercial
ties with the Dutch. Since the 1600s, Japanese administrators had continuous access to developments in Dutch medicine, technology, and general
learning in an arrangement that facilitated Japan's very rapid political and
economic reforms of the late 1800s. The administrators who led a modern
industrial Japan at the start of the 1900s started their lives as samurai who
fought on foot for the *daimyo* of each of Japan's domains-turned-prefectures.
The dramatic shift in clothing from the cloak of a samurai to the suit of a
parliamentarian signaled, alongside a political and economic transformation,
a broader cultural turn away from China.

Japan's turn away from its China-centered political and commercial past
was especially remarkable from this very cultural perspective. The Meiji era
(1868–1912) saw Japan embark on an all-encompassing path to political and
socioeconomic reform that coopted British models of modernization and
simultaneously rearticulated them in the form of a revised classical Chinese

written vocabulary about tradition, order, and progress. It was a model of modernization that would become China's own, one that Sun Yat-Sen would study with his own eyes over the course of his education and travels from British-held Hong Kong to Meiji-era Japan at the start of the 1900s.

For China, however, the replication of that model would take more than a century, and it would only truly accelerate in the 1970s in an arrangement that saw Western powers replicate a model implemented previously in Japan: the transfer of political and technological know-how eastward in a bilateral attempt to build a new Asia in the West's image—that is, in a West-centered global economic and security framework. From the perspective of this approach's critics, where this arrangement has potentially fallen short is in one of its widely anticipated outcomes: like the Japanese Empire of the early twentieth century, China in the early twenty-first century has emerged as one of the world's most formidable military and commercial players, which means policies oriented around economic partnerships have come under renewed scrutiny. The outcome is that the rise of a new global China evocative of an earlier one has pushed Western observers to call for a new "China policy."

DEBATES ABOUT A WESTERN "CHINA POLICY": BETWEEN CONFRONTATION AND COMMERCIAL DIPLOMACY

How the world navigates today's new and emerging Chinese superpower is in some ways unpredictable, but if history offers lessons for the future, then the story of China's first modern global era provides insights. In China's own case, the name of Beijing's state-led international development project—the One Belt One Road initiative—illustrates how Chinese political administrators are interested in repurposing history in the formation of policy.[4] The name "One Belt One Road" evokes the ancient world's storied overland and maritime "silk road," and its use in Chinese diplomacy illustrates how Beijing's growing infrastructure partnerships around Asia's emerging markets draw on a form of Chinese soft power built on a specific China-centered understanding of world history. In other words, Beijing's national administration looks self-consciously to its earlier global history for inspiration and models of soft power as it expands its geopolitical importance throughout parts of Asia, especially Southeast Asia's ASEAN markets (Association of Southeast Asian Nations), where Beijing has again encountered the West.

In the case of the West's most powerful player, the United States, what history tells us about the future of a "China policy" is more elusive, but not entirely so. While Washington's connection with the history in this book is much shorter, the spectrum of positions in the United States' current policies on both China and the ASEAN region evokes the full spectrum of its European predecessors in a way that illustrates the obvious: countries that see themselves as Western, including NATO's leading members in the European Union, have experimented for 500 years with dozens of approaches to engaging China's historical role as a global center of manufacturing, innovation, and productivity. What makes these earlier engagements with China educational for modern observers is how different aspects of the United States' current policies in Asia evoke all of its predecessors, making world history the proverbial window into the future.

On one side of the West's diplomatic antecedents is the early modern Portuguese Empire, which evokes the modern blend of American commercial and military engagement in the South China Sea. Throughout the 1500s and 1600s, the Portuguese were simultaneously cautious around China and aggressive with China's allies. More specifically, in contrast with Portugal's careful negotiations with Beijing and Tokyo was its much more militarily hostile policy further south in the Malay peninsula. Portugal outright conquered the Ming's Melakan ally (1511) in a campaign that Thailand's Ayutthaya Kingdom never attempted for fear of Ming reprisal. The Portuguese, in other words, used a mix of diplomacy and military engagement around the South China Sea to simultaneously maximize their profits in China and minimize the risks to their own Portuguese-held territories across the Atlantic and Indian Oceans. What exposed the limits of Portugal's political and commercial abilities, however, was its growing tensions with Japan in the early 1600s. In Tokyo, the rising Tokugawa shogunate commanded enough political and military force to expel the Portuguese in 1639. The shoguns saw the Portuguese as a blend of merchants, pirates, and a potential military nuisance who could compromise the Tokugawa dynasty's own aspirations of bringing all Japanese domains under the dynasty's rule in Tokyo. The expulsion came some three centuries before American officer Commodore Perry arrived in Tokyo harbor in 1853 to force a new trade deal on the same Tokugawa dynasty. For Portugal, the silver lining of its multifaceted engagement in the region was its continued settlement rights on the Chinese coast, where Portuguese-Chinese bilateral diplomacy allowed the city of Macau to remain a central transit point for Portuguese trade in Asian commodities well into the 1900s.

On the other side of these diplomatic models was Spain's approach in Asia, which evokes modern protectionist policies oriented around producing commodities for local consumption and export rather than relying on imports. More specifically, in the 1500s and 1600s, Spanish administrators charted and mastered the trans-Pacific Acapulco-Manila sea route in a way that facilitated access to Chinese markets without being dependent on it. More specifically, the Spanish conquest of the Philippines secured a back door to Asian markets while still allowing the Spanish Habsburg Empire to build a semi-protectionist economic system oriented around productivity within its own imperial boundaries. The most productive Spanish-held centers were cities like Mexico City and Oaxaca (Mexico) as well as Lima (Peru). On the one hand, the Manila-Acapulco galleons brought Chinese silk and porcelain to centers like Mexico City throughout the 1600s and 1700s, where they became intertwined with the empire's earlier trans-Atlantic ceramic and silk industries linking Mexico with Seville and Granada. On the other hand, wholesalers and silk craftsmen in Spain pressured the government to restrict the import of Chinese commodities to the Americas, where there were already legal limits at the start of the 1600s on the amount of Asian merchandise that could be imported into the Americas via Manila. Spanish legal restrictions on the import of Chinese and Japanese goods into the Americas were in harmony with Madrid's successful construction and expansion of industries like the silk industry in Mexico that could produce and export commodities just as valuable as their Asian counterparts.[5] That is, Spain sought to control the price of their own empire's commodities by preventing the mass import of Chinese and Japanese goods and maximizing the export of their own portfolio of Chinese-like goods: Iberian- and Mexican-made silk commodities, Mexican-made cochineal dyes for silk-based textiles like Venetian velvet, Mexican- and Peruvian-mined gold and silver, Mexican-made chocolate for consumption as a beverage in Europe, and various other profitable empire-made exports that eventually competed in Europe with Portugal's Chinese and Japanese imports.

In many ways, Spain anticipated the later machine-facilitated productivity of the industrial-era British and Dutch, but it had the advantage of a vast and sprawling territory of natural resources as well as a local—specifically, indigenous—labor force. Its approach evokes Western anti-globalization arguments since the 1970s that are in favor of protecting Western manu-facturing and productivity and limiting trade deals with China. Spain was willing to engage the world of China by building a back door to its markets in the Philippines, but it relied primarily on productivity within its impe-rial borders in a way that limited the risks that the Portuguese, conversely, embraced in the latter's sprawling activities from Melaka to Macau and Nagasaki. That Spain was at the head of a massive American empire, one replete with natural resources and an indigenous population that maintained their own pre-Spanish Mesoamerican industries, made exposure to these Chinese commercial and security risks even less urgent.

For the Dutch and British in the 1700s, both powers found benefits in a mix of Portugal's and Spain's approaches on the eve of their own machine-driven factory industrialization. Dutch administrators like entrepreneur Jan Pieterszoon Coen mapped out a plan for commercial and military engage-ment in the South China Sea that was built explicitly on lessons from the Portuguese and Spaniards. For the Dutch, Portugal's model demonstrated the commercial possibilities of securing direct access to Chinese commodi-ties. Spain's model illustrated that it was equally lucrative to find ways of manufacturing commodities within one's own territories, whether in the Southeast Asian sultanates that the Dutch could outright conquer or in Dutch cities. On the Indonesian island of Java, the Dutch managed to manu-facture Arabic coffee in the 1700s using local labor. The move foreshadowed the British transfer of Chinese tea manufacturing secrets to the plantations of British India a century later in the 1800s. Back in the Netherlands, the city of Delft became the center for the manufacture of porcelain-like blue-and-white Delftware ceramics. Delftware was close enough to Chinese porcelain to render the Chinese import superfluous. The rise of Delftware anticipated the development of Staffordshireware in England in the 1800s, when develop-ments in machinery and mass production would facilitate the mass export of western European commodities onto the very Chinese markets that once manufactured items for Western consumption.

The Dutch and British, in other words, synthesized both the Portu-guese and Spanish approaches of building a massive import portfolio and constructing industries within the empire's boundaries that diminished the need for these imports. What distinguished the Dutch and British from their predecessors most clearly was something that also evokes the West's current engagement with China: government administrators relied on the privatized efforts of government-supported companies that were awarded a monopoly, or that were at least subsidized, in the purchase and sale of select goods in certain geographies around the world. These were the Dutch and British East India Companies. Like the powers that governed them back home, both companies were interested in foreign productivity and innovation, and they knew from their Portuguese predecessors that their most profitable commodities would include those of the South China Sea and Indian Ocean—namely, Chinese tea, Chinese and Japanese porcelain, precious metals, and both South and Southeast Asian finished textiles. In the end, through a mix of conquest and trade agreements, both the British and the Dutch managed to carve out a large slice of the Asian economic world by the end of the 1700s. The outcome was not only a turn of Dutch and British material and popular culture towards all things "Oriental" and exotic, but also the start of a profound advancements in innovation and design in Europe itself—especially the use of steam engines for low-cost mass production of Chinese-like commodities—that, in turn, drove the Industrial Revolution.[6] And from these new British and Dutch industrial centers, through the ingenuity of steam technology and factory-centered mass production techniques, porcelain-like ceramics and silk-like textiles could be exported for profit all around the world. For the British, what accelerated these manufacturing advancements was the simultaneous development of an unprecedented level of military might, one that facilitated the possibility of building what became by the late 1800s the world's most powerful global empire—that is, the British Empire. With that might came the authority to accomplish what no European power could previously: forcing China to open its markets to mass-produced European commodities, making China an overnight mass importer of British machine-made commodities.

What makes these older varieties of a "China policy" so evocative of the United States' current policies is how they are driven by the same fundamental question asked by today's policymakers: How will Western powers simultaneously benefit economically from a productive China while also minimizing their dependence on China and any related security risks? Where there are limits to turning history into a window for the future is in one of the many new dimensions of this question today. While the West studied Chinese innovation throughout the Age of Discovery and the Enlightenment, the Industrial Revolution saw the tables turn: since the Opium Wars, China has emulated the West's high-tech advancements in a process that accelerated in the 1970s and that drew in part on neighboring Japan's nineteenth-century industrial reforms. Since the late 1800s, British interest in helping industrialize both China and Japan has evolved against the backdrop of competition over economic influence in Asia, particularly with the rise of new global players. By the mid-1900s, the most important of these new global players was the Soviet Union, whose rivalry with the United States and United Kingdom motivated a new Western partnership with China that evoked the same patron-client partnerships that Western countries cultivated with Japan in the late 1800s. In Japan's case, Japanese industrialization facilitated the rise of the Japanese Empire that found itself on the losing side of World War II and that was rebuilt in the 1950s and 1960s but—in accordance with postwar treaties—without its military industry.

The West's agreements with China since the 1970s were similarly oriented around industrializing Chinese cities, but they never came with limitations on the development of a modern high-tech Chinese military industry. The emphasis, rather, was on economic partnerships focused on building China's own high-tech manufacturing know-how so that a postindustrial West could benefit economically from Chinese manufacturing and labor. The move came with the enthusiastic support of Western policymakers, corporations, and shareholders, with economists and policymakers celebrating the merits of freer trade, offshore outsourcing, and Cold War–era security. Critics, in contrast, warned of the long-term outcome of trade agreements that were unbalanced in the way they remained protectionist of local industries on the Chinese side while parallel industries in the United States and United Kingdom collapsed. Other critics pointed to long-term security concerns. In the end, some fifty years after the first Sino-American diplomatic meetings of the Nixon and Ford eras, China has managed to recenter itself both economically and militarily in an Asian economic world where broader advancements in a variety of new industries—like renewable energy—have become potential models for a new American and British post-factory high-tech reindustrialization.

Against this backdrop, current American, European Union, and Brexit-era British debates about trade with China and the wider Asia-Pacific world echo the debates of Western predecessors: Should American policymakers emulate the Portuguese of the 1600s and, through careful diplomacy, profit from economic partnerships with a productive China as it has since the 1970s? Or rather should the United States begin emulating the British of the 1800s by building—or in today's context, building anew—infrastructure for the production of goods and services that can correct its current trade deficit with a manufacturing superpower? Is there a model in the Spanish example of relying on natural resources and industries that are already available within one's own political borders? Is there something to learn from the Dutch diversification of commodities, from its sale of imported Chinese-manufactured tea to Delft-manufactured pseudo-porcelain?

The United States' current "China policy," in sum, evokes all of its predecessors' models of engagement, but there is one arena where it departs: a continuing modern trend in overlooking the recent and long-duration history of innovation throughout Asia that has only recently begun to capture popular imagination. Whether fearsome lion or a paper tiger, China is a historical center of innovation in the realm of design and manufacturing, and as in the case of all innovation, a history of culture lies underneath. That history includes centuries of political culture across dynasties and state administrations, intellectual culture oriented around books on aesthetics, popular culture built on language and social customs, and material culture oriented around design in everyday life. The Iberian-sponsored Jesuits were masters in understanding this history of innovation and culture, as were the many Dutch and British innovators who traveled to China and discovered the objects and manufacturing techniques that they found useful for their own industrial futures. It is this understanding of Chinese innovation and culture that remains missing in the writings of Western observers today, and it forms the heart of this book's analysis of China since the Great Ming and the making of the modern world.

WRITING GLOBAL HISTORY FROM AN ASIA-CENTERED PERSPECTIVE

From the tales of Zheng He's storied cargoes filled with silks and camphor to the life of the Italian-born Jesuit Matteo Ricci in Beijing, many of the figures in this book have been seen before in historical narratives about global navigation since Columbus. Some appear in chronicles written by their contemporaries, while others appear in studies written by historians interested in the lessons history offers today's observer. Among the most influential of these historians is Peter Borschberg. Borschberg's analysis has demonstrated how the modern economy came into existence in large part following centuries of global exchange in Southeast Asia. His research demonstrates how trade partnerships like ASEAN are as much a shift in the global economy as they are a revival of past trade networks.[7] Andre Gunder Frank's analysis of global economic history likewise illustrates how the modern world economy in many ways has its origins in Asia.[8] Janet Abu-Lughod's work offers a similar contribution with an emphasis on connections between the Middle East and its eastern frontiers. In agreement with Chinese works on global history that see the Middle East as both Europe's neighbor and Asia's western periphery, Abu-Lughod has shown how the Dutch and British were historical newcomers to an ancient set of socioeconomic systems centered in Asia.[9]

This book builds on the analysis seen in past works on global history with a new emphasis on how history illuminates the current and future geopolitical landscape. What follows in this book's remaining chapters is the story of how China went from the storied exporter of the world's rarest commodities in the Ming era (1368–1644) to the largest importer of machine-made British exports by the end of the Qing era (1644–1912) to, today, a resurgent manufacturing superpower in the aftermath of its industrial transformation (ca. 1970s–present). This book tells the story of how western European mariners went from pirates to trade partners in the eyes of Asian administrators, and how these administrators found themselves coopting European models of modernization by the early 1900s in an attempt to extricate themselves from a geopolitical landscape that the West came to dominate. As this landscape continues to be reshaped in light of the European Union's slowed growth and the continued emergence of Asia's tiger economies since the 1970s, it is more important than ever to tell the story of global exchange since the Great Ming and the making of the modern world.

CHAPTER 2

Global Beijing under the Great Ming

How did China under the Great Ming (1368–1644) become a global power? The story of Beijing's global turn during the Ming era is connected with developments in both Europe and in China itself. More than a century before the Age of Exploration, Beijing's Ming dynasty was in the process of consolidating its place at the center of Asia's overland and maritime trade routes—that is, the legendary silk and spice routes of the ancient world. The Ming commissioned a series of diplomatic expeditions across all three of its frontiers: the khanates of Central Asia across the Great Wall, the sultanates of Southeast Asia across the South China Sea, and the shogunates of Northeast Asia across the Sea of Japan. The outcome was the remarkably transoceanic cultural orientation of Ming politics and trade in the 1500s, when Spanish and Portuguese mariners began arriving in centers like Melaka, Macau, Manila, and Nagasaki. These cities became Europe's back doors to the Chinese commercial worlds, and by the 1600s, a rising Russian empire cultivated its own overland route to China via the khanates of Central Asia. A closer look at the Ming's connections with its three frontiers in the 1400s—Central Asia, Southeast Asia, and Northeast Asia—illustrates precisely how China went global just prior to the arrival of European mariners in the 1500s, and how the Age of Exploration's construction of new transoceanic trade routes from Europe to Manila and Macau in effect extended the geographical

reach of Chinese politics and material culture to its final historical frontiers: western Europe and the Americas.

ORIGINS OF THE MING'S TRADE WITH
CENTRAL ASIA AND THE MIDDLE EAST

When the dynasty of the Great Ming rose to power in China in 1368, it
competed with several dynastic states that were well established in the region
and that shaped the Ming's interest in global exchange. The most powerful
were the Yuan, whom the Ming replaced in Beijing. The Yuan dynasty was
one of four Mongol dynasties descended from the grandsons of Genghis
Khan (d. 1227). One of the main legacies the dynasty left was a renewal of
overland exchange across Central Asia. This renewal, and more specifically
the ability of Italian powers to gain direct access to Central Asia via the Black
Sea, earned the Mongol era the term *Pax Mongolica* (Mongol Peace) among
European writers. The term echoed the so-called *Pax Romana* of the ancient
Roman Empire, which consolidated enough of the Mediterranean coastline
under a single centralized administration to build a semi-centralized trade
system. There were parallels in how European merchants saw trade across
the emirates and sultanates of the Abbasid Empire in the 700s C.E., which
stretched from Iberia and North Africa to Egypt, Iraq, and the Indian
subcontinent.

From the vantage point of Beijing, the key outcome of the Mongol Yuan
era of the 1200s was the rise of new, or rather renewed, overland connections
with Central Asia and the Middle East. Under earlier dynasties, especially
the Song (960–1279), the movement of trade networks and commercial objects in and out of China often took place along the coast. In the 900s, for example, Quanzhou and Guangzhou represented the cultural crossroads where
Middle Eastern Muslim merchants took up long-term residence for activities
in diplomacy and commerce. Under the Yuan in the 1200s, inland regions
like Yunnan just north of Thailand—the Ming's western frontier—became
the new heartlands of Muslim commercial activities in China. Unlike the
Arabic-speaking Middle Eastern Muslims of Song-era Quanzhou, these
newer Muslim arrivals in the Yuan era were Persian speakers from Central
Asia. This cultural shift in China's Muslim demographic helps explains
why later Ming-era travelers from Central Asia came to encounter polyglot
Persian-speaking Muslims who worked in Ming service in Beijing, and how
Yunnanese admiral Zheng He emerged as a prominent Ming political figure

descended from one of the Yuan era's most famous Persian-speaking Central Asian Muslim families—namely, the family of the Bukharan governor of Yunnan, Nasr al-Din. Nasr al-Din was in charge of imperial finances in the 1250s, and the person who named him governor of Yunnan was the Mongol Yuan emperor himself: Khubilai Khan, the grandson of Genghis Khan. This shift also explains why the most prominent figures in the earlier Song-era administration, especially Pu (Arabic: Abu) Shougeng, came not from inland Yunnan but the coast. A closer look at these Muslim political and commercial networks illustrates how the Yunnanese Muslim administrators who worked in Ming service, including Zheng He, were not a new and unusual phenomenon in the 1400s but rather the most recent manifestation of an older Chinese connection with Central Asia and the Middle East that dated back to the Tang and Song eras. The outcome of this history is that with the arrival of the Ming, two developments occurred that facilitated Beijing's connections with its Central Asian and Southeast Asian frontiers in the 1400s: One segment of these Muslim networks was absorbed in Ming society and, in the case of Yunnanese Muslims, played a key role in the Ming administration in its diplomacy with Central Asian states. Another segment of these Chinese Muslim networks headed to Southeast Asia for permanent settlement among the rising sultanates. Some individual Muslims like Yunnanese admiral Zheng He connected both worlds in a career that was fitting for a global Ming-era diplomat.

Muslim Social Networks in China in the Lead-Up to the Ming Era

Tang-era Muslims settled at the eastern ends of the Central Asian silk routes in cities like Gansu and Shaanxi as early as the eighth century. Among coastal Chinese cities, Muslims settled especially in centers like Fujian and Guangdong.[1] In the Tang period, Muslim merchants were able to secure residency and movement rights through extraterritorial agreements, and they also built mosques in coastal cities like Guangzhou, Quanzhou, Hangzhou, and Chang'an. By the Song period (960–1279), certain developments in diplomacy occurred that made the rise of Persian- and Arabic-speaking Muslims in post-Song Yuan service a commonplace phenomenon. Partly in continuity with the earlier Tang dynasty's (618–907) coastal trade routes, the Song in southern China cultivated international maritime commerce and saw the settlement of various foreign communities along its interior and coastal regions. Song-era Quanzhou specifically saw both the long-term settlement and short-term residency of a variety of Muslim merchants and Muslim community leaders. Song-era gravestones, replete with Muslim names, provide a surviving record of this phenomenon.[2] These gravestones, like the surviving annals of the Ming, point to a process of Sinicization among long-term Muslim resident families who worked in the Song administration. The most famous case is that of Pu Shougeng.

Pu Shougeng was the superintendent of maritime trade at Quanzhou when the Yuan arrived. His family name, Pu, was the Sinicized form of the Arabic *Abu*, meaning "father of." Pu Shougeng was one of the many Song officials who remained in their positions upon the arrival of the Mongols and the establishment of the Mongol Yuan dynasty in Beijing. The Mongol administration in the 1200s absorbed much of Song governance in the aftermath of the conquest, paving the way for a Ming administration in the late 1300s that would synthesize its predecessors' overland and maritime political outlooks.[3] Pu Shougeng was an example of the many residents in late Song-era coastal China who came from Muslim families in imperial service and who remained in imperial service under the Yuan. Under both the Song and the Yuan, this demographic around the South China Sea facilitated maritime trade relations across the Indian Ocean with Arabic-speaking lands, and they commonly held the position of superintendent of trading at the ports. Fujian employed a total of thirty superintendents of trading ships during the Yuan period, and some one-third were Muslims. Under the Yuan, Pu Shougeng, was the supervisor of maritime trade for Guangdong and Fujian, eventually being named vice minister of Fujian.

Pu Shougeng's profile and career as Fujian's Muslim vice minister in the 1200s illustrates the extent that China was at a political and cultural crossroads on the eve of the Ming era, and that the new Ming administration was poised in 1368 to build connections with the Muslim khans and sultans who rose to prominence in Central and Southeast Asia on the eve of Europe's arrival in the region.

What facilitated the Ming's overland connections with these Central Asian khans was the deliberate attempt by Yuan-era administrators back in the 1200s to resettle Central Asian Muslim administrators and merchants in China's interior, especially Yunnan. While the Yuan brought Muslim craftsmen and architects to the region as part of an empire-building technique, other Muslim arrivals such as merchants, tax collectors, and administrators came looking for new opportunities.[4] Some even settled in Goryeo Korea along the Yuan's northeast borders, only disappearing into a larger Confucian Korean future in the era of the Joseon dynasty (1392–1897) and its culturally homogenizing policies. The rise of Yuan-era Muslim administrators like Yunnanese-born governor Nasr al-Din offers a particularly interesting example of Central Asian Muslims becoming, in a sense, Chinese on the eve of the Ming.

Nasr al-Din al-Bukhari was the governor of Yunnan in the late 1200s and was born not in Bukhara but in Yunnan itself. He was the son of Sayyid Shams al-Din Omar al-Bukhari, Yunnan's first provincial governor who was appointed to the position by Yuan Emperor Khubilai Khan. Shams al-Din was also an ancestor of Yunnanese admiral Zheng He, who was born a century later (1300s) and hired by the Ming's Hongwu and Yongle emperors. Shams al-Din, the Central Asian born father of Nasr al-Din, was known by two names: Shams al-Din in Arabic and Persian, and the Sinicized version of the same name that today would sound like *Zhānsīdīng* in modern Mandarin.[5] The reason Shams al-Din and other Central Asian administrators ended up working in Yuan service was because the Mongol Ilkhanids of present-day Iran and Uzbekistan maintained diplomatic and commercial relations with the Mongol Yuan of China. Muslims who originally worked in Ilkhanid service often moved to the Yuan administration. In Shams al-Din's case, his career east of Bukhara took him first to Beijing and then to Yunnan. In Yunnan, he was tasked with building Confucian, Buddhist, and Islamic sacred spaces in what had the intended effect of urbanizing and Sinicizing China's then-frontier and rural regions.

From the perspective of later Ming history, the rise of Yuan-era Yunnanese Muslim political figures of Central Asian ancestry simultaneously echoed the role of Pu Shougeng in Song-era Quanzhou and foreshadowed the career of admiral Zheng He. It also foreshadowed the Ming-era career of a certain Mawlana Yusuf, a polyglot court interpreter in the Ming palace in Beijing whom the Central Asian traveler Ghayath al-Din Naqqash encountered as part of the fifteenth-century embassy from Timurid Samarkand to the Ming capital. Naqqash's story appears in the next chapter. What the Ming-era careers of Zheng He and Mawlana Yusuf indicate is that despite the massive shifts in governance that occurred with the Ming's expulsion of Mongol ruling circles in the late 1300s, Beijing's pattern of employing commonly multilingual Muslims as administrative go-betweens connecting China with Central Asia became a permanent part of Ming diplomacy.

Muslim sources on the eve of the Ming era tells us that the example of the Bukharis in China was far from rare. Rashid al-Din al-Hamadani, a physician employed by the neighboring Mongol Ilkhanid Empire further west, was a witness to this phenomenon. One of his most widely read texts, *Compendium of Chronicles*, offers evidence of a widespread Muslim administrative presence in both inland cities like Zhejiang and coastal cities like Guangdong.[6] Their Persian names indicate origins not only in Bukhara, but also other Central Asian centers like Khwarezm and Khorasan. The pattern of hiring Muslims in Beijing became so embedded in the later Ming era that the most prominent Jesuit scientist during the Age of Exploration, Matteo Ricci, described how Beijing's bureau of astronomy employed many Muslims. That fact must have come as a surprise given his encounter with Muslims in South and Southeast Asia during his trip along the Portuguese trade routes to Macau.

Ming-era Beijing, in other words, was not only situated at the eastern crossroads of the silk and spice routes, but it also embraced its cultural links with those routes. This connection helps contextualize why, in the lead-up to the Age of Exploration, Chinese commodities like porcelain and silk loomed large in the eyes of Iberian monarchs and mariners. Trade along the silk and spice routes was more active than ever in the late 1400s, which meant that cities like Venice, Cairo, and Istanbul were replete with the objects that would come to dominate the portfolio of Portuguese, Spanish, and later Dutch and British business networks. The China that the Iberians would encounter was the same China that hired Central Asian Muslim administrators: it was China under the Great Ming. What facilitated a European-Chinese encounter in Southeast Asia was the fact that the Ming had already commissioned at least one of these Yunnanese Muslim administrators, namely Zheng He, to build political and commercial relationships with the rising Muslim sultanates of Southeast Asia.

MING DIPLOMACY ACROSS SOUTHEAST ASIA'S SULTANATES

The early Ming era saw a transformation of Southeast Asian politics and society that included the rise of Islam in the region and a closer connection between the rising Muslim sultans and Beijing. The sultanates themselves emerged out of the fragmentation of several older maritime states in the region, and they included the famous sultanates of Pasai, Melaka, Banten, and Brunei. Pasai's proximity to present-day Aceh in northwest Indonesia illustrates the region's geographic connections with the Middle East and the Indian Ocean coast. Brunei's proximity to the Philippines, like Melaka's distance from Thailand and Yunnan, points to the sultanates' proximity to China. Banten's location, close to present-day Jakarta, highlights the region's connection with the most strategically important center of Southeast Asia in the eyes of the Ming in the late 1300s and the European navigators of the 1400s: the Spice Islands. Southeast Asia was strategically important to the Ming because of Indonesia's Molucca Islands (Spice Islands) and the region's location at the crossroads of the Indian Ocean and South China Sea—that is, the intersection of commercial traffic coming to China both from the Middle East and from Japan and Korea.

Given Southeast Asia's geographical connections with the Middle East and Indian Ocean coast, it was fitting that the Ming commissioned a Yunnanese Muslim admiral for diplomatic expeditions in the region in the early 1400s. When Zheng He embarked on his voyages, he was accompanied by a Muslim crewmate named Ma Huan. Unlike Zheng He, Ma Huan was a convert to Islam and came not from Yunnan but coastal China. Ma Huan's surviving written observations of Southeast Asia note the presence of Muslims among both Chinese and non-Chinese communities throughout Southeast Asia, including Java. Ma Huan's descriptions of these Chinese Muslim communities in Southeast Asia correlate accurately with historical evidence of the settlement of Chinese Muslims in the Malay Peninsula during the transition from the Yuan to the Ming periods in the mid-1300s. The rise of Islam among Southeast Asian ruling circles, in other words, may have been linked with a broader cultural expansion of coastal China in the 1300s into the worlds of Southeast Asia. Zheng He and Ma Huan's connections with the Ming, with Chinese Islam, and with the Southeast Asian sultanates was likely the tip of the iceberg in this story of Ming China's cultural expansion into the islands of the Malay Archipelago.

What epitomized these connections most was the expeditions' most memorable outcome: the absorption of the Sultanate of Melaka into a kind of patron-client relationship with Beijing that ultimately protected it in the 1400s from invasion by Thailand's Ayutthaya Kingdom. For the Melakan sultanate, a tributary relationship with Ming China offered foreign powers access to precious Chinese commodities like porcelain wares, silk and brocade textiles, calendars, and copper coins.[7] For the Ming, close relations with the Melakan sultanate offered strategic access to the Spice Islands and

Indian Ocean commerce some one hundred years before Iberian mariners established regular shipping routes through the region.

What distinguished the Ming from these later Iberian mariners was, among other distinctions, the scale of the maritime operation and the projection of power it intended. This scale, together with the overall projection of Ming power under the leadership of multiple Chinese Muslim mariners, likely facilitated the growth of Islam's cultural currency within Southeast Asia's increasingly Muslim ruling circles at a time when Muslims from lands further west were already traveling in the region as merchants. Zheng He's fleet was vast, and its memory loomed large enough in Southeast Asian history that it became embedded in a variety of oral traditions. While the exact size of these boats continues to be debated, the scale and sight of the fleet would have been impressive even in modern ports. In contrast with Columbus's three comparatively tiny unaccompanied vessels, Zheng He's fleet led with 62 large treasure ships together with a larger entourage of 225 smaller boats. The highest estimates of the leading boats' length are as high as 400 feet, though they were likely not that long.[8] Still, by comparison, large high-walled Portuguese carracks reached up to 150 feet in length, while Venetian galleys with low walls were slightly longer at 160 feet. The Santa Maria, one of the vessels that carried Christopher Columbus's crew, was just short of 72 feet. The contrast in size offers perspective on what a remarkable sight Chinese ships arriving on tributary missions must have been. The fleet also visited an impressive number of lands during their first four voyages between 1405 and 1421: Vietnam, Indonesia, Malaysia, Thailand, Sri Lanka, India, Iran, Somalia, Kenya, Yemen, and Oman. The variety of ports that Zheng He and Ma Huan visited indicates that the connection between Ming China and the rising Muslim sultanates of Southeast Asia were just one part of a larger diplomatic campaign to connect Beijing with the many ruling circles of the South China Sea and Indian Ocean. The lasting transformation of Vietnam into a center of Chinese political and intellectual culture is perhaps the clearest artifact of Ming history that illustrates best how zealously the Ming turned towards the South China Sea.

The Limits of China's Southeastern Turn during the Ming: Vietnam and Thailand
The Ming's connections with Vietnam and Thailand, located between China and the Southeast Asian sultanates, represented both the limits and possibilities of the Ming's Southeast Asian turn. On the one hand, Vietnam

and Thailand's proximity to southern China meant the Ming would pursue a more aggressive military approach in the region. On the other hand, these were powerful states that would attempt to outmaneuver not only China but also all of the later European arrivals interested in Thai and Vietnamese ports.

More specifically, the same Ming Yongle Emperor (r. 1402–1424) who commissioned Zheng He's travels to Melaka and Mecca also invaded Annam in present-day Vietnam in 1406. The invasion ushered in several decades of Ming domination in the region. The Vietnamese state's conquest of its chief rival Cham in 1471 was facilitated by the fifty-year process of Vietnamese political and military centralization that took place partly in response to Ming presence in the region.[9] By the late fifteenth century, Vietnam had taken over most of Cham, and its administrators managed to placate the Ming emperors by subsuming Vietnam into a tributary relationship with the Ming. One of the most remarkable outcomes of this Ming-Vietnamese connection was the Vietnamese state's assimilation of Confucian political ethics, a phenomenon more common in Northeast Asia. That expansion of Ming-era Confucianism into Vietnam paralleled in many ways the movement of Chinese Muslims to Southeast Asia in the same period.

In contrast with the Ming's abilities in Vietnam were its limits in Thailand. The Ayutthaya Kingdom based in the region developed a complex connection with the Ming that more closely resembled Beijing's patron-client relationship with Melaka. Thailand had an old patron-client relationship with China dating back to the Mongol era and was held back by the Ming from encroaching on the Melakan sultanate by the promise of continued Chinese-Thai relations and the threat of a Chinese invasion similar to the Vietnam example. Annual tribute missions that filled Beijing's coffers remained lucrative. For its part, Thailand's independence throughout the Ming era and into the arrival of European powers in the 1500s meant that its ports could grow into a global center of commerce that rivaled Melaka with a similar mix of merchants coming from the Middle East, the Indian Ocean coasts, China, and Japan.[10]

In projecting Ming power to the closest and most distant reaches of Southeast Asia, in sum, Ming diplomacy accomplished what its administrators sought to achieve: the transformation of Southeast Asia into China's commercial and political backyard. The Ming annals recount the arrival of delegations in Beijing that include the Melakan sultan himself, while

Malay epics offer multiple accounts of Chinese political figures settling in the region and producing local dynasties.[11] It was this set of connections that made China loom so large in the eyes of Portuguese mariners arriving in the Malay peninsula in the 1500s, and it was a similar set of connections that the Ming cultivated in their third frontier—Northeast Asia—that made Japan the most climactic site of Europe's encounters with the Chinese commercial world across the centuries between the Age of Exploration and Commodore Perry's arrival in Tokyo Bay.

THE MING IN GORYEO KOREA AND MUROMACHI JAPAN

Every dimension of the Ming's diplomatic connections with Japan and Korea in the late 1300s pointed to how culturally intertwined cities like Beijing, Seoul, and Tokyo would remain as late as the 1900s during Japan's turn away from China. The legacy of Ming political and intellectual culture, from Confucian social and political ethics to Chan (Zen) Buddhist sacred traditions, looms large even in present-day Korea and Japan. In both countries, sociopolitical reform movements continue their industrial-era debates about the limitations of a once ubiquitous Chinese cultural past in the same way Southeast Asian nations look simultaneously to China and the West as they reinterpret their histories and navigate the world's geopolitical landscape. For the Europeans who arrived in the region during the Age of Exploration, China loomed large in Japan, which meant that diplomatic engagement with both powers went hand in hand. What made Beijing's presence particularly strong in the region was the set of diplomatic overtures that built on a much older history of close connections across Northeast Asia.

When the new Ming Emperor Chu Yuanchang (Zhu Yuanzhang) took the throne in Beijing in 1368, he styled his regnal period the Hongwu (洪武, "Great Martial Power") era. The name he gave his regnal period made him the Hongwu Emperor (r. 1368–1398). This conception of history and time in terms of Chinese ruling periods was shared across Northeast Asia, where the "Middle Kingdom" represented the center of politics and culture well into the 1800s. The Ming made sure to maintain this connection with neighbors like Japan through several diplomatic missions that were contemporary with the actual relocation of Chinese administrators and intellectuals to Japan.

After his ascension, the Hongwu Emperor sent an edict to Northeast Asian states establishing his claim to the throne of the Middle Kingdom (Zhongguo)—that is, China. "We are the ruler of the Middle Kingdom," it read. "When the dynastic fortune of the Song reached an end, Heaven commanded the immortal [*chen-jen*, referring to Khubilai Khaghan] in the desert to enter the Middle Kingdom and become the lord of the empire."[12] The edict explained how this divinely ordained dynastic rule passed from son to grandson for more than a hundred years, but that as the Mongol Yuan's dynastic fortunes diminished, local strongmen vied with local magnates until the Ming family restored order. "The title of the empire has been set as Great Ming," it declared. "The present year has been made the first year of Hongwu."[13]

Since the new Ming dynasty controlled key coastal ports once held by the Yuan and Song, Northeast and Southeast Asian states cultivated diplomatic relations with the Ming in response to the edicts. In the Korean peninsula, the Goryeo dynasty was nearing the final decades of its rule and delayed its recognition of the new Ming dynasty for almost ten years.[14] The survival of the Goryeo dynasty was at least partly based on its role as a client state of the Mongol Yuan, with whom the Goryeo political elite intermarried. The result was that for almost a decade after the rise of the Ming, the Goryeo dynasty precariously managed to engage in diplomatic relations with the Ming while continuing to recognize the Yuan as the imperial sovereigns of China. Evidence of this two-sided diplomatic strategy appears in the Goryeo's surviving official communications, which indicate the year of the letters in terms of the year of the exiled Yuan khan's reigning period rather than the period of the Hongwu Emperor. As mentioned, the name Hongwu identified the period of the first Ming emperor's reign rather than the emperor himself, making 1368 the first year of the Hongwu period and Chu Yuanchang the Hongwu Emperor. More than dynastic minutiae, the correct identification of China's reigning period in Korean and Japanese communications was a key part of the renewal of regional diplomatic relations from one Chinese period to another. The Ming expected Korean diplomatic communications in 1374 to be dated as the sixth year of the Hongwu, but they were instead dated with the respective year of the Yuan ruler. Between 1374 and 1377, more than ten years after the rise of the Ming, Korea attempted to hedge its relations with both the Ming and the Yuan by continuing to recognize the Yuan ruler as "Son of Heaven" in communications with the Ming, even as "Son of Heaven" was the imperial title the Hongwu Emperor claimed to inherit once the Ming captured Nanjing and Beijing.

The outcome was a diplomatic disaster for the Goryeo and illustrated at least one of the many ways China played a dominant role in Northeast Asian politics and culture well into the late 1800s: in a move likely intended to coerce the Goryeo into realigning themselves away from the Yuan, multiple Korean emissaries were imprisoned by the end of their stay in Nanjing. By 1377, the Goryeo officially recognized Ming suzerainty.[15] With the formal recognition of Ming power, the Goryeo sought Ming investiture of authority throughout the early 1380s in order to bolster the legitimacy of the dynasty. By 1392, however, a Goryeo general usurped the throne and established a new dynasty that would survive until nearly World War I: the Joseon, which oversaw a major intellectual and cultural turn towards the Ming.

In accordance with Ming intellectual developments, Korea's Joseon dynasty (1392–1897) were patrons of Neo-Confucian political and social ethics. During much of China's Ming period (1368–1644), the Joseon facilitated a pattern of cultural convergence that cultivated syncretic forms of Sino-Korean arts and literature.[16] Among the early Joseon's most enduring legacies was its cultivation of a dedicated non-Chinese phonetic script—namely, the phonetic Hangul script—that was used together with Chinese ideograms (Chinese: 漢字, hànzì, Korean: hanja, Japanese: kanji) in the formation of an early modern Sino-Korean literary corpus.[17]

Further east from Goryeo Korea, Muromachi (Ashikaga) Japan was in a complex position of simultaneously attempting to establish diplomatic and trade relations with the Ming while also limiting Chinese involvement in Japanese political affairs. An initial period of diplomatic relations was cut short in 1380, when the Ming Emperor suspected that the Japanese were colluding with fallen Ming minister Hu Weiyong (d. 1380) to usurp the throne.[18] Under the third Muromachi shogun, Yoshimitsu (1358–1408), diplomatic and trade relations were restored. Yoshimitsu's reign saw the growth of lucrative tributary commerce with China. Tributary trade, in contrast with private trade, involved China's reception and housing of a foreign embassy that brought in valuable foreign commodities in an official capacity. In return, the embassy left with precious Chinese commodities like silk, porcelain, and tea.

For Joseon Korea and Muromachi Japan, China's tributary commerce amounted to lucrative import trade of luxury commodities that left a strong impact on local material culture and taste, from local porcelain and pseudo-porcelain production to the cultivation and consumption of Chinese tea. In exchange, Chinese tributary embassies brought back Japanese commodities such as silver and Japanese silk. The Portuguese and Dutch would eventually participate in this inter-Asian trade, bringing Chinese silk to Japan in exchange for Japanese silver. For the Ming, this tributary exchange had clear and measurable political outcomes.

Beyond projecting Ming power abroad and bolstering the dynasty's legitimacy in the region, this tributary commerce facilitated several specific diplomatic goals related to borders and security. Most importantly, Muromachi (Ashikaga) Japan's administration agreed to cooperate with the Chinese on limiting piracy along the Chinese coast. By 1403, the shogun Yoshimitsu sent an embassy that attempted to ingratiate the shogunate to the Ming by declaring Japan a vassal or client of China, identifying the shogun as "Your subject, the King of Japan."[19] As in the case of late Goryeo Korea, there were lucrative outcomes: the Ming soon reestablished trade relations, reopening the maritime trade intendancies in Ningpo, Quanzhou, and Canton to Japanese traders in accordance with a system of certifications—the so-called tally (Chinese: 勘合, kānhé, Japanese: kango) system—that ensured that merchants were Japanese-sponsored tribute missions and not smugglers or pirates.[20] For the Ming, the key outcome of stable trade relations with Japan was the commitment of the shogun to preventing smuggling off of China's coast. Under Yoshimitsu, Zen monks played a major role as go-betweens facilitating these diplomatic agreements. Under his successor Yoshimochi, in a move that foreshadowed some of the late Tokugawa debates about Japan's Sinocentricism, the shogun distanced both Japan from the Ming and the shogunate from the Chan (Zen) monks involved in Chinese-Japanese political relations. Despite these intermittent tensions, private trade with China continued through Japan's southern ports in what reflects an enduring commercial connection with Ming China throughout the Muromachi and early Tokugawa periods.

Chinese Intellectual Culture in Joseon Korea and Muromachi Japan

Against this backdrop of Ming diplomatic exchange, what solidified an enduring Chinese cultural impact on modern Korea and Japan was the transfer of specifically Ming-era Confucian ethical philosophy—that is, Ming-era Neo-Confucian sociopolitical ethics—into Korean and Japanese political circles. In the case of Korea, the Joseon dynasty's cultivation of Confucianism correlated with the Ming's own patronage of Confucian political and social ethics. Confucian scholars in Joseon Korea played a role in the Korean administration as advisers, diplomats, and, more broadly, scholar-officials. Joseon founder King Yi Seonggae (Taejo) came to power with the assistance of Jeong Dojeon (d. 1398), a Korean Confucian scholar who helped establish key institutions of governance. Jeong Dojeon was a graduate of the *Seonggyun-gwan*, the highest institution of learning during the Goryeo and Joseon periods dedicated to Neo-Confucian scholar-officials working in Korean civil service. A key figure in the reform of Korean law and political ethics along Neo-Confucian lines, Jeong Dojeon wrote several seminal Neo-Confucian works in the early Joseon period that included *Joseon Kyeonguk Cheon* (*Joseon's Codes for Governing the Country*) and *Kyeongje Mungam* (*Historical Mirror for Managing the World and Saving the People*) that played a role in disseminating the Confucian social ethics characteristic of Joseon Korea well into the twentieth century.[21]

Ming-era Chinese political and intellectual culture became similarly embedded in Japan in the late 1300s and 1400s, giving rise to Japan's mix of Zen Buddhism and Japanese Confucianism in both ruling circles and popular society. Chan (Zen) Buddhist monks close to Japanese political circles cultivated close connections between the two states and facilitated a similar transfer of political culture eastward. Chan (Zen) monks had the strongest knowledge of Chinese language and high culture, which made them appropriate go-betweens in Chinese-Japanese diplomacy.[22] Yoshimitsu's (r. 1368–1394) and his successor Yoshimochi's (r. 1394–1423) respective turns towards and away from close diplomatic relations with Ming China correlated with their respective proximity and distance from Japanese Chan (Zen) monks who played a role as advisers to the shogunal governing authorities (*bakufu*).

In a similar parallel with Ming-Joseon relations, Japanese Neo-Confucian scholar-officials would also eventually play a role in Ming-Japanese diplomacy, but this development occurred in the late Ming period with the transition of Japan from the Muromachi period to the Tokugawa period.[23] In seventeenth-century Edo (Tokyo), the new capital of the Tokugawa shogunate, earlier Kamakura-era and Muromachi-era Neo-Confucianism in Japan moved from the realm of Zen monasteries to the wider political and social world of Japan, including the official academic education of the bakufu's administrators.

Tokugawa-era Neo-Confucian administrators like Arai Hakuseki, a leading mediator of Japan's reception of Chinese political and ethical thought in the early 1700s, was a product of that late Ming-era Japanese naturalization of Neo-Confucianism in Japanese politics and society. Hakuseki was most famous for his interest in Dutch medicine, and his later successor Sugita Genpaku in the 1800s witnessed the proliferation of Dutch learning throughout Japan in the lead-up to its turn away from China and emulation of British industrialization. In the Sinocentric world of Northeast Asia where they lived, however, neither Hakuseki nor Genpaku could predict that the Dutch learning they cultivated would radically contest Chinese cultural currency by the end of the Edo era. It was a contest of cultures in the 1800s with an outcome that overturned the primacy of China dating back to the Ming's zealous diplomatic efforts to center China in the politics and cultures of Asia. In the five centuries since the start of the European Age of Exploration, European military technology had advanced to such a degree that it induced a sense of urgency among late Qing-era and Edo-era Chinese and Japanese reformers shocked by the European transition from mostly careful diplomacy in the 1400s to the diplomacy of gunboat coercion in their dealings with Northeast Asian powers in the 1800s. The once mighty Ming-era Chinese naval force that was powerful enough to dictate Dutch settlement patterns around seventeenth-century Taiwan was, in the late Qing era, scrambling to contain British plans in Chinese ports following the nineteenth-century Opium Wars. By the end of the century, both Qing-era and Edo-era Chinese and Japanese reformers planned ways of reorganizing their respective lands along European political, intellectual, and social models. The degree that Chinese cultural currency was contested in Northeast Asia was unprecedented and even surprising against the backdrop of a half millennium of Chinese cultural transfer westward to Europe. That turn bookmarked the end of a half millennium of China's role in shaping the modern world, but in the words of early twentieth-century Chinese administrators themselves, the eclipse of China was not the end of the Middle Kingdom, and like the industrialized Japanese Empire, an industrialized China was on the horizon.

What follows in the next chapters is a closer look at the stories and accounts of the people who traveled to China and its frontiers following the rise of the Ming and the transition to the Qing (1644–1912), and how they became conduits of Chinese cultural transfer around the world. From Samarkand and Melaka to Macau and Manila, all of the cities where Asian and European merchants set out to engage with China through commerce and diplomacy became transit points for the transfer of objects and images from China to the rest of the modern world.

CHAPTER 3

Picturing China in Persian along the Silk Routes

Ming China left an extraordinary visual legacy across Central Asia and the Middle East. From the manufacture of porcelain ceramics in Syria to the ubiquitous blue-and-white tilework in Turkey's mosques, and likewise from the decorative peonies embroidered in Afghanistan's textiles to the jade in Uzbekistan's and Iran's jewelry, China's impact on the visual landscape of Central Asia and the modern Middle East exhibits both breadth and depth. This impact had ancient origins and was an outcome of exchange along the old silk and spice routes connecting Baghdad with Xian and Quanzhou. But in the days of the Ming, this exchange was mediated by merchants active in several new states: the Mamluk sultanate of Cairo and the Levant, the Ottomans of Anatolia, and most importantly, Tamerlane's Timurid Empire based in Samarkand, Bukhara, and Herat. Like the Ming in China, the Timurids emerged in the 1300s from the ruins of the crumbling Mongol states.

With domains stretching from present-day Syria to Kyrgyzstan near China's western frontiers, the Timurids governed much of Central Asia and the Middle East in the 1300s and left an enormous cultural legacy in the Ottoman Empire. In the realm of visual and material culture, the key to that legacy was its Chinese connection. The series of embassies that were exchanged between the Ming and the Timurid Empire became the basis of a profound shift in the visual aesthetics of cities like Istanbul and Cairo.

Royals and artisans acquired a new variety of Chinese objects that included the ubiquitous blue-and-white porcelains that dominated European popular culture during the Age of Exploration.

Two of the famous travel accounts about Ming China were an outcome of these embassies: Ghayath al-Din Naqqash's (d. 1447) account as an artist and envoy of the Timurids (Samarkand) to Beijing, and Ali Akbar Khitayi's (d. after 1516) account of his trip to Beijing that he published upon his return to Ottoman Istanbul. Taken together, their accounts shed light on enduring channels of cultural transfer and convergence connecting Ming China with Central Asia and the Middle East on the eve of the Age of Exploration. Among the most interesting phenomena they recount is the story of Muslims who played a prominent role in the Ming administration as well as the story of the Middle East's porcelain-oriented ceramics revolution that occurred just prior to Europe's mass production of fine "china." Their stories, which survive in Persian and Ottoman Turkish, form the basis of this chapter's look at the aesthetic impact of the Ming on its Central Asian and Middle Eastern neighbors beyond the Great Wall.

GHAYATH AL-DIN NAQQASH ON CHINA'S FRONTIERS
AND IMPERIAL MUSLIM GO-BETWEENS

Two of the most famous Persian- and Turkish-language travel accounts in China come from the era of Ming diplomacy with the Timurid khanate. Ghayath al-Din Naqqash (fl. 1419–1422), based in Herat (present-day Afghanistan), was a Timurid envoy under Mirza Shahrukh (fl. 1407–1447).[1] Naqqash arrived in Beijing via Samarkand during the reign of the Yongle Emperor (fl. 1402–1424), some one hundred years before Matteo Ricci arrived via Macau. Naqqash's surviving account offers an example of a Central Asian traveler witnessing and marveling at Ming Chinese visual and material culture. His widely transmitted account illustrates how travel narratives transferred the representations and imaginations of China throughout Central Asia and the Middle East long after the post-Mongol decline of the overland silk routes. In his writings, Naqqash makes frequent reference to silk objects in the imperial court at a time when Chinese designs—from peonies to phoenixes and lotuses—were becoming a central part of the language of Timurid and Ottoman textiles and ceramics.[2] The account of a later traveler writing in Istanbul, Ali Akbar Khitayi (ca. 1500–1516), likewise captures a key aspect of this expanding Middle Eastern and Central Asian imagination of Chinese material culture. While Naqqash's account reflects a keen interest in objects like silk, Ali Akbar Khitayi's later account describes the technology of Chinese gunpowder and porcelain production.[3] Ali Akbar was a merchant who completed his travel account in 1516 in Istanbul. His account was enshrined in the timeless legacy of a later writer, the Ottoman chronicler and geographer Kâtib Çelebi, who incorporated Ali Akbar's account into his widely read Ottoman Turkish works.[4] Both Naqqash's and Ali Akbar's writings indicate that commerce and exchange was still afoot across the old silk routes despite the collapse of the Mongols and despite some of the limits the Ming imposed on private nongovernment-sponsored trade.

The narrative these texts overturn is one that has been widely held in the study of world history—namely, that with the end of Mongol rule in centers like Iran and China, the overland silk routes collapsed and China entered into a period of isolation. Europe, according to this narrative, embarked on an Age of Exploration that was driven by privatized innovation and that ushered in ex nihilo the industrial era. In reality, China never entered into a period of isolation during the Ming, and the transfer of objects and innovations across the old silk and spice routes in many ways accelerated in the lead-up to the Age of Exploration. From the Persian- and Turkish-language perspectives offered in these texts, the Ming period did not represent the transitional period between a global Yuan state to a closed Qing state, but rather the crystallization of China's first modern global era

The Exchange of Embassies on the Eve of Naqqash's Trip to Beijing

In the years leading up to Naqqash's trip, there were several Chinese embassies that arrived in Samarkand and Herat.[5] Echoing patterns of Yuan diplomacy with the Ilkhanids, the Ming embassy that arrived in 1417 brought a variety of precious objects to the Central Asian capitals: silks, brocades, falcons, and even embroidered paper. Naqqash's account documents a particular delegation he joined in 1417. It was a delegation that reciprocated a Ming-commissioned one that arrived from China earlier that year. In a reflection of the importance of Naqqash's delegation, several major Timurid politicians sent emissaries to join the trip from Samarkand to Beijing. These politicians include Ghayath al-Din Baysongor, the governor of Herat after 1417 and the younger brother of Timurid khan and astronomer Ulugh Beg.[6] Baysongor's legacy as a major patron of Tabriz-based artists fit the profile of a dignitary interested in the westward transfer of Chinese precious objects.[7] Ibrahim Sultan, another son of Shahrukh who sent an emissary, was the governor of much of Fars from 1415 to 1423. Like Baysongor, he was a patron of calligraphy and other visual arts, even earning a reputation as a calligrapher himself.[8] Amir Shah Malik, a third influential political figure interested in the delegation, was the guardian and tutor of Ulugh Beg, the governor of Samarkand renowned among later Ottoman and Safavid rulers for his polymathic activity as a prolific astronomer and mathematician.

Collectively, the profiles of the Timurid politicians involved in the delegation—administrators with polymathic interests in astronomy, the visual arts, and broader scientific learning—foreshadowed the similar profile of figures like Jesuit scholar-diplomat Matteo Ricci, who likewise developed a keen interest in China and ultimately worked in Beijing. Naqqash, an artist himself, was in like-minded company. According to his narrative, the route that Naqqash traveled from Timurid Herat to Ming Beijing crossed through key centers of earlier Turco-Mongol polities. Beginning in Herat, Naqqash traveled to Samarkand, Turpan, Qomul (Hamil, present-day Hami), and eventually Beijing.[9] After crossing Qomul (Hamil) and the Great Wall, where his embassy was received by a Chinese delegation, Naqqash finally reached Beijing and entered the Ming court.[10]

Mawlana Yusuf and the Legacy of Muslim Administrators in Ming Service

Naqqash tells us that upon entering the palace in Beijing, he was struck by the court's grandeur and the size of the emperor's entourage. The Central Asian delegation was welcomed and asked to deliver official letters from various Timurid rulers, including Baysongor—that is, the brother of Ulugh Beg and patron of Herat's fifteenth-century architectural and artistic revival. According to familiar diplomatic protocols, the Timurid delegation was only permitted to deliver the letter to a courtier of the Yongle Emperor, who would in turn submit it to the emperor himself. Interestingly, that courtier was a Muslim whom Naqqash identifies as a certain multilingual administrator named Mawlana Yusuf Qazi.

> Mawlana Yusuf Qazi, who was one of the officers associated with the [Ming] Khan and held one of the twelve posts of imperial minister, and who knew Arabic, Persian, Turkish, Mongolian, and Chinese, came before the emissaries with several other Muslims who spoke our language and said to them, "First bend down and then touch your foreheads to the

ground three times." The emissaries bowed their heads but did not touch their foreheads to the ground . . . the aforementioned Mawlana Yusuf took the letters from them and handed them to the chamberlain . . . then the emperor came down from his throne and took the letters. Three thousand robes were brought, one thousand short-sleeved garments (*dagala*) and two thousand tunics. The emperor . . . had robes of honor placed on the embassy.[11]

Before inviting the delegation to a feast, the emperor asked about Qara Yusuf, the ruler of the Qaraqoyunlu dynasty of eastern Anatolia who was captured by the Ottomans a few years later. The Yongle Emperor wondered whether Qara Yusuf would be sending an emissary and tribute. The question, and the encounter more broadly, is remarkable yet unsurprising. The allusion to past embassies from eastern Anatolia points to something known in the Ming annals—namely, that the Ming were as active in diplomatic exchange along the Central Asian frontiers as they were across Southeast Asia and Northeast Asia. From Naqqash's account, the Ming were clearly active enough to have built a relationship with individual Turkish ruling circles who were subsumed into Ottoman dominion in the 1400s. Mawlana Yusuf's profile as a Muslim in Ming service is likewise both remarkable and unsurprising. It parallels the legacy of his more famous contemporary Zheng He and his many Yunnanese Muslim predecessors in Ming and early Yuan service.

As the narrative continues, Naqqash offers a closer look at some of the imperial court's visual dimensions, including the omnipresence of silk. Naqqash's analysis foreshadows Magellan's and his Venetian crewmate Pigafetta's observation of silk in the Philippines a century later and their realization that they were in the environs of China. In both cases, their observations illustrate the association of China with innovations in design, manufacturing, and material culture.

Narrating Chinoiserie: Naqqash's Observation of Silk

Naqqash's references to yellow cloths and silks are notable in that they appear throughout the text. One of the first references appears when Mawlana Yusuf delivers Naqqash's letters to the Yongle Emperor.

Then they [the Timurid emissaries] took the letters from His Majesty Shahrukh and His Highness Baysongor and the other princes and amirs [of Timurid Iran], which were wrapped in yellow silk as had been indicated by the emperor's servants—it is the custom of the Chinese to wrap anything that pertains to the emperor in yellow silk.

On the one hand, Naqqash's observation of yellow silk is as expected as his account of the Ming's awareness of individual Turkish rulers. In the longue durée of Chinese history, yellow silk was a widely known aspect of imperial royal symbolism and became a central part of the Southeast Asian sultanates' sacred and royal visual culture. On the other hand, Naqqash pays so much attention to yellow silk throughout the text that there was clearly something remarkable enough about it to catch his attention. When the Timurid letters are delivered to the Yongle Emperor, for example, Naqqash tells us that they are fitted in yellow silk (*parcha-yi atlas-i zurd*).[12] When the embassy first witnesses the emperor's throne and his entourage in the story, Naqqash describes the throne as a triangular platform (*takht-i musallas*) of yellow silk (*atlas-i zurd*) covered with "Cathayan"—that is, Chinese—motifs (*nuqush-i khatayi*) of dragons (*azhd*) and mythical birds (*simurgh*).[13] When the emperor himself appears and everyone falls silent, above the emperor hangs a canopy-like curtain or bower (*sayban*) of yellow silk (*atlas-i zurd*) with four dragons (*azhd*) on it.[14] When the food of the emperor is prepared between seven parasols during the feast, the enclosed area is enclosed with yellow silk.[15] When the emperor issues an edict, it is wrapped in gold (*dar zir girifta*) and tied with a yellow silk cord (*tanab-i abrishami-yi zurd*) together with a ring (*halqa*) and sealed in gold.[16] Later in the narrative, the emissaries discover they have run afoul of the emperor because the horse sent by Shahrukh throws the emperor during a hunting episode. When Mawlana Yusuf then takes them to an enclosure to meet the emperor, the canopies surrounding it are covered in gold brocade and yellow silks.

What explains Naqqash's marked interest in gold and yellow silks with Chinese motifs of dragons and mythical birds? The answer is that during the Ming era, in continuity with the earlier Yuan era, Central Asian sovereigns were in the process of assimilating specific aspects of Chinese design and material culture into their own royal and popular visual vocabulary. Part of what propelled this transfer was the presence of Chinese artisans who were resident in Timurid domains. The Timurid capitals of Maraga and Tabriz had resident Chinese artists in addition to Chinese objects such as ceramics, drawing primers, scroll paintings, and textiles. In this context,

Naqqash's observations offer a textual representation of that cultural transfer as it occurred in real time during this exchange of embassies. And his familiarity with the objects he described, especially yellow silk, fits into a larger familiarity Central Asians in cities like Samarkand had with Chinese objects dating back to the previous Mongol-dominated century.

During the earlier Yuan period, silk was a symbol of imperial authority that was used for tribute, diplomatic gifts, objects of Confucian ritual, ceremonies of imperial investiture, and even currency.[17] The use of silks woven with gold thread (*nashi*) on clothing, tents, and wagon coverings was particularly popular among the Mongols. In the Ming period, yellow silks were used in imperial palaces in continuity with earlier Yuan and Song practices. Ming robes excavated in the late twentieth-century include several so-called "dragon robes," which were yellow silk robes with dragon designs embroidered into a fitted upper garment connected with loose sleeves and a pleated skirt.[18] The bower Naqqash sees, made of yellow silk with four dragons on it, offers parallels to this design. The use of yellow silk textiles to house royal texts also offers parallels with practices popular during the Yuan era. Tibetan Buddhist texts, for example, are preserved and wrapped in yellow silk. The Samantabhadra thangka is covered with yellow silk on the back, which points to its origin in the imperial palace.[19]

Naqqash's interest both in Chinese silks and the designs embroidered on them matched the changing artistic trends of Timurid cities in the 1300s. By the time Naqqash wrote, Timurid ceramics already began to integrate the typically Chinese motifs of peonies, dragons, and scroll patterns into older Middle Eastern arabesque patterns. Timurid textiles likewise saw increased use of Chinese floral and cloud designs alongside older Arabic and Greco-Arabic floral motifs. What survives of Timurid textiles of silk and silk brocade, for example, shows this blend of Chinese and Arabic influences. In parallel with Ming Chinese ceremonial customs, these designs are particularly obvious in surviving paintings of canopies, royal parasols, and tents that the Timurid khans used to address and entertain outdoor audiences. This Timurid Chinoiserie was adapted further by the Ottomans, whose Iznik wares and tiles drew originally on early blue-and-white examples of the kind that decorate the Blue Mosque.

Naqqash, in sum, was both the product of the Yuan and early Ming-era cultural transfer that preceded him and an agent of this cultural transfer as he returned to Timurid Samarkand and Herat with objects and stories of what he encountered in Beijing. In the parallel example of Ali Akbar Khitayi almost one hundred years later (ca. 1500s), this Timurid imagination of China finds a counterpart in a new Ottoman-era picture of Chinese porcelain production and a broader picture of China's place in the world. Ali Akbar describes China as a global power with borders stretching deep into the South China Sea and Indian Ocean, and he represents Beijing as its bustling center.

ALI AKBAR KHITAYI ON BEIJING AS A COMMERCIAL ENTREPÔT AND CHINA'S GLOBAL BORDERS

By 1515, in an era when Timurid intellectuals and merchants were moving westward to Ottoman capitals, a Persian-language writer named Ali Akbar Khitayi was residing in Istanbul writing an account of his trip to China. Ali Akbar Khitayi completed his work the following year in 1516, some ninety-seven years after Naqqash set out for China from Herat and Samarkand. What is notable about Ali Akbar's account is how closely it echoes and further develops Naqqash's picture of Ming China—namely, as a state that was culturally global with commercial connections across all of its frontiers. Ali Akbar's account is extensive, but what is of particular interest is his analysis of China's rare manufacturing commodities as well as the overland and maritime trade routes where those commodities were sold.

Ali Akbar begins his account by explaining that there are three routes from Timurid lands to China: Kashmir, Khotan, and the land of the Mongols. The third, he explains, is the route through the Chaghatai khanate, which he describes as the safest and the one he chooses.[20] From Ali Akbar's very first observations about the watchmen who patrol the routes to the Chinese capital, the reader learns that one of his chief interests is in Chinese material culture. In the context of security along these routes, Ali Akbar observes the use of smoke signals among watchmen to communicate information to the capital with impressive speed. He notes the widespread use of a new technology among these watchmen: handheld firearms (*tufang*).[21] Ali Akbar was not fascinated by the mere existence of this technology as though he had never seen it before. Indeed, by the early 1500s when Ali Akbar was writing, the Portuguese were already employing it and encountered its local use in the Malay world. The Ottomans likewise were equipped with it and used it against the Mamluks. What Ali Akbar was impressed by specifically was how adept the entire Ming armed forces were in the use of these arms, from the corps of Ming soldiers to individual watchmen.[22] He was likewise impressed by the Ming's use of cannons. China was historically the first power to use cannons in armed conflicts. Cannons were stationed on the Great Wall, and Ali Akbar describes how he saw them along the wall as part of China's impressive military defense. In a comment that foreshadows the Qing's expansion beyond the Ming's frontiers, he notes that the Qalmaqs were generally fearful of Chinese arms.

As Ali Akbar moves further into his discussion, he turns his attention to Chinese trade in a way that answers a historical question about Ming isolationism on the eve of the Age of Exploration. As post-Mongol (Yuan) Beijing became the center of a geographically smaller state under the Great Ming, one that finalized the inland Great Wall in its current form and that intermittently instituted isolationist bans on private trade along the coast, was China a closed country upon the arrival of European powers in the 1500s or did it remain a bustling center of global commerce as it was during the earlier Mongol (Yuan) era? Ali Akbar's writing points to the latter picture.

Ming China: Isolationist Country or Bustling Center of Frontier Commerce?

In contrast with the modern picture of an isolated Ming-era China that placed heavy restrictions on private trade, the picture of Ming China in Ali Akbar's account is the image of a bustling entrepôt where everything from Venetian scarlet and diamonds to woolen cloth and jade were traded. Ali Akbar explains how nomadic groups and the world's most enterprising Asian empires brought their precious objects as tribute to China, returning with rare items manufactured in China. This image fits what historians know about private exchange during the Ming era, which economic historians frequently overlook. While the Ming famously restricted private trade, these restrictions were counterbalanced by frequent legal exceptions, the continuous growth of official government-sponsored trade, and a bustling private smuggling culture that operated with government knowledge. Connected with this picture of Chinese trade is Ali Akbar's representation of the borders of Ming China. He explains how they extended into Korea in the Northwest and Sumatra in the Southeast. This picture is historically accurate if one thinks of borders in terms of commercial boundaries, spheres of influence, and political vassalage or clientage. What follows is a closer look at both sides of Ali Akbar's representation of China.

Ali Akbar represents Beijing as a bustling entrepôt of global tributary commerce in a concise summary of the city's commercial situation. He explains that foreigners bring diamonds, woolen cloth, Venetian scarlet, jade, coral, snow leopards, lions, lynxes, and horses, which the Chinese offer to soldiers on the frontier.[23] From the Qalmaqs, the Chinese receive sable fur skins and furless skins native to the steppe as well as ponies and tigers.[24] What Ali Akbar describes merchants receiving in exchange for one lion offers a window into the content of return shipments: three boxes each containing a thousand pieces of satins, velvet, iron stirrups, gold brocade, and sometimes scissors, knives, and needles. A merchant receives fifteen similar boxes in the case of a snow leopard, lynx, or horse. Each merchant also receives eight pieces of clothing and an additional three robes of different colors to provide for two people. They also receive boots and other objects, all of which are lower than the regular selling price. The image of Beijing, in other words, is that of a busy center of exchange where precious local commodities are exported for tributary gifts coming from as far away as Venice. Interestingly, what Ali Akbar identifies as a local commodity depends on how he identifies China's borders, which he surprisingly identifies as inclusive of what were then the politically independent regions of Khotan, Korea, and Sumatra.

Chinese Material Culture as a Set of Visual Cues Illustrating China's Global Borders
Ali Akbar offers a surprisingly accurate geographical picture of the Ming as a politically global dynasty. At a time when Central Asian and Middle Eastern cartographers were still learning the exact contours of China's coastline from the Sea of Japan to the South China Sea, Ming China was a state with twelve districts, stretching from Khotan in the west to Korea (Shilla) in the north and Sumatra in the south.[25] In this section on the provinces of China, the material culture of each province offers the reader a variety of visual cues that include jade, silk, ceramics, and porcelain.

One of the first districts Ali Akbar discusses is Khotan, which he describes as a land of jade.[26] Interestingly, Khotan was never actually subsumed into Ming dominion, only becoming part of Beijing-led rule much later under the Qing. Ali Akbar is aware of this and indicates that Khotan is not quite a province of China but pays homage to Beijing. Ali Akbar more specifically describes Khotan as a kind of frontier or crossroads separating China from Muslim-held regions, specifically identifying it as the province furthest west of China and the region furthest east in "Islam." Khotan, in other words, is the furthest east of the Muslim-governed lands of Central Asia. Jade is Khotan's principal commodity, he writes. Nothing is more expensive than jade, he explains, which is found in two rivers southeast of the city. The Aqqash River produces white jade, while the Qara River produces green and black jade. Pieces of jade are scattered throughout the two rivers across a distance of a ten-day walk. Large pieces go to the state, while smaller pieces move through the channels of private trade.[27]

Ali Akbar's characterization of Khotan as a political and cultural crossroads, together with his analysis of jade as the region's most valuable commodity, is significant in the historical context of Ming exchange because it aligns perfectly with what we know about jade during his lifetime. Sixteenth-century Ming China saw a robust movement of jade westward to cities like Samarkand and Bukhara, and with that movement came the further transfer of Chinese designs and symbols into Central Asian and Middle Eastern Islamic visual cultures. The first example of Central Asian jade lapidaries working on an original jade decorative structure is only recorded at the end of the reign of Timur's grandson Ulugh Beg, the brother of Naqqash's patron Baysongor. Two pieces of jade were imported and used in Samarkand to construct Ulugh Beg's tomb in 1425.[28] Whether jade objects were imported or created locally, designs and motifs commonly evoked the way they were used for imperial purposes in both Khotan and China. In an example of how this cultural transfer proceeded from Central Asia in the Ottoman-era Middle East, the Timurids sent gifts of turquoise and jade to Egypt's Mamluk sultanate, which was in turn absorbed into Ottoman dominion at the start of the 1500s. Timurid gifts were one of the central vehicles for the transfer of jade from China to the Ottomans. Against this backdrop, Ali Akbar's interest in jade, like his deep knowledge of its history and origins, offers a window into the taste and expectations of a typical Ottoman-era merchant active across the markets of the Ming-era silk routes.

Beyond Khotan and its jade, Ali Akbar turns to Korea and Sumatra in an advanced illustration of his familiarity with China's Northeast Asian and Southeast Asian frontiers. Along the northeastern borders, Ali Akbar explains, is Korea (Shilla).[29] There, the imperial treasury gives its soldiers, and likewise the Mongols and foreign Buddhists, thousands of pieces of unbleached silk. He even notes his awareness of Islam in Korea. Among the Koreans, he explains, the Muslims are the least in number but the most honored and well respected. Foreign envoys from Korea receive thousands of pieces of silk that are fashioned into kimonos. In an interesting reference to Japan, he explains furthermore that the Buddhists of the "eastern sun" all wear kimonos. His familiarity with Japan was likely an outcome of the extensive connections Middle Eastern merchants had with the ports of Southeast Asia, especially the ports of Thailand, where Persian-language writers noted encountering Japanese merchants during the pre-Tokugawa Ashikaga era.

Further south along the road to Southeast Asia, Ali Akbar discusses Yunnan as a place of pearls, rubies, turquoise, and other precious stones that are well priced. Beyond Yunnan in Southeast Asia is China's furthest province: Sumatra.[30] The fact that Ali Akbar identifies Sumatra as part of China comes likely from his sense of Indian Ocean geography and from his identification of tributary vassalage with Ming sovereignty. His conception of the area's geography appears to fuse the two sides of the Malay Straits— that is, northern Sumatra and the Malay peninsula—in way that explains how Yunnan pours into Sumatra. Ali Akbar notes that all ships coming from Jeddah and other ports pass through Sumatra on the way to China. In his description of Sumatra, Ali Akbar indicates that the things the Sumatrans bring to China are exactly those of Hind (northern India)—namely, sugar, spices, textiles, and rubies. These are then taken to Beijing, and from there the markets of China. China, in other words, is incredibly vast in Ali Akbar's eyes in terms of the expanse of its frontiers stretching from the borders of Khotan in the interior to the outskirts of Yunnan in the south. From Sumatra, Ali Akbar takes the representation of China's borders to its final destination: Fujian, the heart of Europe's encounter with the Chinese mainland decades after Ali Akbar's return to Istanbul and the long-term settlement of European mariners in the region. The description of Fujian is where his narrative takes the most interesting turn in how it anticipates the same interest in porcelain production shown by later European observers.

Porcelain in the Southeast Asian Gateway to China

Like the European merchants who arrived in China after him, Ali Akbar takes a particular interest in porcelain and its manufacturing process in Fujian.[31] Ali Akbar describes specifically how porcelain is taken from a white opaque rock that is pulverized and put through a sieve. One then soaks this powder in hollow basins in blocks of stone, kneading it with sticks like a launderer. The paste is then put in a second basin, still kneading, and then a third basin, where it is dried, and then again kneaded with hands and feet to form complete porcelain-made objects. Pieces produced in the winter are eventually decorated with winter themes, while those of the summer incorporate summer themes. They are then placed in a giant cast iron oven. When they are purchased, buyers must pay before examining a box of porcelain and must take their chances when it comes to the ratio of perfect and flawed pieces. Ali Akbar points additionally to three distinguishing characteristics of porcelain: it has a natural filtering property that detects poison by changing color or shattering, it does not age or wear, and it cannot be scratched.

Why does Ming porcelain inspire so much of Ali Akbar's interest given that indigenous Ottoman, Timurid, and earlier Abbasid traditions of emulating porcelain through slipware existed as early as the Tang and Song dynasties? The answer is connected to how this enduring Middle Eastern tradition of emulating Chinese porcelain, which continued well into the late Ottoman and Safavid eras, never eclipsed interest in original Chinese-made porcelain pieces. What made original Chinese porcelain a high-priced and rare commodity was not only the fact that the manufacturing process remained a secret until the industrial era, but also that Ming-era trade restrictions limited the amount of jade and porcelain that could be exported outside the contexts of diplomatic gift exchange and tributary exchange. The result was a culture of Middle Eastern and Central Asian porcelain emulation that, for centuries into the Ming and Qing eras, continued to draw on Chinese models but that coexisted with a tradition of collecting rare Chinese originals. In the Ming era, Chinese originals took on a specific form that came to dominate the global porcelain and pseudo-porcelain aesthetic: blue-and-whites. A brief look at these parallel traditions of emulating and collecting Chinese porcelain helps contextualize why Ali Akbar was so fascinated by porcelain despite his clear familiarity with it, and why Dutch merchants a century later were able to pass Iranian pseudo-porcelain blue-and-whites as genuine Chinese blue-and-whites on the Dutch import markets. In the centuries leading up to the Ming, a ceramic revolution took place across the Middle East and Central Asia that was an outcome of continuous exposure to Chinese porcelain. By the 1500s, this revolution took on its most enduring aesthetic in the form of the Ming-era blue-and-white palette that was the form of porcelain first encountered by European merchants. These merchants, in turn, became agents of Europe's own ceramics revolution in the lead-up to the proliferation of pseudo-porcelain blue-and-white

Delftware and Staffordshireware on the eve of the Industrial Revolution. A closer look at the story of Ming blue-and-whites offers a broader window into the visual dimensions of Ming China's impact on the modern world.

THE ISLAMIC WORLD'S PORCELAIN REVOLUTION AND THE GLOBAL RISE OF MING BLUE-AND-WHITES

The Ming period saw the start of a new convergence of Middle Eastern and European cultural histories that reflected the impact not of the older Roman, Abbasid, or Mongol Empires but rather the impact of China. It was during the Ming when an ancient Middle Eastern and Central Asian tradition of collecting and emulating Chinese porcelain began to intersect with a parallel modern European tradition. In other words, the Ming era connected two global ceramics revolutions that were an outcome of Chinese innovation: one Middle Eastern and the other European. What makes the first essential for understanding the second is how closely they resembled one another, and how they illustrate the way Europe during the Age of Exploration was in the process of becoming integrated into older forms of global exchange and innovation.

Following the Safavid dynasty's capture of Iran from the Timurids in the 1500s, Iran's local ceramics industry had become so sophisticated in the ability to emulate genuine porcelain that the Dutch East India Company's merchants began buying Iranian-made pseudo-porcelain wares from coastal Iran in the 1600s and passing them off as originals in European sales inventories. A century later, while the Dutch and their British rivals continued importing genuine porcelain as a luxury item, an industry of European-made varieties of pseudo-porcelain was in formation that would drive Europe's Industrial Revolution: Delftware in the Netherlands and Staffordshireware in England. Both industries became a formative part of the Industrial Revolution once advances in mass production and manufacturing allowed Europe to compete with and, eventually, eclipse Chinese porcelain production. That is, the European mass production of pseudo-porcelain became so sophisticated in its resemblance to genuine Chinese-made porcelain and its economical production costs that it began, in reverse, to flood Asia's ceramics import markets in the early 1900s together with European-made silk-like textiles with the help of new trade deals after the Opium Wars.

At the start of this story about the Middle East and Europe's shared Sinocentric aesthetic convergence is the story of a shift in ceramics design that occurred in the heartlands of early Islam—specifically in Baghdad and

Basra. That revolution saw eighth- and ninth-century local potters emulate Chinese porcelain coming from three sources: northern China's Xing kilns producing white wares, northern Zhejian's Yue kilns producing celadons, and Hunan province's Changsha kilns commonly producing polychrome wares. All three varieties of porcelain were present in the shipwrecked cargo of the Arab dhow ship discovered in 1998 that was on its way back from China. All three formed the early Islamic world's image of China.

This Tang-era Arab dhow ship, discovered off the coast of Belitung island in the Java Sea, had an intact cargo of some 70,000 pieces of ceramics from China, much of which now sits in Singapore's Asian Civilizations Museum.[32] The ship itself was a ninth-century Arab dhow vessel that was fifty-eight feet long and twenty-one feet wide, and its planks were tied together using coconut fiber. What the ship's cargo indicated was that in the 800s, Arab merchant vessels had begun to carry ceramics, mass-produced in China, through Southeast Asia for Middle Eastern and Central Asian markets. The ship's cargo illustrates that long before the notion of a household kitchen using porcelain and pseudo-porcelain came into practice in Europe, and long before elite households and palaces displayed shelves of fine china throughout the modern West, households in Iraq and Iran were already collecting fine Chinese porcelains for decoration and daily use back in the 700s and 800s.[33]

The reign of Harun al-Rashid (786–809) is one of the first literary references to the arrival of these white wares from China, coming as gifts to Baghdad from the governor of Khurasan around present-day Afghanistan and Iran. The inability to produce porcelain is what explains the proliferation of a native Iraq-based approach to using a white slip over earthenware. The ninth-century Tang shipwreck came from this period. By the twelfth century, local potters in Iraq, Iran, and Syria had perfected their pseudo-porcelain wares in what came to be known as fritware. They used a complex technique of blending a variety of ingredients, applying a white slip, firing at high temperatures, and adding an afterglaze with designs under the glaze that effectively evoked genuine Chinese porcelain. As early as the eighth and ninth centuries, local versions produced in Basra had become almost indistinguishable from Chinese originals.[34]

Against this backdrop, what was unique about the Ming period was how a particular aesthetic in porcelain and pseudo-porcelain manufacturing was about to go global, reaching as far as London and Amsterdam: simple blue-and-white porcelain, which became the dominant design of pseudo-porcelain ceramics in Dutch, British, and French palaces and households. Interestingly,

the emergence of Ming-era Chinese blue-and-whites was itself partly an outcome of a cultural transfer in reverse from the Middle East to China, and the
city where these cultures converged was the legendary center of Jingdezhen.

The Rise of Jingdezhen and the Global Proliferation of Blue-and-Whites in the Ming Era

The Ming-era acceleration of Jingdezhen's development as a center for blue-
and-white porcelain production has its origins in the early Mongol Yuan era.
In 1278, the Yuan dynasty set up a porcelain bureau to regulate the official
kiln in Jingdezhen. They assigned officials to regulate both the taxation of
private ceramics manufacturers and the quality of the clay and glazes intended
for official imperial use. The use of cobalt blue coming from Iraq and Iran
in Yuan-era Jingdezhen comes as no surprise, as the managers of the bureau
were a diverse group from the frontier and neighboring regions: Mongolians,
Nepalese, and various Muslims from Central Asia. By the end of the Yuan
period, just as Iraq and Iran inspired some of the shapes and designs of products made in Mongol-era China, so those products in turn went westward to
inspire Ilkhanid and later Timurid products in Iran. The city of Samarkand
as a major point of cultural transit between China and the Middle East during
the late Yuan and early Ming period illustrates the continuity of exchange
along the silk routes across the ancient, medieval, and early modern periods.

Upon the rise of the Ming, the new administration kept many of these
structures of production and commerce in place. China under the Yuan
was a global crossroads in continuity with the earlier Song and Tang eras,
and it remained so when the first Ming Emperor came to power (1368–1398).
The Hongwu emperor ordered the construction of an imperial factory in
Jingdezhen on Pearl Hill (Zhushan) close to the Yuan-era Porcelain Bureau.
The people who worked there included both skilled workers with multiyear
contracts and unskilled labor forces who worked in the firing process. Making ceramics required one of two types of clay: official imperial clay (guantu)
or the more popular clay that could be used for commercial purposes. The
former came from Macang Mountain until 1583, when Gaolin became the
new source. The workers there came from all around China and eventually
established guilds, determining everything from the specifications in size
and type of wares to salaries and workday hours. In this way, Jingdezhen
became a major commercial center, attracting groups of merchants from
places like Guangdong and Fujian.[35] The city, thus, became the center of

the local elite working in consumer and export production, with designs for foreign export eventually incorporating not only Middle Eastern, Southeast Asian, and Northeast Asian designs, but also Dutch designs ordered by the Dutch East India Company in the 1600s.

By the Ming period, in other words, the reception of Chinese ceramics and porcelains in Muslim centers in the Middle East and Central Asia was an established phenomenon dating back to pre-Ming centuries. What gave Chinese-made porcelains novelty during the Ming period, therefore, was the transfer of specifically blue-and-whites to Europe at a time when Middle Eastern forms of blue-and-white pseudo-porcelain were becoming almost indistinguishable from Chinese originals. It was against this backdrop that Iranian blue-and-whites were passed off as Chinese blue-and-whites on Dutch markets at a time when Europe was finally becoming integrated into the older ceramics revolutions of the silk and spice routes. Iran in the 1500s was under the rule of the Safavids (1501–1736), who captured most of present-day Iran and Afghanistan from the Timurids. The Safavids were the chief competitor of the Ottomans in the Middle East, and while the Ottomans developed their own blue-and-white Iznik ceramics inspired by Chinese and Timurid models, the Safavids developed a unique copy industry that fed the insatiable European taste for Chinese porcelain.

Ali Akbar's fascination with the actual process of creating ceramics in Southeast China, therefore, did not come from having never seen Chinese designs before. Rather, it came from the novelty emerging from the parallel existence of local Islamic Chinoiserie ceramics industries and the omnipresent collection of Chinese originals. It was this same coexistence of an emulation industry and culture of collecting originals that made European owners of Delftware and Staffordshireware in the 1800s avid collectors of rare Ming blue-and-whites. Whether at Ardabil or Topkapi, original Ming ceramics were not simply a sign of luxury, preciousness, or the sacred. They were also, among their buyers and consumers, a visual and material marker of one's elite familiarity with Ming China's rare commodities across centuries when elite households and palaces from the Middle East to Europe imagined China as a center of innovation and design. The inability of artisans around the world to replicate porcelain production outside of China and later Japan became the key dimension of porcelain's allure and mystery.

Naqqash and Ali Akbar's travel narratives, in sum, demonstrated a deep fascination with Ming China as a center of global commerce and culture, and the transmission of these narratives in Persian and Ottoman Turkish ensured that there would always be a textual and visual imagination of China that corresponded with the stories these Chinese objects told. Interestingly, their writings foreshadowed written Iberian representations of China as a center of innovation and design following the arrival of the Spaniards, Portuguese, and their Jesuit clients in Southeast Asia in the 1500s.

FIGURE 1.1.　The trade agreements that developed between Beijing and the West in the 1970s evoked those of the late 1800s, but the role of manufacturing exporter had been reversed. Back in the 1800s, the conclusion of the Opium Wars and the ratification of the Treaty of Nanking saw China become an importer of a variety of machine-made Western goods that were manufactured in the United States and the United Kingdom, especially textiles. The Treaty of Nanking also saw the establishment of British and American extraterritorial enclaves in Shanghai—that is, the Shanghai International Settlement (1863–1941) complete with Western tribunals. Thirty years after the enclave was officially closed, three successive US presidents—namely, Presidents Richard Nixon, Gerald Ford, and Jimmy Carter—laid the groundwork for a new era of political and economic relations with China. In this new era, China would become a new high-tech industrial manufacturer for Western import markets. This newer period of relations was developed through a series of diplomatic meetings with Chinese head of state Deng Xiaoping (center). Secretary of State Henry Kissinger (1973–1977), previously National Security Advisor (1969–1975), was one of the key architects of both the policy move and these meetings. Gerald Ford (left) and First Lady Betty Ford (right) traveled to Beijing in 1978 for a state visit, while British Prime Minister Margaret Thatcher visited in 1979. In the case of both the United States and the United Kingdom, one of the outcomes of these meetings was the controversial acceleration of Western deindustrialization and offshore labor outsourcing in accordance with economic theories in favor of globalization and an expanded services sector. Forty years later, as China has emerged as the world's foremost manufacturing power, the policies of that era have become the subject of heated debate among policymakers and economists alike. On the one hand, China's role is not unprecedented, as it evokes the days of Ming and Qing preindustrial manufacturing in the 1500s and 1600s. In those days, Western business networks imported Chinese textiles, tea, ceramics, and scent before learning to manufacture similar items themselves by machine in newly industrialized Europe. On the other hand, China's role is unprecedented in at least one key way: China's current iteration of manufacturing know-how, and specifically its high-tech machinery and growing use of robotics, has its origins in the intellectual transfer eastward that occurred in the 1970s and 1980s. A middle player that facilitated China's current rise was Japan, with its much older and longer history of industrialization dating back to the modern Japanese Empire.

Source: Gerald R. Ford Library/Wikimedia Commons. Public domain. https://commons .wikimedia.org/wiki/File:Gerald_and_Betty_Ford_meet_with_Deng_Xiaoping,_1975_ A7598-20A.jpg

FIGURE 1.2.   In the early 1800s, Chinese merchants like Wu Bingjian (English: Howqua) amassed an extraordinary amount of wealth in the import-export world of Guangzhou. The so-called Canton System restricted official import-export exchange with Western countries to the port of Guangzhou, where a Chinese *hong* was assigned to each of thirteen warehouses to facilitate trade. Wu Bingjian was the most powerful among them in the decades connecting the two Opium Wars. Restrictions on trade with the West were significantly loosened in the aftermath of the Second Opium War, when whole districts of Chinese coastal cities came under international control. The Treaty of Nanking, ratified in the aftermath of the Opium Wars, gave the British and other Western powers extraterritorial settlement and legal privileges in port cities like Shanghai. The seaside district known as the Bund, for example, once included a quarter for Westerners that was established in 1845 and that remained in place in different forms as late as 1941. Western control over this quarter came to an abrupt end at the height of the Japanese Empire's conflict with the United States during World War II and in the final years of the Chinese civil war. Shanghai's more recent connections with Western residents is connected with the rise of modern Shanghai since the 1970s as a center of Chinese technology, telecommunications, and manufacturing.

Source: The Metropolitan Museum of Art. Public domain. https://www.metmuseum.org/art/collection/search/10478

FIGURE 1.3.   Since the transformation of its economy in the 1970s and the establishment of trade partnerships with the Americas and the European Union, China has emerged as the leading manufacturer of exports like electric vehicles. Bogotá, Colombia (above), is the world's largest importer of electric vehicles that are used for public transit. The same company that makes these vehicles, BYD, also produces mass transit vehicles in industrialized cities like Stockholm. Neighboring Southeast Asia has likewise become a global exporter of electronics since the 1970s and, like China, is the center of innovation in industries like biotechnology and renewable energy. Since the 2000s, these industries have begun to catch up with their counterparts in Japan and the West, leaving some entrepreneurs in the United States looking eastward for cues in innovation. Taken together, the rise of China, the so-called Four Asian Tigers (Singapore, South Korea, Taiwan, Hong Kong), and the "tiger cub" economies (Malaysia, Indonesia, Philippines, Thailand, Vietnam) have renewed popular interest in understanding the global economy from an Asia-centered perspective. From the perspective of global history, Western trade and security agreements with the ASEAN members states in many ways evoke an earlier era of European negotiations with the kingdoms and sultanates of Southeast Asia during the heyday of the Age of Exploration.

Source: BYD Colombia/Wikimedia Commons. https://commons.wikimedia.org/wiki/File: Autobuses_el%C3%A9ctricos_BYD_en_Bogot%C3%A1.jpg. Creative Commons (CC BY-SA 2.5)

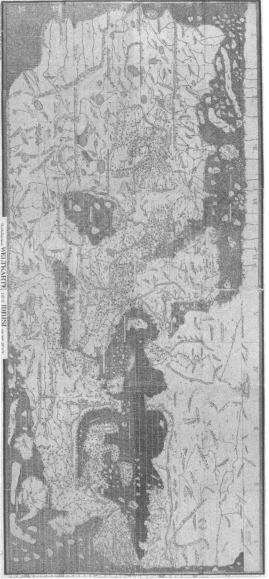

FIGURE 2.1. The world, as European and Chinese cartographers knew it in the 1400s, was still imagined the way Middle Eastern cartographers had mapped it back in the 1100s: the eastern Atlantic coast, the Mediterranean Sea, and the Indian Ocean were the dominant maritime regions, making trade with China possible only via the overland silk routes and the maritime spice routes. In the lead-up to the Age of Exploration, few European merchants traveled directly to China, and those who did went overland through Central Asia. Venetian merchant Marco Polo traveled along the overland silk routes to Dadu (present-day Beijing), where he met Mongol Emperor Khubilai Khan in 1269. A representation of his trip appears in Majorcan cartographer Abraham Cresque's *Atlas català* (Catalan Atlas, 1375). There was a third route westward across the Atlantic, but it remained uncharted. The fact that the oceans furthest west and east were distinct—that is, the Atlantic and Pacific—likewise remained unknown, at least outside the Mesoamerican empires. The most advanced map of the twelfth century (above), Muhammad al-Idrisi's originally south-facing (flipped) *Tabula Rogeriana* (Map of Roger) of 1154 (above), became the basis of European maps used as late as the 1450s on the eve of the Age of Exploration. Venetian monk Fra Mauro's map was similar, but it attempted to represent visually the world's spherical dimensions in what amounted to a two-dimensional globe. Chinese, Korean, and Japanese maps were similarly based on Middle Eastern cartography, but they used much larger dimensions to represent China and the Indian Ocean. Although Middle Eastern merchants had extensive travel experience throughout Southeast Asia and the Chinese coast during the Tang era (ca. 618–907) and Song era (960–1279), Arabic-language cartography was still more accurate in its representation of the Mediterranean coastline than of the Indian Ocean and South China Sea. Later maps of the Age of Exploration represent Southeast Asia and the East Asian coastlines with much greater accuracy in accordance with the Jesuit-led synthesis that developed between European cartography and Chinese land surveys. Those Chinese surveys drew in part on some of the observations made by Yunnanese admiral Zheng He and his crewmate Ma Huan, Muslim mariners in Ming service, during their diplomatic expeditions in the 1400s across the ports of Southeast Asia, the Indian Ocean, East Africa, and the Middle East.

Source: Wikimedia Commons. Public domain. https://en.wikipedia.org/wiki/Tabula_Rogeriana

FIGURE 2.2.   Muslim Yunnanese admiral Zheng I Ie's expeditions saw the expansion of Ming-
era diplomacy and commerce throughout the South China Sea, Indian Ocean, and the Arabian
Sea. Southeast Asia, especially in the island of Java, saw a growth in families with Chinese
patriarchs and Javanese matriarchs. These families came to be known by a variety of terms
including, most recently, Peranakan, Baba-Nyonya, and Kiau-Seng. While most present-day
Peranakan families are not Muslim, historical evidence indicates that many of the earliest
families were Muslim and were absorbed into the expanding Chinese-influenced Muslim
cultures of early modern Southeast Asia. This photograph captures the wedding scene of a
couple from Penang: Chung Guat Hooi (left), the daughter of Kapitan Chung Thye Phin, and
Khoo Soo Beow (right), the son of Khoo Ieng Pan.

Sources: Lukacs/Wikimedia Commons. Public domain. https://en.wikipedia.org/wiki/
Peranakans

FIGURE 2.3.   Korea's Joseon dynasty (1392–1910), which succeeded the Goryeo, rose to power in the early Ming era and remained in place well into the 1900s. Like Japan's Tokugawa shoguns, the Joseon cultivated a close political and cultural connection with the Ming, absorbing China's Neo-Confucian political and social ethics as well its Chan (Japanese: Zen, Korean: Seon) Buddhism. King Yi Seonggae (Taejo), pictured above, came to power with the assistance of a Korean Confucian scholar who helped establish Korea's early modern institutions of governance. The scholar, named Jeong Dojeon (d. 1398), was a graduate of the Seonggyun-gwan, the highest institution of learning dedicated to Neo-Confucian scholar-officials working in Korean civil service. A key figure in the reform of Korean law and political ethics along Neo-Confucian lines, Jeong Dojeon wrote several seminal Neo-Confucian works in the early Joseon period that included *Joseon Kyeonguk Cheon* (Joseon's Codes for Governing the Country) and *Kyeongje Mungam* (Historical Mirror for Managing the World and Saving the People). These works, which were characteristic of Ming-Joseon relations, played a key role in popularizing the Confucian social ethics characteristic of Joseon Korea well into the twentieth century. In a notable sign of the older Mongol Yuan-era legacy of culture in the region, there were Muslims living in Korea at the time of King Taejo, while the Joseon's mapmaking tradition similarly drew on China's Sino-Islamic cartographical heritage. Today, after Korea's industrialization and the turn from Buddhist and Confucian traditions to Protestantism, the legacy of Confucianism looms large in debates about social reform.

Sources: Wikimedia Commons. Public domain. https://commons.wikimedia.org/wiki/ File:King_Taejo_Yi_02.jpg

FIGURE 3.1. The Hongwu Emperor (above) was the founding emperor of the Ming and played a key role in maintaining Beijing's connections with Central Asian and Middle Eastern states in the aftermath of the Mongols' political decline. He was also responsible for cultivating the career of Yunnanese Muslim admiral Zheng He in the 1400s. Together with his crewmate Ma Huan, also Muslim, Zheng He's expeditions to the sultanates of Southeast Asia took shape during the era of the Yongle Emperor, who received embassies from the Timurid khanate beyond the Great Wall. Central Asian traveler Ghayath al-Din Naqqash met the Yongle Emperor in Beijing's imperial district—the Forbidden City—during the Timurids' diplomatic exchange with the Ming. His observations of golden yellow silks and tapestries correspond with surviving representations of Ming emperors (above) and empresses, including Empress Xu. Gold also dominates the surviving color palette of various thrones in the Forbidden City, which were built during the Ming era. It was this same emperor who commissioned Yunnanese Muslim admiral Zheng He's expeditions to Southeast Asia and the Indian Ocean. Zheng He's legacy as a Muslim in Ming service echoed Naqqash's observation of polyglot Muslims working in diplomatic capacities at the court in Beijing. The interest of Central Asian, South, and Southeast Asian Muslim rulers in diplomatic exchange was represented in Ming-era paintings that depicted the reception of gifts in China from abroad. In one example, an illustrated Chinese manuscript represents the gift of an African giraffe from Malindi sent by the ruler of Bengal (Saif al-Din Hamzah Shah) to the Yongle Emperor. The gift was evocative of Mamluk Egypt's near contemporary gift of a giraffe to the menagerie of the Medicis in Florence. During this era, corresponding with Zheng He's travels throughout Southeast Asia and the Indian Ocean, giraffes came to be identified with the ancient Chinese mythological creatures known as Qilin. The cultures of the Ming's frontiers, in other words, were shaping China as much as the reverse.

Source: National Palace Museum/Wikimedia Commons. Public domain. https://commons
.wikimedia.org/wiki/File:A_Seated_Portrait_of_Ming_Emperor_Taizu.jpg

FIGURE 3.2.   Beijing's connections to Central Asia and Southeast Asia indicated that despite the Ming's turn to the seas, trade and diplomacy with Central Asian states was still central to Ming foreign policy. Still, Ming security concerns along the western frontiers motivated the construction of the Great Wall (above) in its present form. Almost all the wall's brick and stone in its current state dates back to the Ming era (1368–1644). Central travelers like Ali Akbar Khitayi were among the first writers to describe the Great Wall in languages like Persian, Turkish, and Arabic. Lands west of the wall became part of modern China during the Qing era.

Source: Walkerssk/Pixabay. Free for public use, no attribution required. https://pixabay.com/photos/the-chinese-wall-china-wall-in-china-2174275/

FIGURE 3.3. In the early Ming era, Central Asian Muslim travelers like Ghayath al-Din Naqqash had a deep interest in Chinese material culture, especially textiles and ceramics. The transfer westward of these objects through cities like Timurid-era Samarqand (1370–1507) had a tremendous impact on the material culture of the Ottomans after their capture of Istanbul (1453). The blue-and-white pseudo-porcelain Iznik ceramics that dominate the Blue Mosque's design in Istanbul draw on this influence. This transfer westward of Chinese porcelain dated back to the heyday of exchange between Abbasid Baghdad (est. 761) and China during the Tang and Song eras. The use of porcelain and pseudo-porcelain in the Middle East offered an aesthetically pleasing alternative to the use of precious metals, which was widely used in palaces for ewers and other wares. As early as the ninth and tenth centuries, almost a millennium before the development of pseudo-porcelain in Delft (Netherlands), artisans in Iraq learned to emulate genuine imported Chinese porcelain using a clay-based material and tin glaze. Iraqi potters mastered the art of emulating porcelain's luminous qualities using sophisticated firing and glazing techniques, even decorating pseudo-porcelain earthenware with minimalist ornamentation evocative of Chinese designs. The most famous example (above) dates to the ninth century, with an inscription that reads "happiness" (*ghibta*) in cobalt blue. The two-way movement of designs and ornamentation reached new heights in the Ming era, when Chinese artisans began to incorporate Arabic calligraphy into Jingdezhen-made porcelain. The most famous examples of Chinese porcelain with Arabic inscriptions date back to the reigns of the Yongle Emperor (1402–1424) and Zhengde Emperor (1502–1521) and were kept at the court in Beijing. It was during these periods when the Chinese emperors employed Muslims in the court and cultivated continued diplomatic relations across the silk and spice routes to the Middle East. One of the most famous examples has the word *purity* written in the center. Arabic inscriptions on other pieces included words like *prosperity* and *sweetness*. All Zhengde-era court pieces include the Chinese inscription "Crafted during the reign of the Zhengde Emperor of the Great Ming Dynasty." The best preserved examples can be seen in museums like the Metropolitan Museum of Art in New York and the National Palace Museum in Taipei.

FIGURE 4.1   In an illustration of Ming China's early connections with Southeast Asia's sultanates, the mausoleum of Bruneian Sultan Abdul Majid Hassan is located not in Brunei but Nanjing (above). During the Ming era, a variety of Muslim sultanates flourished in Southeast Asia in centers like Pasai (Sumatra), Melaka (Malay Peninsula), Banten (Java), Brunei (Borneo), and others. The rise of Muslim sultanates across islands of the former Srivijayan and Majapahit empires is shrouded in mystery. Southeast Asian Islam has long been seen as an outcome of cultural exchange with Muslim merchants from South Asia and the Middle East. Recent research demonstrates, however, that the oldest centers of Islam in Southeast Asia are connected with the arrival of Muslims from China. These Muslim arrivals include Muslims from the Yuan-era Chinese coast who fled the arrival of the Ming. Many Muslims still living in Ming China in the 1400s, including Zheng He and his crewmate Ma Huan, remained connected with military and administrative circles in continuity with their Yuan-era predecessors. This picture of Muslims working in Chinese imperial service in the 1300s and 1400s, together with the history of Chinese administrators and political exiles traveling to Southeast Asia, fits new evidence of Southeast Asian Islam having both Indian Ocean and Chinese origins. In accordance with this Chinese connection, it is unsurprising that the legacy of Zheng He's voyages looms large in oral histories of Islam throughout Southeast Asia. Palembang on the island of Sumatra, across the Melakan strait from the Malay peninsula and the city of Melaka, was one of the oldest centers of Islam in Southeast Asia and had an early commercial and diplomatic connection with the Ming. The city, like Melaka, is home to some of the oldest mosques in the region.

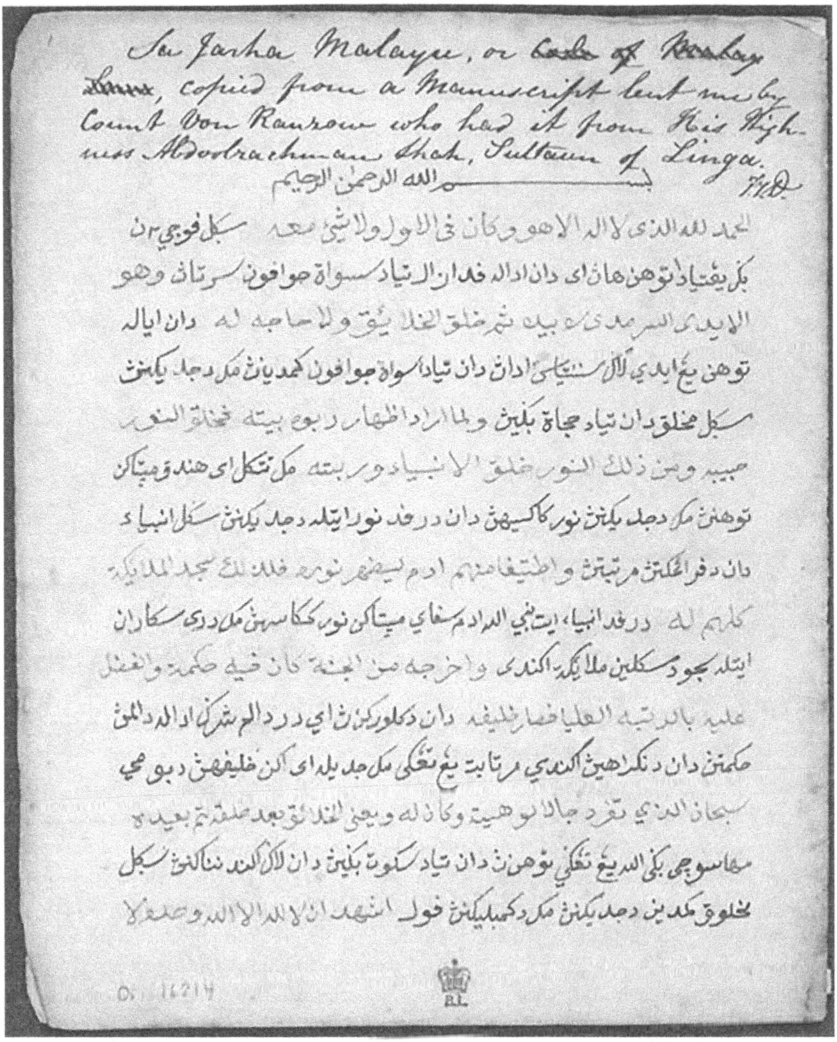

FIGURE 4.2. Like the *Undang-Undang Melaka* (above), one of the Sultanate of Melaka's early legal codes, the legend of Hang Tuah was written in Malay using a form of the Perso-Arabic script. Known as *jawi*, the script became the standard form of writing in Malay and various Southeast Asian languages by the fourteenth and fifteenth centuries. *Jawi*'s use in Malay replaced the earlier Brahmic Pallava script, which is related to the Telegu-Kannada alphabet of southern and coastal India. The Perso-Arabic script continued to be widely used in texts like biographies as late as the 1800s. By the end of the 1800s, the impact of British administration introduced the use of English as a language of learning, and by the 1900s, the Latin script was used for writing Malay. Many older Malay manuscripts were brought by British administrators to London. There, collectors built libraries of originals and copies and began to study the historical contents of the texts. Some of their notes in the margins can still be seen (above).

Source: British Library, Or.16214, f.1r. Public domain. https://blogs.bl.uk/asian-and-african/ 2013/11/two-malay-manuscripts-from-wales.html

FIGURE 4.3.   Like the courtly spaces of the Malay Peninsula, some of Southeast Asia's earliest mosques reflect the region's historical symbiosis of Sumatran, Javanese, and Chinese architectural and ornamentation styles. The mosque of Madura (above) features multitiered roofs and pavilions that are common architectural elements in Sumatra and Java. Its color palette features the bold yellow and gold colors common in Chinese architecture. Among the most famous mosques that feature this kind of cultural synthesis is Masjid Tengkera in Melaka. Its minaret, built in the form of a pagoda, evokes the use of a pagoda in Chinese mosques from Yunnan and Ningxia to Guangzhou. The memory of past connections between Islam in Southeast Asia and Islam in China are maintained in part through objects like the Cakra Donya bell, a gift of Zheng He to the sultan of Pasai that was passed over centuries through the hands of multiple administrations: the Sultanate of Pasai, the Sultanate of Aceh, the Dutch administration, and modern Indonesia where it remains in the Aceh Museum.

Source: astama81/Pixabay. Free for commercial use, no attribution required. https://pixabay.com/photos/masjid-architecture-mosque-madura-198176/

CHAPTER 4

Trading with China in Malay along the Spice Routes

W hen the Portuguese and Spaniards first arrived in the South China Sea, the commercial worlds they encountered in centers like Melaka and Manila were already deeply intertwined with the politics, economy, and cultures of Ming China. How did the Ming manage to build these connections on the eve of the Iberians' arrival, and what motivated the Iberians to look to the South China Sea in the first place given their profitable access to Middle Eastern and Italian middlemen?

The transformation of Southeast Asia into a global hub of transoceanic commerce has its origins in a series of developments that crystallized in the 1400s. It was at the end of this century when the European Age of Exploration took shape, and it was also in this century when the Ming embarked on their own set of maritime expeditions to build diplomatic relations throughout Southeast Asia. One of the most interesting windows into the convergence of these two developments is the writings of the Malays themselves. Their representations of China, including Chinese royal figures living in the Malay peninsula, blend with an early look at the Portuguese as pirate-like characters trying to insert themselves into local commerce. The picture these texts paint of Malay-Chinese connections illustrate why Southeast Asia became so central to European interests in Chinese commodities.

This Malay representation of a global Ming China comes from a set of fifteenth-century Malay-language epics that offer colorful narrative

47

representations of Chinese-Malay connections: specifically, the *Hikayat Raja Raja Pasai* (*Chronicle of the Kings of Pasai*) and its references to Chinese villages and martial arts teachers, the *Hikayat Hang Tuah* (*Chronicle of Hang Tuah*) and its tale of the warrior-ambassador Hang Tuah's diplomatic missions to coastal India and Beijing, and the *Sejarah Melayu* (*Malay Annals*) with its lively stories of Chinese-Malay marriages and diplomatic go-betweens. Despite their legendary semifictional orientation, all three epics represent Chinese-Malay connections in ways that match evidence in Chinese texts of the time, especially the writings of Zheng He's crewmates and the Ming annals.[1] A closer look at these texts illustrates just how deeply the sultanates of Southeast Asia became embedded within the political and commercial world of China on the eve of the Age of Exploration, when Southeast Asia became the global crossroads of the world's encounters with Ming and later Qing China.

HIKAYAT RAJA RAJA PASAI IN A CHINESE CONTEXT

Historical Context: Chinese Muslims in Sumatra

Hikayat Raja Raja Pasai (*Chronicle of the Kings of Pasai*) dates to the fourteenth century or earlier and is one of the oldest historical chronicles written in Malay. One of the two surviving manuscripts of the text, British Library Or. 14350, offers a glimpse into the interconnections between Ming China and the Malay peninsula from the sultanate's earliest years in the late 1300s. The manuscript is collated with and is preceded by a text known as the *Hikayat Raja Handik* (*Chronicle of the King of the Trench*). This second text relates the sacred story of the Battle of the Trench in early Islamic historiography. This latter text offers historians Malay-language evidence of how Muslim sacred history developed a growing Southeast Asian audience of various backgrounds.

Specifically, the start of the *Hikayat Raja Handik* shows that the text was addressed to a mixed audience of listeners and readers that included Malays, Makassarese of Sulawesian origin east of Borneo, and most significantly for the current study, Chinese listeners.[2] Why were Chinese among those addressed in a Malay-language story about early Islam? One answer emerges in the writings of Zheng He's crewmates, who noted the existence of Chinese Muslims on Sumatra and its northern port of Pasai. Ma Huan's travel account, *Ying-yai Sheng-Lan* (*The Overall Survey of the Ocean's Shores*), notes two interesting resident populations around the ports of Java, a geographical neighbor of Sumatra to the south. The first group of Muslims Ma Huan observed were Muslims of "western lands," meaning the Middle East and the Indian subcontinent. The second group of Muslims Ma Huan found were "Chinese" that included arrivals from "Canton, Quanzhou, and Quanzhou." Critically, Ma Huan indicates that many of the second group—that is, the Muslims from China—include those who "fled and now live in this country." Among them, he explains, are those who "follow the Muslim religion, doing penance and fasting."[3]

Ma Huan's observations offer a fascinating firsthand account of the history of Muslims in Yuan service who fled during the fall of the dynasty for fear of Ming retribution. Historical evidence corroborates Ma Huan's observations: with rise of the Ming, many Yuan-era officials both in inland China and along the coast headed for Southeast Asia, while others remained. Zheng He (d. 1435), the Yunnanese Muslim who worked in Ming service and who traveled with Ma Huan, came from one of the families that stayed. Zheng He was a descendant of Bukhara-born Yuan-era governors Sayyid Ajall al-Din (d. 1279) and his Yunnan-born son Nasr al-Din, and he lived at a time when Central Asian merchant and political families in former Yuan service were becoming increasingly Sinicized under the Ming in terms of names, networks of kinship, and language.[4] Muslims with names like Hasan, Husayn, and Mahmud took the abbreviated transliterated names Ha, Hu, and Ma during the Ming era. Ma Huan's own background as a Muslim, though of recent convert origins in his case, fit this naming pattern. Interestingly, Ma Huan's observations point to a phenomenon that is only recently beginning to be discovered: that among those who fled China during the fall of the Yuan and arrival of the Ming were Muslims who played a role in the spread of Islam in Southeast Asia.[5] The Chinese named as part of the audience of the *Hikayat Raja Handik* likely numbered among these Ming-era Chinese Muslims.

Given how the *Hikayat Raja Handik*'s mixed audience indicates cultural proximity between Chinese and Malay speakers in Southeast Asia, what does the longer text collated with the manuscript—namely, the *Hikayat Raja Raja Pasai*—have to say about China's presence in Southeast Asia in the 1400s and 1500s? This longer text tells us that China was both politically foreign and culturally local in a way that illustrates the movement of Chinese social networks around the South China Sea during the Ming era.

China as a Foreign and Local Presence in Sumatra

The *Hikayat Raja Raja Pasai* is a collection of early Malay narratives that tells the origin stories of the Sultanate of Pasai, one of the oldest Muslim sultanates in Southeast Asia. Pasai is located today in northern Sumatra close to Aceh and just across the Melaka Strait from Melaka. The text bolsters the past legitimacy and glory of the rulers of Pasai by emphasizing how the court unified disparate communities of northeastern Sumatra—including both upstream and downstream communities—under court authority in the port city.[6] The texts date back to the 1400s and, looking back, represent Pasai's origins in the 1200s and 1300s. Like the *Hikayat Raja Handik*, the *Hikayat Raja Raja Pasai* similarly represents a Southeast Asian world where Chinese and Malay-speaking communities had close commercial and cultural connections. This picture fits what we know about the region in the early 1400s.

By the time the text began to circulate in its current form (ca. 1400s), the nearby Ming dynasty and neighboring Sultanate of Melaka were at the height of their power and political-commercial exchange. At the time, northern Sumatra—home of Pasai—was a center for the production of pepper. Like the spices of the Spice Islands (Moluccas), pepper in Sumatra was pivotal to commerce between the Indian Ocean and South China Sea. Pasai, like Melaka, was closely intertwined with trade routes linking local merchants in Southeast Asia with both China and Indian coastal cities. That connection explains why Pasai and Melaka were the crossroads of multiple cultures. In this commercial world, the movement and acquisition of textiles became a particularly significant marker of social status and courtly rank. These textiles additionally competed with silver and gold in terms of value.[7] Where this pepper, cloth, and silver moved is clear based on a quick look at the polities that the Pasai kingdom had to contend with both on Sumatra and abroad. Locally, the rulers of Pasai arranged the equivalent of a mutual nonaggression pact with the local rulers of Barus in western Sumatra.[8] In eastern Sumatra, Pasai's rulers arranged a marriage with the ruling circles of the Islamic port of Perlak. Abroad, several powerful neighbors numbered among the geopolitical actors that simultaneously facilitated and delimited Pasai's political and commercial activities.

Sumatra's historical connections with commerce in China and the Indian Ocean are represented clearly in *Hikayat Raja Raja Pasai*, and specifically in the text's discussion of the various local communities—Chinese included—that paid homage to the sultan. At the start of the text, we learn that the Pasai's neighbors include kingdoms in Thailand, China, Java, and India, and that the Pasai kingdom had to contend with these powers when cultivating trade relations in the region. These powers first appear in the text when the son of the sultan of Pasai promises not to abandon his subjects upon the completion of a trip away from the kingdom. The prince indicates that his loyalty to the kingdom comes not out of fear of his people, but rather from his commitment to having "no mind to be a traitor." As their protector and patron, he explains, it was in his power to betray his people, and if he did, the people of Pasai would be powerless against him and against the kingdoms of Siam (Thailand), China, Java, and Kalinga (Deccan India). The sultan chooses patronage because of his fidelity to his people. In his comments, we learn more about the political worlds that surround Sumatra, which in turn sheds light on the communities active in Sumatra.

> My comrades, hold your peace, all of you. I have no mind to be a traitor. If I wished to be a traitor . . . not even the whole of Pasai would prevail against me; if against Siam not even the whole of Siam would prevail against me; if against China not even the whole of China would prevail against me; if against Java not even the whole of Java would prevail against me; if against Kalinga not even the whole of Kalinga would prevail against me.[9]

China, in other words, is represented accurately in this epic as one of the key players in the region that is a clearly foreign political entity. The text's further references to China, however, build a picture of Chinese culture that is far more intertwined with the life of Pasai. That local picture first appears in the story of Ali of *kampong china*—that is, Ali of the Chinese village.

China as a Local Presence: Ali the Pendikar of Kampong China and Chinese Material Culture

Early in the text, after learning about the sultan and his loyalty to his communities, readers are introduced to the local leader of the Chinese village (*kampong china*)—namely the *pendikar* Ali. We learn that Ali was a master of a *silat*-like martial art and a member of the Pasai prince's royal entourage. In the ceremony where this *pendikar* Ali is summoned by the sultan's son to prepare for the reception of foreign dignitaries from India, the narrative makes extensive reference to courtly Malay materials and designs with conspicuously Chinese dimensions that reflect what Ming texts corroborate about Chinese-Malay courtly exchange. Both of these Chinese-Malay connections appear in the story of the sultanate's preparations to receive foreign dignitaries from "Kalinga"—that is, coastal India.

The story introduces Ali of the Chinese village in a story about the reception of Indian emissaries. When a delegation of dignitaries from Kalinga (coastal India) arrives in the Malay peninsula with a warrior, the sultan of

Pasai feels compelled to demonstrate the sultanate's own military prowess. Prince Tun Beraim Bapa, the sultan's son who referenced China and Java earlier, is tasked with the duty of demonstrating the skills he has learned from his teachers.

> Listen all of you, my old friends and brothers in arms. I have sent word to call you together because His Highness has received a visit from certain foreigners. Their leader is a champion warrior from Kalinga who has come here to pick a fight. For in his own country there is no one to match him in cudgel and dagger play.[10]

The description of the warrior's military prowess as "cudgel and dagger play" points to the fact that they are not planning on engaging in a duel, but rather a competition of military demonstration, performance, and ceremonial. Interestingly, what Prince Tun Beraim Bapa plans to offer the visiting dignitaries in the text closely resembles *silat*, a historical Malay term for the surviving martial arts of Sumatra and the Malay peninsula. What makes this connection notable is *silat* in Southeast Asia is historically intertwined with both Indian and Chinese martial arts.[11] In the text, echoing historical evidence, the description of the sultan's preparation for the military display and its actual performance similarly point to Pasai's cultural connection with China.

Specifically, the first reference to China in this part of the narrative appears in the list of companions and teachers of martial arts. In order to gather the right men for his martial arts display, Prince Tun Beraim Bapa asks for "my old friend the Pendikar of Pulau Kukur" as well as "my friend the Pendikar of Bangka," "my friend the champion of Langgar," "my brothers in arms Malik Akasan and Ali the Pendikar of *kampong china*," and finally "Tun Bijaya Pangiran" and "Rawana Permatang with their fighting-men."[12]

Who exactly was the *pendikar* Ali of *kampong china* who was among these masters of martial arts? In Malay, the term *kampong china* refers to a Chinese settlement or village. *Pendikar* literally means warrior and was among terms of authority granted by the sultan alongside similar terms in Malay like *orang besar* (great man) and *orang kaya* (man of wealth).[13] Why, then, was there a Chinese village in Pasai and why was it under the authority of someone named Ali?

One strong possibility is that Ali was a Muslim head of a Chinese village that included both Muslims and non-Muslims. Several pieces of evidence point to this likelihood. Upon their arrival decades after this text was in circulation, the Portuguese wrote maps of Melaka that referred to several Chinese villages (*kampong china*).[14] The reference to *kampong china* in this text likely refers to one of these settlements. Moreover, while the reference to a village master named Ali might indicate a local associate of the Pasai sultan assigned to the village, the history of semiautonomous communal governance in the Malay sultanates suggests that Ali shared the cultural background of Pasai's Chinese settlement. Evidence for this possibility includes the previously mentioned narrative of Zheng He's Muslim compatriot Ma Huan, who wrote of Chinese Muslim communities during his travels to Southeast Asia.

Whether or not the Chinese village and its leader Ali did indeed include Chinese Muslims, Prince Tun Beraim Bapa's close association with the village's *pendikar* nonetheless points to an enduring Chinese social presence in the port city that undoubtedly bridged the city with commerce in the South China Sea. Tun Beraim Bapa's reference to the *pendikar* of Bangka, a neighboring island, is similarly noteworthy from the perspective of Pasai's connections with China. Bangka (present-day Bangka-Belitung province) lies on the other side of the Strait of Melaka and was noted in Fei Xin's *The Overall Survey of the Star Raft* (星槎勝覽) as a major site of commercial exchange between the Indian Ocean and South China Sea commerce.[15] Historical evidence corroborates this picture of an early Chinese commercial presence in Bangka during the Ming era. This presence comes as no surprise given Bangka's proximity to Melaka, where the history of Chinese settlement is best documented. The fact that the *pendikar* of Bangka likewise participated in these military preparations together with the *pendikar* Ali of the Chinese village points to a variety of figures with close cultural proximity to Southeast Asia's Chinese communities in the Sultanate of Pasai.

Tun Beraim Bapa's entourage, in other words, was characterized by a certain cultural mix that reflected Chinese social proximity to the Malay sultans in the 1300s and 1400s. As the text continues to tell the story of Prince Tun Beraim Bapa's preparations for the martial arts demonstration, we learn more about the impact of Chinese royal ceremonial on the developing material culture of the Malay sultanates.

Chinese Dimensions of Prince Tun Beraim Bapa's Malay Ceremonial

The way that China is integrated into the story of Tun Beraim Bapa's military display itself is twofold: the royal material culture and ceremonial associated with the clothing of the event, and the martial arts form that is

displayed at the culmination of the scene. In the first case, when Tun Beraim
Bapa opens a chest of clothing for himself and his companions, he pulls out
a headdress and robe for himself illustrative of his royal rank. In the case of
the headdress, the narrative describes it with imagery that strongly evokes
Ming royal clothing. The clothing is described as:

> a cloth of fine yellow silk [*lia ben-ben*] with the back in iridescent colors, the
> border neatly worked—in gold thread with a trellis pattern of . . . gold,
> the fringe decorated with tinking bells; a coat shimmering like the rays of
> the sun . . . buttons encased in gold and bespangled with myriads of scarlet
> gems; a headcloth the color of *china kepaluan* with jewel-encrusted edges of
> gold and fringes of pearls; a shining waist-belt and armlets; bracelets in
> the form of dragons, [their bodies] in seven coils; a *keris* inlaid with pre-
> cious stones mounted in a scabbard of gold. A sash held the sword, which
> could flash like lightning. He wore a jeweled guard . . . and had a golden
> bow slung from his left shoulder . . . his coat flashed in the colors of the
> rainbow.

There are three elements in the prince's royal clothing illustrative of cultural
connections with China. The first and clearest is the set of "bracelets in the
form of dragons." In the Central Asian material culture of the late Yuan
and early Ming period, Chinese dragons became a central motif in what art
historians have described as an Islamic Chinoiserie—that is, the assimilation
and emulation of Chinese art forms and talismanic symbols.[16] *Hikayat Raja
Raja Pasai*'s reference to Tun Beraim Bapa's early Ming-era use of dragons in a
royal context closely parallels contemporary Timurid integration of dragon
motifs in royal regalia. The possibility of Chinese cultural transfer either
directly across the South China Sea or through Central Asian intermediaries
like Timurids and Safavids is demonstrated by the narrative's two references
to that world—namely, the text's reference to Samarkand as a center of learning and Persia as a source of thoroughbred horses.[17] The similar appearance
of dragons in royal ceremonial in the Sultanate of Pasai, noted in this text,
points to the impact of Chinese material culture on Muslim ruling circles
across both the overland silk routes to Central Asia and the maritime spice
routes to Southeast Asia during the Ming era.

The second element of the prince's royal clothing that illustrates a Chinese cultural connection is the color of the headdress. The text indicates

that the cloth used is jewel-encrusted with gold and pearl elements and is the color of *china kepaluan*. While the exact color of *china kepaluan* is unknown, the very name of the color points to a specifically Malay form of Chinese clothing design. *China kepaluan* likely refers to a royal Malay color palette drawing on Chinese courtly culture. The fact that the main cloth is made of "yellow silk" suggests that *china kepaluan*-colored textiles are a form of yellow, a royal color used in Chinese ceremonial.

Where the text offers a third piece of evidence of a Chinese design influence on Malay royal clothing is the description of the headdress. The text indicates that the main cloth used for the headdress is a cloth of "fine yellow silk" with gold embroidery. Like the use of dragons, the royal use of yellow silk in Ming China was a known part of Chinese courtly culture, and the Timurid diplomat and artist Ghayath al-Din Naqqash's (fl. 1419–1422) previously discussed travel narrative to the Ming court made this explicit point. Naqqash's observations of the court were replete with references to yellow silk: the fittings used by Ming officials to wrap letters, the Ming throne's triangular platform and its yellow silk covering with "Cathayan" motifs of dragons and mythical birds, the canopy-like curtain or bower of yellow silk with four dragons on it hanging above the emperor, the enclosed area close to where the emperor's food was prepared that was covered with yellow silk, the yellow silk cord used to tie together the emperor's edict, and at the end of the narrative outside the court, the gold brocade and yellow silks used to cover the emperor's enclosure. Naqqash's observations in the 1300s were contemporary with the writing of *Hikayat Raja Raja Pasai*, underlining the fact that the Pasai prince's gold-embroidered yellow silk headdress that incorporated the color of *china kepaluan* was a product of this growing Ming-era Chinese-Malay cultural proximity.

Hikayat Raja Raja Pasai, in sum, points to a variety of Chinese dimensions of royal Malay material culture at a time when the newly Muslim sultanates were just beginning their rise to prominence on the eve of European arrival in the region. This Chinese-Malay connection in material culture parallels the picture it paints of Chinese-Malay social proximity in the entourage of the Malay sultan. Both pictures echo historical evidence of Ming China's growing role in the development of Malay political and social life under the sultanates. Where this picture of a Chinese-Malay cultural symbiosis finds additional contours is in another contemporary Malay text: the *Hikayat Hang Tuah* (*The Chronicle of Hang Tuah*). The chronicle tells the epic tale of the

Malay peninsula's most revered legendary warrior and his curious trip to the Ming capital. It also, notably, offers an early picture of the Portuguese not as a group of sophisticated merchants based in Macau—a later image specific to the 1600s—but rather as disorganized seafaring pirates.

HIKAYAT HANG TUAH: CHINESE PROJECTIONS OF KINGSHIP AND DIPLOMATIC CULTURE FROM VIJAYANAGARA TO MELAKA

The *Hikayat Hang Tuah*, like its more famous counterpart *Sejarah Melayu (Malay Annals)*, offers a glimpse into the way Ming political and material culture looms large in the background of Malay epic tales. Both texts are associated with the Sultanate of Melaka. Melaka was and remains situated on the Malay Peninsula's western coast and on the east side of the Strait of Melaka across from Sumatra island. The Sultanate of Pasai's location in northern Sumatra meant that the two sultanates were neighbors in the 1300s and 1400s. Like Pasai, Melaka is represented in these texts as a city at the maritime crossroads of China and the "land of Kalinga," that is, the Indian subcontinent. In contrast with Pasai's connection with China, Melaka's political connection with Ming-era China was historically more direct according to evidence in Ming historical records. Representations of this proximity are offered in both the *Hikayat Hang Tuah* and *Sejarah Melayu*.

The Grandeur of Malay, Indian, and Chinese Kingship during the Early Portuguese Encounter

The legendary warrior Hang Tuah's visit to India on behalf of the sultan of Melaka, together with his subsequent visit to China on behalf of India, offers the reader an interesting glimpse into Malay representations of China as a growing regional player. Interestingly, the narrative represents the prestige of the three kingdoms according to a graded rank. While the previously discussed *Hikayat Raja Raja Pasai* represented both "Kelinga" (coastal India) and China as powerful players on a par with Majapahit-controlled Java, *Hikayat Hang Tuah* represents the "land of the Keling [people]" as actually less powerful than both China and the Melakan Sultanate. In a comparison of the two texts, the "land of the Keling" in this narrative somehow declines in a rank of kingship to a position equivalent with or even subordinate to the prestige of a Malay sultanate, which in turn is characterized as having political parity with China. The Portuguese, meanwhile, make an appearance in this text but are far from powerful colonizers. The text represents them as a nuisance who are equivalent neither to the sultan of Melaka nor even the traveling military entourage of Hang Tuah. The Portuguese, according to the text, are rather a group of uncouth pirates. These comparisons of rank in kingship that elevate Chinese kingship, together with reference to the Portuguese as pirates, are introduced in the story of Hang Tuah's visit to India on behalf of the sultan of Melaka.

Hang Tuah's Visit to India

The text tells us that upon Hang Tuah's arrival on the Indian coast as an emissary of the Malay sultan, he is received by the harbormaster, or *shah-bandar* in Persian and Malay. The harbormaster announces his intention to take Hang Tuah to Nala Sang Guna, the regional governor. After serving Hang Tuah and his entourage a feast, the harbormaster begins the journey. "Come, my sons, let's go to Nala Sang Guna." With matching honorifics, Hang Tuah responds, "Please lead the way, my father."[18]

When they explain their presence to the governor, the narrative represents the kingdoms of Bijaya Nagaram (Vijayanagara) and Melaka as near equals. The governor asks, "What brings my two sons here to Bijaya Nagaram under the orders of the Sultan of Melaka?" Hang Tuah's answer indicates a level of familiarity between the Malay and Indian kingdoms, which will contrast with Hang Tuah's later representation of China as an empire of unmatched grandeur later in the narrative. "We are here on the orders of his majesty the Sultan of Melaka," Hang Tuah responds, "to bring a letter as a token of his love and concord between the Sultan of Melaka and His majesty Kisna Rayan, for His majesty desires to hear news of his brother."[19]

When the governor instructs the harbormaster to allow the Melakan vessels to dock for several days, he offers his respect to the Melakan sultan. "It is advisable that the harbor master allow the boats from Melaka to drop anchor besides the boats of the Portuguese, for the sultan of Melaka is the elder brother to His majesty Kisna Rayan."

In the encounter with the Portuguese, the narrative offers an additional dimension of this representation of ceremonial rank, where the Portuguese are depicted as quarrelsome outsiders below the sophistication of the Melakans and devoid of any chivalry. When the Portuguese missions see that the Melakans are "highly honored" by the kingdom, "They became extremely angry." The boat's passengers attempt to order Hang Tuah away. "Do not moor your boats in our place. We do not like that." Hang Tuah responds, "If you wish to pick an individual fight or fights in equal numbers, we are ever ready," but that, "It is not good to become embroiled in a fight in another's country. But afterwards when we are on our return journey, then you can block our path."[20]

Upon Hang Tuah's arrival at the fort of Bijaya Nagaram, the narrative offers a representation of the court's visual language that is sharply distinct from the kind of images of yellow silks and yellow-tasseled umbrellas associated in Malay epics with Pasai, Melaka, and China. The fort of Bijaya Nagaram is surrounded by walls that are "pure as combed cotton" and doors with carvings of "magnificent animals on what seemed to be jacinth"—that is, a kind of reddish gemstone. On another level of the structure, there are animals carved on what appear to be black marble "as dark as the shiny wings of the beetle," and on another level Hang Tuah "could read the story of the *Ramayana*," and on another level still, "the drama of Pandawa Jaya" played out in an elaborate carved scene. On the highest level were "carved animals of the jungles with doors of copper and pinchbeck." When Hang Tuah is eventually invited as a guest of the court, the king Kisna Rayan is described sitting on a golden throne, "inlaid with precious stones and draped with ropes of pearls."[21]

Despite visual cues in Kisna Rayan's court that sharply contrast with the yellow silks and dragons of the Melakan sultanate and Ming China, the narrative nonetheless connects Kisna Rayan and the sultan of Melaka through close ties of princely kinship: Kisna Rayan and the Melakan sultan come from the same family in Bukit Sang but rule different kingdoms that have grown apart diplomatically. The text explains that their shared father or ancestral patriarch is the king of Bukit Sang. This connection appears, among other places in the text, when the locals wonder why the Malay delegation is received with such fanfare in the Indian kingdom. When locals come out to the streets to witness the procession of Hang Tuah's entourage and ask why the letters of Melaka are such an important topic of the day, one observer responds by asking how it could be any other way, given that "our Raja [Kisna Raya] is descended from the Malay rajas."[22] In agreement, another remarks, "We heard that the raja of Melaka is the elder brother of our Raja; that's the reason."

In agreement with the narrative's representation of shared Indian and Malay ancestry, the Malay epics trace the ancestry of the Malay kings to the kings of Seguntang Hill (Bukit Seguntang), which Hang Tuah identifies as the royal ancestors of Kisna Raya of Bijaya Nagaram. The outcome is *Hikayat*

Hang Tuah's interesting representation of the Indian and Malay kingdom's virtual parity in royal prestige. In representing Kisna Raya as the younger brother of the sultan of Melaka, however, that parity appears slightly skewed in favor of the Malay sultan's greater grandeur. This picture will contrast with Hang Tuah's grandiose representation of China upon his departure from the Indian coast.

Before traveling to China, however, the reader is given another glimpse into the Indian and Malay kings' proximity in familial kinship and the Malay king's more elevated royal prestige. This picture appears in a conversation between Kisna Raya and Hang Tuah about Hang Tuah's own heritage once the latter surprises the court with his ability to speak the local Indian language fluently. Taken aback by Hang Tuah's linguistic talents, the Indian king asks about Hang Tuah's ancestry. Hang Tuah answers that he is of Malay ancestry, but that "when your servant was young, I traveled to Majapahit [Java] and studied the Keling language under a teacher; that's how your servant came to acquire something of it, My Lord."[23] "Laksamana" he replies, "how fortunate and blessed are we that you are able to speak our language and are here in audience with us." Upon hearing a pledge of loyalty from Hang Tuah, he asks, "Do tell us Laksamana, what news do you bring of our father on Seguntang Hill and of my elder brother in Melaka?" Upon indicating that Hang Tuah is bringing "good news" from Melaka, Kisna Rayan anticipates the warming of relations after an earlier period of diplomatic coldness: "Is it true that my brother [the sultan of Melaka] wishes to collaborate with us, and that is the reason why the Laksamana and Maharaja Setia have been dispatched hither to us? When we were in Melaka, we had differences with him. Nobody except the *bendahara* and the fishermen were on my side. I feel it in my bones that the arrival of the Laksamana is indeed almost like the visit of our father on Seguntang Hill and our elder brother from Melaka, and seeing the Laksamana and Maharaja Setia is like seeing the Bendahara Paduk Raja and the fisherman."[24] Hang Tuah and Maharaja Setia were then given full suits of the golden costumes worn by Kisna Raya himself. Though Hang Tuah delivers the letter to Kisna Raya with submissive graciousness, he indicates that it is the sultan of Melaka who is the royal elder bestowing a favor on a younger brother, offering to reconcile diplomatic discord.

With this representation of the Sultanate of Melaka's royal superiority over Bijaya Nagaram, the narrative turns to Hang Tuah's visit to China on behalf of Kisna Raya. In the case of China, the narrative represents the kingdom as almost otherworldly while nonetheless ascribing to Hang Tuah a surprising degree of cultural proximity and familiarity with the Chinese royals. That is, in contrast with *Hikayat Raja Raja Pasai*'s picture of a Malay sultanate—the Sultanate of Pasai—rising to prominence in a world of powerful Indian, Chinese, and Javanese empires, *Hikayat Hang Tuah* represents the Sultanate of Melaka as a well-established kingdom superior to the Indian kingdom and on a par with China. This picture comes together below.

Chinese Kingship and Hang Tuah's Familial and Cultural Proximity to China

With the thawing of India and Melaka's relations, Kisna Raya then addresses the Bendahara Hang Tuah and asks him to travel to China:

> "We wish to send a mission to China, whom shall we order?" The Bendahara raised his hands, "Daulat, my Lord, in my humble opinion, sending a mission to China is indeed a tremendous undertaking, for the Emperor of China is a great king. We should not send anyone as ambassador: a person who may not be able to secure a meeting with the Raja or even with his minister." Kisna Rayan then enquired, "Laksamana, may we send you to China?" The Laksamana bowed low, "Daulat, My Lord, why should Your Majesty not send me to China? Even if it were to Rome Your Majesty may command me, for any one of Your majesty's missions is also the mission of your brother, the Sultan of Melaka; and I'm a servant to your majesty's brother.[25]

Before visiting China via Nagapatam, Hang Tuah announces to the court his intention of visiting the temples and mosques of the land. On the way, they again encounter the Portuguese, whose pirate-like presence offers additional entertainment for the reader. "Hey there, you Malays and Kelings, do not anchor here so close to our captain's galleon. When he arrives he will open fire on all your boats."[26] Comically, the story indicates that "the Malays all laughed at the threats and they dropped anchor alongside the galleon." The Portuguese soldiers, enraged, shout, "You Malays and Kelings are an absolute disgrace! You are just bent on picking a fight with us, for you find yourselves in the majority."[27]

Once in China, Hang Tuah learns that he is unable to meet directly with the Ming Emperor, and that the delegation will be limited to meeting four Chinese ministers: Wong Kim Seng, Pa Shin Nga, Lu Ti, and Sim Pai

Qip.[28] In other words, the narrative's first representation of China's royal prestige in rank appears in the diplomatic protocol of foreign dignitaries: Hang Tuah's entourage is unable to meet the emperor or even lay eyes upon the Ming throne. This picture contrasts with Hang Tuah's casual proximity to the Indian king.

Once in the court, however, the image of Chinese kingship's other-worldliness gives way to a picture of Hang Tuah's familiarity with Chinese language and culture. Speaking to the Maharaja Setia and his men, Hang Tuah indicates:

> My Lords, we shall now be proceeding into the great audience hall of the King of China, please remember not to roll up your sarongs. Other than that, there are indeed many wonderful and rare inventions which we shall never have seen, for the Chinese are ingenious in numerous fields." The Maharaja Setia enquired, "Where did my Lord hear about this?" The Laksamana explained, "From an old Chinese man whom I have adopted as my father in Melaka; he was the one who told me.[29]

Interestingly, the narrative reveals that Hang Tuah had a close family connection with an "old Chinese man" whom he had adopted as his father back in Melaka. The reference to an elderly Chinese man as an adoptive father echoes the reference in *Hikayat Raja Raja Pasai* to the *pendikar* Ali of *kampong china*, who was Tun Beraim Bapa's teacher. Despite Hang Tuah's familiarity with Chinese culture, he remains bound by strict diplomatic protocols in the court that the Ming Emperor nonetheless relaxes.

When the emperor hears that Hang Tuah's mission is to "confirm the friendship" between the two kingdoms—that is, China and the Indian kingdom on whose behalf Hang Tuah and his entourage have come—the emperor is delighted and summons Hang Tuah for a direct conversation. "Summon the Keling mission here before me; we wish to speak to them directly," the Ming Emperor indicates, and proceeds to bestow upon Hang Tuah and his entourage a gift of costumes, gold, and silver.[30] Despite Hang Tuah's direct conversation with the Ming Emperor, the restriction against looking directly at the face of the emperor endures in this part of the encounter. This restriction is clear from the story of the banquet that follows.

In accordance with Hang Tuah's commitment to Kisna Raya that he not return without having seen the emperor with his own eyes, Hang Tuah devises a plan to look up at the Ming throne during the banquet without getting caught. Hang Tuah realizes that certain types of cuisine, especially long uncut vegetables, require him to lift his head to consume them. "At the moment of the feast, I shall be able to see the countenance of the emperor," Hang Tuah says to himself. He instructs the banquet planner of the dietary restrictions of his entourage, indicating that curries should be prepared of shoots of vegetables and fruits to the exclusion of meat and fish: "These are the ingredients of the curries they cook. The vegetables are left uncut, so that they are long. This is how we eat."[31]

During the banquet, Hang Tuah and his entourage are welcomed and served their meal while the emperor is seated on the throne. Then at the right moment, holding a pair of golden chopsticks, Hang Tuah picks up a long watercress and raises it to his forehead to steal a glance at the throne of the emperor. Hang Tuah finally beholds the emperor in that moment seated on the throne, "the Chinese Emperor sitting in the jaws of the golden dragon with scales made of nine sorts of precious stones, on a throne studded with glorious gems, overhung with ropes of pearls, as a candle in a lantern, shining as the moon on the fourteenth night."[32] In a moment of misfortune, Hang Tuah is seen lifting his gaze to observe the throne by the emperor's ministers, and he even locks eyes with the emperor himself.

The emperor, his four ministers, and the emperor's heralds all witness Hang Tuah's movements and draw their swords. Luckily, the emperor intervenes and shows his forbearance: "Heralds, do not execute him. He is a wise man who wishes to serve his master: it is difficult to find a servant and warrior the like of Laksamana."[33] The emperor is not displeased by the incident and, to the contrary, instructs his servants to offer the delegation gifts: "Four Ministers, bestow gifts of fine suits upon all the envoys from Keling with all due ceremony."[34] Hang Tuah and his entourage are given costumes, and the Malays in his entourage specifically are gifted each with more than seven complete Chinese suits that they will take back with them to Melaka.[35]

In this visit to China, the narrative of *Hikayat Hang Tuah* offers the text's clearest picture of the Malay sultanate's connection with Chinese courtly culture. The narrative situates Hang Tuah, a legendary Malay hero and representative of the sultan of Melaka, in close proximity with China both in terms of Hang Tuah's familial kinship ties—his adoptive Chinese father—and in terms of the Melakans' exceptional diplomatic proximity to the Ming Emperor. The text represents Hang Tuah's direct conversation with the emperor and the special gifts given directly to the Malay representatives as an exceptional break from typical Ming customs in dealing with foreign delegations. Malay epics build this image of Chinese-Malay proximity further in the story of the Melakan sultanate offered in the *Sejarah Melayu* (*Malay Annals*).

SEJARAH MELAYU: CHINESE KINGSHIP AND MATERIAL CULTURE IN PALEMBANG AND MELAKA

The *Sejarah Melayu*, the so-called *Malay Annals*, depicts a Malay political and cultural proximity to China that echoes the spectrum of connections found in *Hikayat Raja Raja Pasai* and *Hikayat Hang Tuah*. This proximity is particularly prominent in the stories of Chinese and Malay royal intermarriage. One of the first indications of this connection in royal kinship appears in the reference to the reigning kings of Palembang. The text indicates that they are descendants of a Chinese nobleman who settled in Palembang during a period when China and King Sang Sapurba developed a close relationship. The text indicates that this Chinese-Malay marriage, in turn, led to the settlement of Chinese courtiers in the Malay Peninsula. The *Sejarah Melayu* also tells the enduringly famous story of Chinese princess Hang Li-Po's marriage with the Melakan king, and in particular the diplomatic dimensions of the marriage. In the Ming era, the political marriage of Chinese princesses with foreign monarchs occurred across both Central Asia and across the South China Sea. In the former case, which appears to have been more common, Chinese royal marriages were arranged within the framework of a Chinese political theory that deemed nomadic frontier groups culturally unsophisticated yet militarily formidable enough to be recognized in alliance. This text similarly ascribes to the Chinese emperor a belief in the necessity of arranging a marriage with the Malay sultans, but in this case the emperor is described as believing in the Malay sultanate's cultural sophistication, political prestige, and most interestingly, the Malay court's superiority specifically in terms of sacred miracle performance. This last image represents the Ming Emperor as a sovereign who was impressed by the spiritual cultures of the Malay sultanate and, perhaps, attempts to place the sultanates on a par with the Ming by comparing China's temporal sophistication with the Malay sultanate's spiritual sophistication as a Muslim center. What follows is a closer look at these close connections between Ming

China and the Malay world in *Sejarah Melayu*, beginning during the reign of Sang Sapurba of Palembang.

Chinese Emperors of Malay Origins, Malay Sultans of Chinese Origin

The *Sejarah Melayu* begins by describing a series of incidents in Palembang that point to a growth in Malay-Chinese political connections in the 1300s. It tells the story of a Malay ruler who was an ancestor of the sultans of Melaka and who married a Chinese princess. That is, the Malay sultans are of Malay and Chinese ancestry.

Specifically, the text explains that during the reign of Sang Sapurba of Palembang (southern Sumatra) in the late Srivijayan period (650–1377), the Chinese emperor developed great respect for Palembang's ruling dynasty after learning of their ancestry in Alexander the Great. In other Malay texts, Alexander the Great is *Iskandar Zulkarnein* "of both Rum (Greece, Anatolia) and Iran," which points to how Malay epics echoed Arabic and Persian epics that similarly represented Alexander the Great as a respected ancient royal ancestor of certain ruling circles.[36] In the *Sejarah Melayu*, the Chinese emperor understands the prestige of the Palembang ruler's ancestry and requests the hand of Sang Sapurba's daughter in marriage. The emperor sends a letter to Palembang together with a large entourage of Chinese men and women, including a particular Chinese nobleman.

> They reached Palembang and delivered the letter of the Raja of China in the most respectful manner, in the hall of audience. The letter was read and comprehended, and Raja Sangsapurba consulted with his warriors whether it would be proper or improper. They were all of the opinion that if the request were not complied with, the safety of country would be endangered. "Besides," said they, "there is no greater prince than the raja of China, nor of more noble extraction, whom she could get for her husband, nor is there any country greater than the land of China." "Then," said Sangsapurba, "if you approve it, we will grant his request, in order to promote the friendship between the Malay and the Chinese rajas."[37]

The reason the Malay king complies with the request is a combination of Malay recognition of the grandeur of Chinese kingship and kinship as well as the threat of political fallout and repercussions if the Malay king refuses. When the Chinese emperor marries the daughter, named Sri Devi, she is treated especially well "due to her rank and family" and "produced a son, from whom are descended the royal race who reign in China at the present time."[38]

Sang Sapurba of Palembang, in other words, is the shared ancestor of the current Malay and Chinese kings according to the narrative. Malay and Chinese kingship during the reign of Sang Sapurba of Palembang and in future generations, therefore, have a certain parity in terms of ceremonial prestige, and they are moreover intertwined in terms of royal genealogical pasts and future kinship through the shared figure of the Palembang king's daughter Sri Devi.

What cements the relationship of Malay and Chinese kingship and its shared ancestry is the marriage of this Chinese nobleman who remains in Palembang. Upon arrival, the Chinese nobleman cultivates a connection with the king of Sang Sapurba so closely that he marries Sang Sapurba's adoptive daughter. Against this backdrop, the more famous story of Chinese princess Hang Li-Po represents the culmination, rather than the foundation, of the narrative's representation of connections between Chinese and Malay kingship. In this latter story of princess Hang Li-Po, the epic likewise offers a familiar window into the visual dimensions of this connection between the Sultanate of Melaka and Ming China.

The Story of Hang Li-Po

The *Sejarah Melayu* recounts the story of Hang Li-Po, a Chinese princess sent by the Ming to marry the Sultan of Melaka, Mansur Shah, to boost diplomatic ties between the two kingdoms. The story is told in the context of the intermediary role of the Malay ambassador to the Ming, Tun Parapati Puti, while he was in China. The text indicates that as Tun Parapati Puti was about to return, "the raja of China, judging it proper to ally himself with the raja of Melaka," asked Tun Parapati Puti to "have the raja of Melaka pay me a visit, so that I can have my daughter Hang Li-Po marry him." Tun Parapati Puti replied, "The raja of Melaka cannot possibly leave the kingdom as it is surrounded by enemies, but if you would do a favor to the raja of Melaka, allow me, the Malay ambassador, to conduct your daughter, the princess, to Melaka."[39]

When Tun Parapati Puti reaches Melaka, Sultan Mansur Shah is informed that the ambassador has returned and has brought with him the princess of China. Sultan Mansur Shah "was greatly delighted, and he went himself to receive the princess to the isle of Pulu Sabot." The story describes how pleased Sultan Mansur Shah was by the Ming's marriage proposition. "Having met her with a thousand tokens of respect, he conducted her to the palace, and the sultan was astonished to behold the beauty of the princess of China, and he said, in the Arabic language, 'Oh fairest of created creatures, may God the creator of the world bless you.'" In what seems to correlate with the reference to the sultan's bilingualism in Arabic, the sacred language of Islam in Malay texts, the story explains how the Chinese princess eventually became Muslim together with the entourage of some five hundred courtiers that came from China. What follows is a closer look at the two previously mentioned aspects of this story—its visual cues and the historical notion of Chinese royalty marrying into frontier kingdoms.

When the letter from the Chinese emperor arrives in Melaka, the embassy brings as gifts an interesting mix of items: needles, silks, a form of brocade, as well as "a great variety of articles" that can be found "nowhere else."[40] The narrative's reference to a gift of golden needles points to the historical reality that Ming Chinese artisans were indeed increasingly intertwined with the textile and tailoring industries of Southeast Asia after the fifteenth century. Gifts of metal specialty exports like needles along with silks and brocades points to that movement of Chinese design and manufacturing into Southeast Asia—particularly in courtly circles—in a phenomenon that echoes the earlier Song-era and Tang-era export of ceramics and silk commodities across the South China Sea. In the case of metal specialties manufacturing, Shanxi in northern China was a center of iron that was one of the main sources of iron specialties exports, including scissors, dating back to the Tang.[41] Tang-era scissors manufactured in Shanxi were a major Chinese import globally and were even featured in Chinese poetry. The scissors used in China came largely from Shanxi and were only destroyed as a local export in the late 1800s with the flood of cheap foreign scissors into the Chinese market.

The gifts are significant as they point to growing Melakan-Ming ties in material culture. On one level, the golden needles represent a form of power according to the emperor himself, who explains that every needle represents a subject. That is, the Chinese emperor is a powerful monarch ruling over a vast number of royal subjects. On another level, a gift of needles—together with silk and brocade—fits more broadly in the historical legacy of Ming China both as a source of textile artisans moving to the Malay sultanates and as a manufacturer of special metal commodities for Southeast Asian silk production. The visual cues of Hang Li-Po's marriage to a Malay sultan accurately depicts in literary terms the historical reality of this Chinese-Malay cultural transfer during the fourteenth and fifteenth centuries.

The second dimension of this embassy indicative of the Malay peninsula's changing relationship with China appears in the marriage itself, and specifically in the concept of a Ming Chinese emperor marrying a princess to a foreign dignitary. The marriage of Chinese princesses to foreign political rulers has a long and storied history from the Han dynasty through the Tang dynasty and was a formal and informal part of imperial statecraft. This practice, known as *heqin* ("peace marriage") was instituted during the Han dynasty's alliance with the Xiongnu pastoral nomads (ca. 202 B.C.–220 C.E.).[42] Under the Tang, this approach was aimed at securing alliances with various neighboring states that included the nomadic Khitan people of northern China, who eventually formed the Liano dynasty. During the Yuan period, some seven Yuan princesses were married to Korean princes and kings. The Ming period, meanwhile, did not see the imperial employment of this policy and even saw an example of a Ming imperial prisoner—namely, the Zhengtong Emperor—refusing marriage with an Oirat princess whom the Oirat ruler Esen Taishi wanted to install in Beijing in a kind of reverse marriage alliance aimed at pushing frontier royalty into the Ming imperial court.[43]

In this regard, the case of a Ming princess sent to the Malay world to marry a vassal king evokes the idea of the Malay peninsula as a kind of maritime frontier rather than an overland frontier. Instead of a Chinese dynasty offering their princess to a nomadic group to keep the peace, a Chinese dynasty offers their princess to a client state to solidify its foreign alliances. This kind of empire-building approach evokes the Yuan-era princesses' marriages with the Goryeo Korean princes and the later Qing princesses' marriages with Central Asians. The *Sejarah Melayu*, in other words, offers a picture of the Sultanate of Melaka as part of Ming China's frontier and as a state that was powerful or influential enough to merit *heqin* marriage. Interestingly, this image of Melaka as a Chinese frontier is one substantiated by historical evidence. We know that the Ming and Melaka had a kind of patron-client relationship, one that played a role in preventing Ayutthaya's (Siam) conquest of its southern neighbor. It is an image seen also in the writings of Ali Akbar Khitayi, who represented

Sumatra just across the Malay Straits from the Malay peninsula as part of China's frontier.

Taken together, the narratives of China offered by Central Asian visitors Naqqash and Ali Akbar offer an interesting parallel with the Malay epics and the travel narratives of Zheng He's crewmate Ma Huan. In the aftermath of the collapse of the Srivijayan and Majapahit Empires across Southeast Asia, the region's core islands—Borneo, Sumatra, Java—were the heartlands of rising Muslim sultanates that cultivated close political and commercial connections with the Ming. That Malay and Chinese ruling circles likely married, at a time when Muslims and non-Muslims were arriving in the region from China, comes as no surprise. In this world of increased Chinese-Malay connections, perhaps most surprising is the picture of the Portuguese. By the end of the 1500s, their initial appearance in the region as pirate-like figures was about to give way to the story of an ambitious European power with plans to conquer Southeast Asian islands and negotiate for trade privileges with the Ming.

CHAPTER 5

Europe's Search
for the Spice Islands

The story of Iberia's arrival in the South China Sea is a tale of treach-
erous sea expeditions, grandiose aspirations of world conquest, and
the unlikely long-term settlement of Portuguese mariners and their
families on China's Macau peninsula. In its origins, it is the story of an
attempt by European royals and mariners to find a new route to the Spice
Islands that bypassed the wealthy port cities of the Italian peninsula and
the Middle East.

The late fifteenth century saw the monarchies of Iberia fund maritime
expeditions across the Atlantic and Indian Oceans to reach Southeast Asia's
lucrative Spice Islands. One of the goals was to sideline the Italian republics,
which held a monopoly over Chinese and Indian commodities through their
close commercial relations with the Arabic- and Greek-speaking eastern
Mediterranean ports. A full century before the Iberians set sail for the South
China Sea, the Venetian and Genoese republics held ports as far east as the
Black Sea's Crimean Peninsula, where merchants traded in commodities
produced in Ilkhanid Iran and Yuan China. By 1492, with the Crowns of
Aragon and Castile's political union and subsequent baptism of economically influential Iberian Muslim and Jewish networks, Aragonese King Ferdinand II and Castilian Queen Isabella I agreed to a new and potentially
lucrative venture: funding a Genoese-led expedition westward to Asia, which
famously landed in the Americas.

By the time Spanish merchants reached and conquered Manila across the American Pacific in 1571, newly Habsburg-led Spain dominated a previously uncharted trans-Pacific trade route connecting Acapulco in Spanish Mexico with Manila. The Portuguese, who pursued a rivaling route into the southern Atlantic across Africa's Cape of Good Hope, were the Spaniards' main competitors in the region. By 1557, the Portuguese secured long-term settlement rights in Macau through direct negotiations with Ming China. They then carved out their own place in the region's inter-Asian trade networks, connecting Nagasaki with Portuguese-held Melaka and, further west, Goa along the coast of Kerala.[1] Far from unaware of these developments, Ming China's administrators already demonstrated their own maritime pretensions in Southeast Asia a century earlier. Portugal's conquest of the Sultanate of Melaka in 1511 was, in fact, a direct affront on the Ming-Melaka's political relationship. While the powerful Ayutthaya Kingdom of Siam (1350–1767) chose not to challenge China in the Malay peninsula, Portugal's simultaneous boldness in capturing Melaka and the strategy of treading carefully in Macau demonstrated that European powers were centuries away from being able to challenge China's military and cultural dominance in the region.

The Spanish conquest of Manila was no less complex given how the city, like Melaka, was at the political and commercial intersection of China and the Southeast Asian sultanates. Interestingly, the sultanate that had political ties with Manila in the 1500s—namely, the Sultanate of Brunei—was one of the few sultanates to elude European conquest altogether. A closer look at how the Spaniards and Portuguese managed to chart new maritime routes to Manila and Macau illustrates how the Age of Exploration's search for the Spice Islands quickly transformed into a search for China and the start of a half millennium of Chinese cultural transfer to Europe.

THE ROADS TO CHINA: MADRID TO MANILA, LISBON TO MACAU

Both Spain and Portugal set out to bypass Venetian trade routes to Asia by exploring Atlantic routes westward and southward, respectively.[2] The career of Ferdinand Magellan (Portuguese: Fernão de Magalhães) represents the typical story of mariners working for both Crowns. In Magellan's case, he moved from Portuguese to Spanish service in search of a patron to invest in his journey. Magellan was born around 1480 into Portuguese nobility. By the 1490s, he was serving the Portuguese military in pursuit of the Spice Islands around the Moluccas. When Magellan asked for government funding to explore a shorter westward route to the Moluccas across the Atlantic, the Portuguese Crown refused. Magellan turned to the Spanish under Charles I and to a German banking family, the Fuggers, who loaned the Habsburgs vast sums under Charles I's grandfather and hoped for returns on their investment in Magellan's voyage.[3]

In 1520, Magellan's crew managed to cross from the Atlantic to the Pacific through a strait in present-day southern Chile that his crew called the Patagonian Straits. Once beyond the strait, they proceeded across the open seas in hopes of making landfall within a few weeks or months. In March of 1521, those who survived among the crew, suffering illness and battling starvation, finally spotted what they expected to see months earlier: land, specifically the islands around Guam. According to the crew member who lived to give the most descriptive account of the voyage, the Venetian Antonio Pigafetta, relations with local islands turned thorny after crossing Guam.

Antonio Pigafetta (d. 1531) recounts that the native Chamorros brought provisions to Magellan's crew by boat and, in turn, took items from Magellan's ship.[4] What may have been a barter-like maritime custom was, in Magellan's eyes, theft. His objections escalated quickly. Magellan violently ordered the Chamorros off the ship. Magellan's crew then attacked the island while looking for a missing skiff that the Chamorros had taken in flight. What began as a friendly encounter ended with Magellan's crew fleeing the island in haste to continue their expedition to the Moluccas.

The trip to the Spice Islands ran into another detour in early 1521 when one of Magellan's crewmates spotted a boat on the horizon. The ship came from the island of Suluan, and within a few days, the crew was offered a meeting with the chief (*datu*).[5] Magellan's next moves paved the way for a less than warm reception for Spanish vessels that followed years later. Magellan attempted to get involved in a local rivalry between the chief of the Suluans on Cebu Island, on the one hand, and the chief of the neighboring island of Mactan, on the other. According to Pigafetta's account, the crew attacked Mactan and was met with more than a thousand islanders who fought under the authority of their chief Lapu-Lapu. By the end of the scuffle, Magellan was fatally wounded.[6] Magellan had managed to survive an uncharted voyage across the Atlantic and Pacific, but the mission's missteps close to the Philippines cost him his life.

The Sultan of Brunei

Juan Sebastián Elcano (d. 1526), a Spanish explorer of Basque origins, was the crewmate who eventually took over Magellan's role and headed southward for Borneo. It was there where he met Matanda, who would reappear in Spanish legends later as the Raja Matanda. In this more famous role, Raja Matanda was one of three rulers around Manila involved in the loss of the city to the Spanish some fifty years later. In his first encounter with the Spanish, however, Matanda was the head of the sultan of Brunei's naval forces. The encounter occurred after Magellan's surviving crew members spent two days on the island kingdom of Brunei.

In Brunei, Pigafetta offers one of the earliest glimpses of Spanish exposure to Chinese and Indian Ocean commodities on their way to meet the king.

> When we reached the city, we remained about two hours in the prau until the arrival of two elephants with silk trappings (*corperti de seta*), and twelve men each of whom carried a porcelain jar covered with silk . . . to carry our presents . . . during the night we slept on cotton mattresses, whose lining was of taffeta and the sheets of Cambaia (*li linsoli de cambaia*).[7]

In his reference to a "porcelain jar covered with silk," Pigafetta demonstrates that he was undoubtedly familiar with the Chinese export during his time in Brunei. Even though a local European industry of manufacturing pseudo-porcelain ceramics only developed in the eighteenth century, fifteenth-century Ming porcelain was part of the courtly material culture of the Italian city-states. These city-states included Pigafetta's native Venice, capital of the Venetian Republic (697–1797). Mamluk gifts of porcelain to the Venetian doge in 1461 were part of a larger history of Mamluk-Italian exchange, which included Mamluk gifts to the Medicis of Florence.[8] Pigafetta's interest in both Chinese porcelain and silks, therefore, is unsurprising.

Pigafetta's observations of the Brunei Sultanate's Chinese-influenced courtly culture continue as the group comes closer to the island kingdom's throne room. They walk through halls "adorned with silk hangings, and two windows, through which light entered the hall and [adorned] with two brocade curtains."[9] When they are finally given an audience with the king, Pigafetta's account offers a window into the diplomatic dimensions of the kinds of material exchanges that took place during the expeditions of the Spanish and Portuguese in the South China Sea.

We told the king [of Brunei] that we came from the king of Spain (*Spagnia*), and that the latter desired to make peace with him and asked only for permission to trade. The king told us that since the king of Spain desired to be his friend, he was very willing to be his, and said that we could take water and wood and trade at our pleasure. Then we gave him the presents, on receiving each of which he nodded slightly. To each one of us was given some brocaded gold cloth and silk, which were placed upon our left shoulders where they were left but a moment. They presented us with refreshments of cloves and cinnamon (*garafolli et cannella*), after which the curtains were drawn to and the windows closed.[10]

The mixture of Pigafetta's observations of brocaded silk, cloves, and cinnamon captures the extent that Borneo was situated at the crossroads of China and the Indian Ocean. It also captures how large China increasingly loomed in the Spanish expedition to the Spice Islands. Upon returning to the governor's house, the travelers are welcomed with lavish meals where porcelain serves multiple purposes. Nine men arrive with wooden trays, each of which contains "ten or twelve porcelain dishes full of veal, capons, chickens, peacocks, and other animals, and fish."[11] Each guest drinks from "a porcelain cup the size of an egg."

Pigafetta ponders the historical and cultural dimensions of porcelain upon encountering it again in the open waters off the coast of Brunei. Upon leaving the island kingdom, they encounter several squadrons (*scandroni*) of ships that he later identifies as junks (*junci*)—that is, the ancient Chinese freight ships that came to be known in fifteenth-century Malay and Javanese as *jong* ships.[12]

One of those junks carries as much cargo as a ship . . . their porcelain (*la porcellana*) is a sort of exceedingly white earth which is left for fifty years under the earth before it is worked, for otherwise it would not be fine. Fathers bury it for their sons. If venom or poison is placed in a dish made of fine porcelain, the dish immediately breaks.

Pigafetta ruminates over the special properties of porcelain. The refinement process is so sophisticated and complex that it takes several decades, and the resulting porcelain even carries a certain reactive property that responds to poison. The lore of porcelain breaking when filled with poison reappears in the writings of Pigafetta's younger relative Marco Antonio, who notes that dishes brought by a Persian ambassador to Ottoman Sultan Selim II had the special property of breaking when filled with poison.[13] This picture of porcelain and its unusual qualities closely mirrors the previously seen writings of Ali Akbar Khitayi, who noted in Istanbul that the porcelain he encountered during his trip to Beijing had a special filtering property that detects poison by changing color or shattering. As Pigafetta continues his description of the junks and their operators, he again identifies two perennial dimensions of the political landscape of the sixteenth-century South China Sea: Muslim merchants and Chinese kingship.

> The money made by the Moors [*li morj*] in those regions is of bronze [*metalo*] pierced in the middle so that it may be strung. On only one side of it are four characters, which are letters of the great king of China. We call that money *picis*. They gave us six porcelain dishes for one *cathil*, which is equivalent to two of our *libre* (pounds).[14]

Pigafetta paints a picture of a vibrant inter-Asian commercial scene that included Muslim merchants trading in Chinese currency who were active between China's southeast coast and the island kingdoms of Borneo. The story of Muslim merchants close to the Chinese coast was an old one, but there was a new element that the Spanish expedition identified: Muslim political networks connecting the Philippines with the rising sultanates of Southeast Asia. The first of Manila's rulers whom they encountered was Raja Matanda, the onetime commander of Brunei's naval forces.

Manila's Rajas and the Conquest of the Philippines

Raja Matanda was also known as Ache, and he was related to the two other rulers in the environs of Maynila. Matanda was simultaneously the uncle of Raja Sulayman and cousin of Raja Lakandula.[15] Ache, as the Spanish expedition knew him, was also related to the Sultan of Brunei. While in Borneo, where the young Prince Ache Matanda was active, the Spaniards thought they were under attack by an approaching squadron of junks and ended up capturing the future raja, not knowing yet that the young mariner was a relative of the sultan of Brunei and a commander of one of the sultan's naval forces. When the Spaniards captured "Prince Ache," they described him as the son of the king of the Luzon island where Maynila—and present-day Manila—was located. Some fifty years after Magellan and Elcano's arrival in the region, during Miguel López de Legazpi's conquest of the Philippines in the 1570s, Prince Ache would resurface in Spanish writings as Raja Ache "el Viejo." This Raja "el Viejo" was one of three rulers governing the regions in and around Maynila during Spain's conquest. Raja Ache would negotiate with de Legazpi during the Spanish conquest of the Philippines, while his nephew Raja Sulayman would continue to resist. During the earlier expedition under Elcano, we learn that the future Raja Ache Matanda lived a fascinating youth.

During the earlier encounter under Elcano's leadership, Pigafetta's shipmate Rodrigo de Aganduru Moriz recorded and left a detailed account of the young prince's background and connections with rulers in the region, including the Sultan of Brunei.[16] This Rodrigo tells us that Ache's mother ruled Maynila and that his cousin was the ruler of neighboring Tondo, the future Raja Lakandula during de Legazpi's conquest. In the context of competition between Maynila and Tondo, Ache Matanda sought support from the sultan of Brunei, his maternal grandfather, and became the head of the sultan of Brunei's naval force.[17] Ache's connections with Brunei included his plans for marriage with a relative in Borneo.[18] It was in this historical context that Ache was around the southern coast of Borneo during the arrival of Magellan's expedition.

As mentioned, Ache Matanda would not resurface in Spanish sources for another fifty years as an older man unwilling to resist de Legazpi's plans on Maynila. In the interim, Spain had sent Ruy López de Villalobos, who is credited with first using the name "the Philippine islands" (*las islas Felipinas*) for the islands in honor of King Philip (Felipe) II.[19] The actual capture of the Philippines occurred during de Legazpi's expedition.

Miguel López de Legazpi's conquest of the Philippines occurred after a thirty-year career in Mexico City. A mariner from the Basque city of Zumarraga, de Legazpi was sixty-two years old when he prepared to embark on an expedition across the Pacific in 1564. The expedition, which began in Acapulco, was commissioned by King Philip II and his viceroy and reached the island of Cebu in 1565. Over the next five years, de Legazpi and his men moved around the islands, establishing pacts with some villages and destroying others. By 1570, de Legazpi began to eye the Luzon island where Manila Bay was located. Juan de Salcedo and Martín de Goiti, de Legazpi's *maestre de campo* (field marshal), led the second of three expeditions to Manila.

The sight of Japanese and Chinese traders around Manila Bay appears to have prompted de Legazpi to consider moving the base of his Philippines operation to Luzon island. Hernando Riquel, one of the expedition members, recorded the group's observations, including their encounters with Chinese and Japanese merchants. In the first encounter, a group of the Spanish vessels at the head of the expedition happened upon a group of large Chinese vessels on one of the rivers leading to Manila Bay. Riquel recounts how, to the dismay of the expedition captain further behind, the Spaniards up front ended up engaging and capturing several Chinese ships after assuming that a Chinese attack was imminent.

> The soldiers searched the cabins in which the Chinese kept their most valuable goods, and there they found silk—both woven and in skeins— gold thread, musk, gilded porcelain bowls, pieces of cotton cloth, gilded water-jugs and other curious articles . . . earthen jars and crockery, large porcelain vases, plates, and bowls, and some fine porcelain jars, which they call *sinoratas*. They also found iron, copper, steel, and a small quantity of wax, which the Chinese had bought.[20]

The Spaniards found the typical portfolio of Chinese exports, including silk and porcelain as well as gold commodities. The expedition's encounter with the Chinese close to Manila Bay offers an eyewitness window into some of the dynamics of Chinese cultural transfer between China's port cities and the Philippine islands on the eve of Spanish conquest. In parallel with Chinese-Malay exchange, Chinese-Philippine exchange saw the local use of Chinese manufactured goods as symbols of political power and social status, particularly as bodily ornaments, wealth objects in households, and burial accompaniments.[21] De Legazpi was interested in these commodities and in establishing close connections with the Chinese and Japanese traders the crew spotted in Manila Bay.

Unsurprisingly, when the expedition's leaders caught up with the front vessels and found that they had captured several Chinese ships, they were not pleased. Juan de Salcedo, de Legazpi's adult grandson, as well as Martín de Goiti, a soldier, were part of the expedition's leadership and were particularly displeased.

> Captain Juan de Salcedo arrived with the rear-guard of the *praus* after the soldiers had already placed in safety the goods taken from the Chinese

ships. He was not at all pleased with the havoc made among the Chinese. The master-of-camp (*maestre de campo*), Martín de Goiti, who had remained behind with the large ship, showed much more displeasure, when he heard of the occurrence. As soon as he was able to cast anchor with the junk in the river of Bato, he made all haste to make them understand that he was sorry for their misfortune, and that they had [however] done wrong in sallying forth against the Spaniards. Nevertheless, he said he would give them, besides their freedom, a ship, in which they might return to their own country without any hindrance—besides whatever was necessary for their voyage. This was highly appreciated by the Chinese who, being very humble people, knelt down with loud utterances of joy.[22]

The expedition leadership's commitment to cultivating positive relations with the Chinese stands out in contrast with their more aggressive approach to diplomacy and conquest seen throughout the islands. It also echoes the contrast between the aggressive Portuguese conquest of the Melakan Sultanate and the more careful Portuguese diplomacy with the Ming in Macau. The difference speaks in part to the perception of the Ming's military might and its lucrative trade connections. The possibility of trade with Chinese and Japanese merchants was one of the main reasons for the expedition's fundamental interest in sailing as far into Luzon island as Manila Bay. Indeed, by this point in the expedition's voyage to Manila, the future of the Philippines as a crossroads of Chinese, Southeast Asian, and Spanish American commerce was increasingly apparent to figures like de Legazpi with his thirty years of experience working in Mexico.

In an interesting illustration of how the Spanish expedition imagined the complexity of Chinese shipping technology back in the sixteenth century, the Spaniards discovered that the mechanisms of the Chinese vessels were beyond their repair expertise when they offered to repair the damage.

Seeing that the sails, masts, and rigging of the vessels were so different from ours that none of his men had any knowledge of them, the master-of-camp thought best to ask the Chinese to send three or four sailors with the junk to Panay, in company with some friendly Moors of Luzon, who were with the Spaniards. The Chinese very willingly agreed to that and provided the required men. Thus the ship was dispatched with twelve Luzon Moros, four Chinese, and four Spanish soldiers of the guard.[23]

With the Spanish expedition unable to work with Chinese shipping technology, a mix of Spaniards, local Muslim merchants, and Chinese headed to the port of Panay with the Chinese cargo. This encounter took place during the second of three expeditions to the island of Luzon, where Manila was located, up the Pasig River.

Sources offer contrasting accounts of how relations between the Spaniards and the rulers of Manila broke down, but by May of 1570, Martín de Goiti's men attacked Maynila and subsequently retreated to de Legazpi's vessels.[24] The possibilities of a lucrative Spanish-held commercial base in Luzon island prompted de Legazpi to order an additional expedition and to join it himself in 1571.

As mentioned, Raja Ache Matanda, whom Magellan's men met fifty years earlier off the coast of Borneo, was one of the three rulers in power upon de Legazpi's arrival. Raja Matanda and Raja Sulayman were based in Maynila, while Raja Lakandula was based in Togo, now a district of Manila. By June, Raja Matanda and Raja Lakandula had submitted to Spanish authority. By 1572, the Manila galleons between Acapulco and Manila had taken shape, connecting these Chinese markets with Spanish Mexico and the ports of Spain.

The following decades of the Acapulco-Manila galleons saw a seasonal arrival of some forty ships with a capacity of more than 350 tons. The cargo included commodities from China as well as regional commodities brought to China from centers including Melaka, Patani, the Moluccas, and Japan.[25] Aboard the Acapulco-Manila galleons westward, the Spanish brought bullion in the form of American gold from Mexico and silver from Peru to pay for the Chinese commodities, and the profits came from the customs duties. From Canton and Amoy came silks, porcelains, and other precious Chinese commodities that were brought across the Pacific to the Americas and Spain. The first immigrants from China in the Americas arrived along this route. The galleons would continue until 1815, the year of the last galleon to make the Acapulco-Manila trip.

PORTUGAL'S ARRIVAL IN ASIA

Contesting Spain's Gains in the South China Sea

While Spain was commissioning Magellan's expeditions and eventually securing an uncharted trans-Pacific trade route from Acapulco to Manila, King Manuel of Portugal dispatched Diogo Lopes de Sequeira (d. 1530) southeastward from Lisbon to the Indian Ocean to gather information on Chinese commerce in Madagascar and Melaka. The orders were to secure trading posts through diplomacy and to avoid provocations, but the outcome was a war with the Sultanate of Melaka in 1511 and a subsequent clash with the sultanate's patron state: Ming China. Though the Ming administration originally eschewed trade with the Portuguese for several decades, regional merchants demonstrated a variety of responses. Merchants from the Ryukyu kingdom in Okinawa (1429–1879) turned increasingly towards Patani on the eastern side of the Malay Peninsula, bringing the city into more frequent contact with the many nodes of the Ryukyuan trade network: Japan, Korea, China, the Philippines, Java, and Sumatra.[26]

Chinese merchants involved in private commerce throughout these nodes of exchange were a mixed group and reacted to the arrival of the Portuguese differently. Some Chinese merchants, including Fujianese, appear to have withdrawn from trade in Portuguese-held Melaka in favor of commerce with Javanese, Malay, and Gujarati merchants in other ports.[27] Others in Siam, Melaka's competitor, continued to trade in Portuguese Melaka after the sultanate's fall. In other words, while all networks were affected by the Portuguese conquest of Melaka, they navigated the shifting political landscape of the South China Sea in ways that reflected their pre-conquest patterns: turning away from certain commercial nodes and doubling down on others depending on conditions of security and access.

For the Portuguese themselves, questions of security and access were specifically about access to Ming China's ports, where the Portuguese were officially excluded since the conquest of Melaka. By 1557, however, in response to Portuguese assistance against piracy off coastal China, the Ming extended trading rights to the Portuguese in Macau.[28] By 1580, the Portuguese secured trading rights in Nagasaki, ushering in the start of a Portuguese dimension to the Chinese-Japanese inter-Asian trade in silk and silver commodities.[29]

Additional administrative and settlement privileges in the Japanese coastal city were partly facilitated by the short-lived rise of Catholicism within the Nagasaki feudal lord's (daimyo) family. The daimyo's exposure to Catholicism began with the activities of Portugal's scholar-diplomat clients: the Jesuits. A look at the Jesuits' role in the next chapter, including their legacy as vehicles of Chinese cultural transfer to Europe, requires an understanding of why they arrived in the Forbidden City via the Goa-Macau route in the first place. Their Spain-sponsored Franciscan and Benedictine co-religionists, in contrast, often took the Acapulco-Manila route. The contrast in trade routes correlated with the division of Spain and Portugal's commercial interests in dividing the world in two.

Dividing the World in Two: The Union and Division
of the Crowns of Spain and Portugal

Across the Pacific and Indian Oceans, respectively, Spain and Portugal were becoming part of the commercial world of sixteenth-century Ming China. Economically, they accomplished what the Venetians wanted to achieve but never quite could: the bypassing of the Middle East for direct access to the Spice Islands of Southeast Asia and the precious commodities of China. In terms of diplomacy and its cultural outcomes, the sixteenth century saw an emerging parallelism between, on the one hand, Venice's exposure to Ottoman political and social life in Istanbul and, on the other hand, the Iberians' exposure to Chinese political and social life in coastal China and—among the Jesuits—even Beijing.

The outcome of this exchange was the beginning of a long and enduring transfer of Chinese material and intellectual culture, together with an even grander imagination of China, back to Europe. This Chinese cultural transfer occurred along the return trip of the Lisbon-Goa-Macau and Seville-Acapulco-Manila trade routes, traversed by the many mariners, Jesuits, Benedictines, Franciscans, ambassadors, and adventurers who reached the gates of China and, in the Jesuits' case, who worked and socialized right in Beijing's Forbidden City.[30] This cultural transfer westward, however, was the not the intended goal of Iberian ruling circles. What they aspired to was something that they fulfilled, and that the British were closer to accomplishing on the eve of Chinese and Japanese modernization: the political and cultural domination of this Sinocentric world of Asia. The terms of this aspirational domination were formulated in a treaty signed between the Spanish and Portuguese monarchies at the end of the 1400s just after the monarchies instituted an all-Catholic Iberia policy and centralized their respective political authority in the peninsula.

According to the terms of the treaty, the world would be divided into two spheres: a Portuguese sphere to the east and a Spanish sphere to the west. What threw this plan into chaos was, first, the fact that those two worlds ended up meeting in Macau and Manila, and second, the union of the Portuguese and Spanish Crowns in 1580. What follows is a brief look at both dimensions of Iberia's aspirational domination of Asia and its unintended consequence of bringing Asia to Europe.

The Brief Union of Spain and Portugal and Its Repercussions in Asia

The union of Portugal and Spain is the complex story of intermarriage between the royal families of Portugal, Aragon, Castile, and the Habsburgs of the Netherlands in the 1500s. The Crowns of Aragon and Castile, under Ferdinand and Isabella respectively, were famous for their joint conquest of the Nasrid emirate of Granada in 1492. The union of Spain with Portugal and the Netherlands decades later relates to the background of the monarch who, in the late 1500s, emerged as the inheritor of the Portuguese, Spanish, and Dutch royal lines—namely Philip II (r. 1556–1598). Philip was the name-sake of the Philippines, which received its new moniker after de Legazpi's conquest. Philip's ancestors include Ferdinand and Isabella of Aragon and Castile back in 1492.

In the late fifteenth century, King Manuel I of Portugal married one of the daughters of Ferdinand and Isabella—namely, the Aragonese-Castilian princess Maria. Together, Maria and Manuel I had a daughter, Princess Isabella of Portugal. Meanwhile, Ferdinand and Isabella's other daughter—Maria's sister—was Aragonese-Castilian princess Isabella II, who was there-fore the aunt of Maria's daughter Princess Isabella of Portugal. This aunt, Aragonese-Castilian princess Isabella II, married the Habsburg prince Philip and had a son Charles V, who was raised in the Netherlands and inherited the Habsburg throne. Princess Isabella of Portugal and Charles V, children of sisters Maria and Isabella II, were therefore cousins and grandchildren of the famous Ferdinand and Isabella. The two—Princess Isabella of Por-tugal and Emperor Charles V—married, making them Empress Isabella and Emperor Charles V.

Their son, Philip II of Castile, was thus the Spanish-Dutch Habsburg Emperor via his father Charles. On Philip II's mother's side, when his grand-father Manuel I of Portugal did not leave an heir, the crown bypassed Philip II's mother Empress Isabella and he himself was crowned King of Portugal while also ruling as Habsburg Emperor.[31]

It was this Philip II of Portugal and Spain and the Netherlands who, under the terms of the union of the Spanish and Portuguese Crowns in 1580, was forced to negotiate with Iberia's nobility in order to preserve Spain's and Portugal's respective autonomy over their decades-old empires across the

Americas, Indian Ocean, and South China Sea. Legally speaking, Philip II imposed restrictions on trade and travel between Portuguese Macau and Spanish Manila. Theoretically, Portuguese merchants in Melaka and Macau would not cross eastward into Manila and compromise the Spaniards' share of profits from Chinese commerce. Likewise, Spanish merchants would derive their commercial profits from the trans-Pacific Acapulco-Manila galleons and would not rely on Portuguese Macau and Melaka for profits. In practice, however, smuggling flourished between Portuguese Macau and Spanish Manila, and the Portuguese made a variety of efforts to block out the Spaniards from local commerce. What facilitated Portuguese commerce's dominance over Spain in Asia was the fact that the treaty that divided the world in two ultimately excluded the Spanish from what became the most lucrative centers of the South China Sea that the Dutch eventually dominated in the seventeenth century.

More specifically, Portugal and Spain divided the world into two Iberian spheres of influence twice, and it was the second division that saw the exclusion of Spain from much of the South China Sea. As mentioned, Portugal and Spain first divided their holdings across the Atlantic in 1494 in the Treaty of Tordesillas before reaching Asia.[32] The long-term outcome was the preservation of Portuguese sovereignty over Brazil in South America and, on the eastern side of the Atlantic, much of the African coast. The treaty protected Spain's holdings north and west of Brazil, which explains the Spanish names associated with cities of the American west coast prior to their Anglicization under British rule. Once the Portuguese crossed the Cape Route to reach the Spice Islands via Goa and Melaka in the early 1500s, and once Spanish vessels reached the same islands through the Pacific Route via Acapulco and Manila, the Portuguese protested at how far Spain's westward share would reach into Portugal's east (*oriente*). Spain's claim over the Philippines since the arrival of Magellan in 1521 constituted a breach of Portugal's aspirational Asian dominion. Likewise, Spain's incursions into Southeast Asia were a breach of the treaty.

By 1529, the treaty was revised in Saragossa. Charles V, in need of finances, agreed to accept 350,000 ducats in return for giving up to Portugal any rights Spain claimed over most of Southeast Asia, with Spain being assigned everything east of a certain position in the South Pacific.[33] The Philippine islands were theoretically part of the Portuguese sphere of influence according to the treaty. In practice, the Portuguese relinquished their claims over the Philippines to Spain, but the Portuguese held tightly to their resistance against Spain making inroads into China. Moving beyond diplomatic negotiations with their Iberian neighbors, the Portuguese resorted to art of the monopoly, using their positions in Nagasaki and Macau to exclude their Spanish competitors from the market for a variety of East Asian commodities.

Portuguese merchants diverted Chinese trade away from Manila towards Macau by paying higher prices and making themselves the illegal middlemen of an illicit Macau-Manila smuggling trade.[34] Aware of the formation of a broader Portuguese monopoly over European inter-Asian trade in the South China Sea, seven Spaniards petitioned for trading privileges in Macau in 1591 in order to access those diverted goods themselves rather than paying raised Portuguese smuggling prices. The efforts were futile the more Portuguese merchants were able to dominate multiple nodes of inter-Asian commerce in the South China Sea west of Manila.

The outcome for Spain was the limitation of its global trade network to the Acapulco-Manila galleons, making the Americas the center of its trans-Pacific and trans-Atlantic imperial trade network. Manila as Spain's western periphery became something of a specialized port in the Spanish Empire that received Chinese merchants from Fujian and their commodities, including silk, and brought them back eastward. In Manila, the commodities were taxed, and as mentioned, Spanish merchants paid for the Chinese commodities with American silver and gold that went back to Fujian. Chinese commodities were transferred to the previously discussed galleons that took them to Mexico, Peru, and in some cases Spain.

What drove Spanish commerce towards a more exclusively American trade network to the exclusion of deeper engagement with the South China Sea and Indian Ocean was not only the Portuguese monopoly between Macau and Manila, but also the Spanish colonial policy of preventing private Asian trade sales in the Americas from compromising the profits of continental Spain's export industries to the Americas. That is, like the later British Empire and in contrast with Portugal's far more diffuse and decentralized empire, Spain aspired to a more centralized imperial economy based in Spain, where continental goods could flood the empire's market. In the case of silk, the Spanish Crown never tried to establish a trading colony in China that would bypass Fujianese silk merchants because the Crown preferred to export its own Spanish silk to the Americas rather than encourage a taste for Chinese silk among Spanish Mexico's silk manufacturers.[35]

Among the most important outcomes of this Iberian race to Asia were its cultural outcomes. While the sixteenth century saw a massive influx of Europeans across the coasts of China, from the South China Sea to the Sea of Japan, it also saw a major transfer of culture in the reverse direction. During the entire period of Portuguese and Spanish political expansion in the region, merchants and administrators brought back to sixteenth-century Lisbon and Seville a variety of commodities, newly created maps, and written accounts of their travels around China. With the arrival of Jesuit scholar-diplomats in Beijing via Macau, this cultural absorption and exposure to the Sinocentric world of East Asia extended to include Chinese intellectual culture, from the Chinese language to Confucian ethics. Within just a few decades of the Iberians' arrival in Asia, in other words, the stage was set for an increasingly complex and enduring imagination of China across Europe that situated China and the South China Sea—flanked by the Indian and Pacific Oceans—at the heart of a global Sinocentric maritime world.

CHAPTER 6

A Sino-Jesuit Tradition
of Science and Mapmaking

The original idea behind having Jesuit scientist-theologians come to Macau to systematically master the Chinese language was the brainchild of Alessandro Valignano (d. 1606), who drew on the earlier cultural accommodationist approach of Jesuit cofounder Francis Xavier (d. 1552). Born in Naples in 1539, Valignano was ordained as a member of the new Society of Jesus in 1566 at the age of twenty-seven.[1] Valignano came in September 1578 to Macau, and it was Valignano who requested that Jesuits from Portuguese India travel from Goa to Macau to study Chinese. Michele Ruggieri (d. 1607), a fellow Neapolitan with a demonstrated ability in learning languages, traveled to Macau to take on the task.[2] Because Valignano was leaving for Japan just before Ruggieri arrived, he left Ruggieri some instructions for the task, and it was Ruggieri who asked the renowned Sinologist Matteo Ricci to join from India. Together with Rudolfo Acquaviva, Ruggieri and Ricci were part of the same group of Jesuits who made the trip from Lisbon eastward via Goa in 1578. In 1579, both Ruggieri and Ricci were in Macau learning Chinese while Valignano was in Japan studying Japanese. By the end of the century, the Jesuits helped pave the way for a massive transfer back to Europe of ideas, images, accounts, and maps related to their enduring experiences in China and Japan. This cultural transfer would contextualize the rise of a kind of philo-Chinese period in Age of Exploration-era and Enlightenment-era European material and intellectual cultures.

THE POLITICS OF JESUIT LEARNING IN JAPAN:
PORTUGUESE MARINERS, JAPANESE DAIMYOS,
AND THEIR SHARED JESUIT CLIENTS

Alessandro Valignano (d. 1606), also known during his lifetime by a Chinese moniker (范禮安, Fàn Lǐ'ān), entered Japan for the first time in 1579, some thirty years after his predecessor Francis Xavier (d. 1552) came to Japan. Xavier, a founding member of the Society of Jesus, traveled throughout the Portuguese trade routes of the Atlantic, Indian Ocean, and South China Sea in the early 1500s. The lore and memory of Xavier's linguistic obstacles motivated Valignano's famous vision of developing a dedicated Japanese language curriculum for Jesuits in Macau, where they simultaneously mastered Chinese.[3]

Xavier's earlier mission to Japan followed an encounter in Melaka with a certain Anjiro, a former samurai and fugitive from Japan's Satsuma Domain.[4] Coincidentally, some three centuries later, many of the most prominent Westernizing political reformers of the Meiji era began their careers as samurai in this very same Satsuma Domain. Back in the sixteenth century, however, the entirety of Japan was barely within the scope of European imagination. What little Xavier knew about the land came from the Portuguese merchants who had only recently arrived there. Writing to his Jesuit peers back in Europe, Xavier's travel accounts offer a glimpse into his earliest plans to travel to Japan.

> I have lately heard of the country of Japan, which lies beyond China more than six hundred miles. They tell us that the inhabitants are very clever, very desirous of learning not only religious truth, but also the natural truths which are a part of education. The Portuguese who have come back from Japan tell us this, and indeed it is proved well enough by certain Japanese themselves, who last year came with me from Melaka to India, and who lately have been made Christian at Goa in the College of Santa Fe. You will be able to see this well enough from the account of Japanese matters which we have sent you, which we got from Paul the Japanese, who is called Paul of the Holy Faith, a man really of very excellent virtue and perfect truthfulness.[5]

Paul of the Holy Faith was Anjiro, the Japanese samurai from Satsuma who adopted a baptized name upon conversion. In Portuguese Melaka,

Anjiro had learned enough Portuguese to communicate with Xavier. On his way back to Japan, Anjiro brought Xavier, who was accompanied by two other Jesuits and two additional Japanese travelers. Xavier arrived in 1549, but his difficulty learning Japanese meant that his attempts to make diplomatic inroads and to introduce his faith found limited success.

Xavier's ship first arrived in Japan in 1549 but was only allowed to call at the port of Kagoshima on the island of Kyushu. By late 1550, a little over a year after his arrival, Xavier was in Anjiro's hometown of Yamaguchi just north of Kyushu island. By March of 1551, following a failed trip to meet the emperor in Kyoto, Xavier approached the daimyo of the province, Ouchi Yoshitaka (d. 1551). Xavier was given permission to preach following his second trip to the daimyo, when he opted for the persona of a wealthy ambassador as opposed to a supplicant. The daimyo was overthrown in 1551, leaving Xavier to turn to daimyo Otomo Sorin (d. 1587) of neighboring Bungo province.[6] Sorin allowed Xavier to preach and, through Xavier, even cultivated connections with the Portuguese in Goa and the Papal States, sending embassies to both. Among the outcomes of daimyo Sorin's diplomatic ventures was the acquisition of a Portuguese breech-loading swivel gun, which remains in Tokyo. Early Jesuit-Japanese political exchange, in other words, developed in correlation with the development of Portuguese-Japanese diplomatic relations and a nascent Japanese absorption of European military technology. By the end of Xavier and Sorin's exchange in the late 1570s, Sorin adopted Catholicism, becoming part of the short-lived phenomenon of late Muromachi-era, early Edo-era Catholic daimyos.

In continuity with the political access that came with Xavier adapting to Japanese diplomatic protocols, Xavier made inroads with the Shingon monks of Japanese Buddhism by somewhat unintentionally adapting aspects of Christian theology to Buddhist theology. Relying on an interpreter, Xavier explained the theology of *deus* in Latin using the Japanese term *dainichi*, the celestial Buddha.[7] However, Xavier later backtracked and rejected this conflation, scandalizing his once receptive Buddhist interlocutors. The significance of Xavier's original conflation of *deus* with *dainichi* was that his efforts fit into a long-term and enduring pattern of Jesuits adapting Christianity to Northeast Asian concepts and customs rather than attempting to Latinize their Japanese and Chinese interlocutors as part of the mission. Xavier even allowed Jesuits to wear orange robes like the Buddhists. This adaption was further developed in the careers of Michele Ruggieri (羅明堅, Luó Míngjiān) and Matteo Ricci (利瑪竇, Lì Mǎdòu) in China but was temporarily rejected in the interim years during the brief tenure of the Portuguese Jesuit Francisco Cabral (d. 1609) in Japan. Upon his arrival in 1570, Cabral prohibited the use of orange robes among the Jesuits in a break from Xavier's earlier approach.[8] When Valignano arrived in 1579, the Jesuit mission in Japan returned to Xavier's attempt to harmonize Jesuit and Japanese modes of learning, placing new emphasis on Jesuit study of the Japanese and Chinese languages.

Xavier and Cabral's contrasting perspectives on appropriate Jesuit-Japanese cultural encounters shed light on a broader European debate about Northeast Asian cultural currency, one that profoundly shaped Asian cultural transfer to Europe in the sixteenth century. At the heart of this debate was the following question: Were Jesuits to adapt their intellectual customs and social practices to Chinese and Japanese modes of living and learning, did this adaptation imply a recognition of China and Japan's intellectual and social sophistication? For the Jesuits who pioneered the Western study of Chinese and Japanese, especially Valignano and more so Ricci, the answer was yes. For other mendicant orders like Spain's Franciscan clients in Manila, the Jesuits' position was religiously problematic and compromised the Catholic faith by assimilating it into Chinese and Japanese sociolinguistic cultural practices.[9]

For the Portuguese mariners and administrators stationed in Northeast Asia, who were in practice the Jesuits' patrons, this question about the comparative cultural currency of Latin Europe and Sinocentric Northeast Asia was less important than its political and commercial outcomes: intimate Portuguese diplomatic relations with powerful Japanese daimyos and with the Chinese emperors. Jesuits Xavier, Valignano, and Ricci were simultaneously scientist-theologians and scholar-diplomats, and their close connections with Japanese daimyos translated into an enduring Portuguese advantage over their Spanish rivals in accessing Asia's Sinocentric political and commercial networks. However, there was an unintended outcome of these deep connections and the cultural symbiosis that emerged with the rise of Catholic daimyos: the rise of a bloc of Portuguese-allied Catholic daimyos on the losing end of the rising Tokugawa clan's successful push to bring the daimyos and their domains under the central authority of the new Edo-era (1603–1868) Tokugawa shogunate in Tokyo. What follows is a closer look at these political outcomes and how they came to an abrupt halt on the eve of the Tokugawa clan's expulsion of the Portuguese and negotiation with the newly arriving Dutch.

The Portuguese Fallout with Japan on the Eve of the Edo Era

The sixteenth-century history of the Jesuits' diplomatic connection with various Japanese daimyos, together with its political outcomes of a close but short-lived Portuguese-Japanese commercial connection, illustrates the extent that the Portuguese encounter with Japan was a deep and multifaceted one that represented the starting point of a long-term, two-way cultural transfer between southern Europe and Northeast Asia. From a European perspective, the Portuguese arrival in Macau and Nagasaki marked the beginning of a continuous transfer of visual, textual, and material representations of China and Japan westward. From a Japanese perspective, in contrast, what began as the Muromachi-era transfer of Portuguese religion, language, and military technology to Japan was abruptly reoriented during the Tokugawa-led Edo era (1603–1868). Most of the Edo era saw the Tokugawa government oversee an explicit cultural filtering process that began with the expulsion of the Portuguese and banning of Catholic learning among the newly Catholic daimyos, and that continued with the cultivation of specific modes of Dutch learning—namely, medicine and technology, made available by the Dutch in Nagasaki following their successful negotiation of settlement privileges in the early Edo era. Interestingly, some two and a half centuries later, Dutch medicine and technology, especially military and industrial technology, played a central role in the late Edo-era administrative and popular overture to European models of political and military reform leading into the Meiji era (1868–1912).

In the earliest era of this Jesuit-facilitated Portuguese-Japanese encounter, what emerged was a variety of Portuguese military connections with specific daimyos, many of whom converted to Catholicism at different points in this alliance. The most notable of these Portuguese-allied daimyos was Omura Sumitada (d. 1587), who controlled Nagasaki and converted to Catholicism early in his relations with the Portuguese. Sumitada granted the Portuguese partial administrative control of Nagasaki in 1580. What turned out to be a short-lived milestone in Portuguese political connections in Northeast Asia came some seventeen years after Sumitada first welcomed the Portuguese to Yokoseura in 1563, which followed the expulsion of the Portuguese from Hirado two years earlier by the local daimyo.[10] Sumitada converted to Catholicism early on in 1563, the same year he relieved the Portuguese of trade duties in Yokoseura for a period of ten years in order to cultivate trade around the harbor. Within months, Sumitada oversaw a steady increase in shipping traffic connecting Yokoseura with the Portuguese settlement in Macau.

After the destruction of Yokoseura, Sumitada cultivated Nagasaki as an alternative port. When the Ryozoji clan attacked Nagasaki in 1578, the Portuguese helped push them out of Sumitada's domain. Two years later, Sumitada turned part of the administration of the port over to the Portuguese, thus advancing the province's trade advantage over other provinces. For individual Japanese daimyos, in other words, political connections with the Portuguese correlated with a variety of long-term economic and military benefits in an environment of fierce competition between daimyos and their domains. That these close political connections correlated with growing cultural connections, including the conversion of individual daimyos to Catholicism, was not immediately scandalous in the Japanese political scene. What made it problematic enough to stir up massive armed Japanese push-back was when these Catholic daimyos formed a kind of political bloc, one that was ultimately on the losing end of the rising Tokugawa clan leadership's efforts to bring all of the domains under the authority of a new Tokugawa-led shogunate in Tokyo several decades after the Portuguese settled in Nagasaki. What made them a kind of political bloc was a process in the 1560s and 1570s that saw several newly Catholic daimyos simultaneously form alliances with the Portuguese and with one another.

This bloc of Catholic daimyos came to be known in Japanese as the *kirishitan* (吉利支丹) who, as mentioned, converted at a variety of stages during their political relationships with the Portuguese[11] While daimyo Omura Sumitada—in charge of Nagasaki—converted in 1563 at the start of his political and commercial alliance with the Portuguese, daimyo Otomo Sorin converted in 1578 at the culmination of this alliance. Sorin was Jesuit cofounder Xavier's previously mentioned Japanese patron.

Arima Harunobu (d. 1612) was the third of the influential Portuguese-aligned daimyos of the late sixteenth century. In the 1570s, the same Ryuzoji clan that would eventually attack Sumitada-led Nagasaki in 1578—the year the Portuguese defended Nagasaki and were rewarded with trading privileges—was the same Ryuzoji clan advancing on Harunobi's provinces. Within the clan, it was specifically Ryuzoji Takanobi, the Japanese daimyo of Hizen province, who advanced on Harunobi's province unaware of Harunobi's connections with the Portuguese. As in the case of Sumitada's reliance on the Portuguese to repel the Ryuzoji from Nagasaki, Harunobi likewise relied on the Portuguese to secure weapons. By 1579, some sixteen years after Omura Sumitada was baptized by his client Xavier in 1563, Harunobi was baptized by Valignano.

Paradoxically, by 1580, Xavier and Valignano's approach of assimilating Catholicism in a Japanese sociolinguistic context, which facilitated various political and commercial milestones for the Portuguese, became in the late 1500s one of the key Japanese pretexts for expelling the Portuguese altogether. This clash occurred under the politically unifying force of Toyotomi Hideyoshi (d. 1598) and his ally Tokugawa Ieyasu (d. 1616), before whom the alliance of Portuguese-supported Catholic daimyos constituted a rival losing bloc. The success of Hideyoshi's unification of Japan on the eve of the Tokugawa-led Edo era meant the abandonment of Catholicism among the remaining Catholic daimyos and the expulsion of the Jesuits.

By 1613, echoing the momentum of a variety of earlier tensions that included Franciscan-Japanese and Benedictine-Japanese friction, and in continuity with the overall consolidation of authority in Japan, Tokugawa Ieyasu—founder of the Tokugawa shogunate in Tokyo and Hideyoshi's ally—issued the Christian Expulsion Edict in 1610. While the newly established Dutch East India Company (1602–1799) managed to negotiate settlement and trading privileges in Nagasaki in place of the Portuguese, ushering in a protracted transfer of Dutch medicine and technology into Japan through the intellectual interests of Arai Hakuseki (d. 1725) and other Neo-Confucian scholar-officials, the legacy of the Jesuits' Northeast Asia mission largely continued in neighboring China. In Macau, diplomat and scientist-theologian Matteo Ricci developed Valignano's approach of cultural adaptation so deeply that the Ming dynasty invited him to Beijing to develop his work on maps and astronomy, while Rome withdrew its support for the Jesuits in Northeast Asia altogether in light of Ricci's controversial advocacy of Catholic-Confucian religious syncretism. As in the case of Japan, the Jesuits' Portuguese patrons were less concerned about the complexities of Church-Jesuit relations than they were about the outcomes of Ricci's cultural access: the strengthening of Portuguese-Ming relations, particularly in light of the tensions of Portuguese-Japanese tensions in the decades leading up to the Edo period. By the end of Ricci's career and that of his late Ming-era and early Qing-era successors, and with the rise of Dutch long-distance shipping carrying multilingual Jesuit mapmakers and translators back and forth from Asia, both southern and northern Europe emerged on the receiving end of a major transfer of images and knowledge about China, Japan, and the Sinocentric world of East Asia.

BEIJING'S JESUIT MAPMAKERS: MATTEO RICCI AND
HIS SUCCESSORS IN THE FORBIDDEN CITY

Among the many businesspeople and administrators who made the trip to Macau on their way to China and Japan, two Jesuit scholars stand out: Michele Ruggieri and Matteo Ricci. Both Jesuits and their successors left monumental legacies in transferring their encounters and imaginations of China back to Europe through a variety of largely Dutch-published works.[12] Ruggieri was known in China as Luo Mingjian. Ricci was known as Li Madou or, more honorifically, Li Xitai.

While Ruggieri's and Ricci's respective legacies in China were similar, their pathways to China were slightly different. Ruggieri was a doctoral graduate of the University of Naples in civil and canon law, and he went on to work in the administration of Philip III, the son of Philip II of Spain and Portugal. Ruggieri was ordained as a priest in 1578, the same year he left for Goa (Portuguese Estado da Índia) with several other Jesuits. One was Matteo Ricci, who eventually joined Ruggieri in Macau later. Ruggieri arrived in Macau in 1579, while Ricci arrived in 1582 on Ruggieri's request. Rudolfo Acquaviva, a fourth Jesuit, remained in the Indian subcontinent, proceeding to the Mughal Empire. Acquaviva was even invited to the court of Mughal Emperor Akbar and participated in the debates and assemblies of the famous *Ibadat Khana* in an episode illustrative of how deep Jesuit connections went across Asia.[13]

Ruggieri, Ricci, and Catholic-Confucian Cultural Convergence

In the case of Ruggieri and Ricci in Ming China, what was notable about their careers in comparison with Valignano in Muromachi Japan was how close the two reached to the highest levels of power in Ming China. There was also a certain parallelism between the Jesuits' projects in China and Japan in terms of their respective attempts to adapt to what the Jesuits' imagined to be Chinese and Japanese cultures, from language and clothing to customs and, most controversially, values. In the last case, given how Confucianism shaped those values in China, the Catholic-Confucian cultural convergence that emerged in the writings of Ricci sparked the same theological controversy back in Rome that inspired Cabral's earlier condemnation of Jesuits wearing orange Buddhist robes in Japan. As discussed, Xavier took the first steps towards a Jesuit accommodationist approach to teaching Catholicism in China and Japan. Like his critic Cabral, papal authorities asked whether the Xavier-era and later Ricci-era examples of Catholic-Buddhist and Catholic-Confucian cultural convergence compromised the values of Catholicism and ascribed an undue amount of truth to Asian spiritual traditions.

Between Ruggieri and Ricci, it was Ricci's career that was in many ways more remarkable because of its location: the court of the Ming Emperor in Beijing itself. Equally remarkable was his ability to implement a project of Catholic-Confucian cultural convergence, a project that he implemented in collaboration with newly Catholic Chinese scholars and officials like Xu Guangqi, Li Zhizao, and Yang Tingyuan.[14]

Ricci's story in Beijing began in 1582 in Macau, where he joined Ruggieri with the encouragement of Valignano. By 1601, some twenty years later, Ricci was in Beijing working for the Wanli Emperor, who was interested in Ricci's knowledge of astronomy.[15] The Wanli Emperor simultaneously employed Muslim astronomers who achieved a certain political prominence during the earlier Mongol era of exchange between Ilkhanid Iran and Yuan China.

Upon Ricci's arrival, in the same way that Xavier and Valignano endeared themselves to Japanese Buddhists and adopted their clothing and language, Ricci likewise experimented with the language of Chinese Confucian doctrines as a lexical medium for articulating Catholicism in China. While Xavier described God in accordance with the language of the celestial Buddha, Ricci described God as the "lord of heaven," which overlapped syntactically with the notion of the divine heaven of Chinese religions. The culmination of this synthesis was Ricci's eight-chapter *The True Meaning of the Lord of Heaven* (*Tianzhu Shiyi*), which argues for the harmony of Christianity and Confucianism in contrast with Buddhism.

Ricci's surviving *The True Meaning of the Lord of Heaven* was completed in 1603 and illustrated the breadth and depth of his learning.[16] As a mathematician, Ricci offered arguments previously seen in medieval Latin and Greco-Arabic works for the necessary existence of the Creator, whom he identified with the Confucian Lord-on-High or Emperor Above (上帝, *shàngdì*) and with the related divine term Heaven (天, *tiān*). Also in agreement with select

Catholic and Muslim theological positions that were in wide circulation in Latin, Ricci argued against commonly Neoplatonic ontological theories—especially the notion that individual souls are part of one conjoined pre-eternal universal soul, an idea echoed in Neo-Confucianism and Buddhism and that potentially compromised the belief in a Creator who created the world in time out of nothing (ex nihilo).[17]

Where Ricci positioned Catholicism and Confucianism in especially close harmony was in ethics, making Confucius and Mencius his textual interlocutors and the intellectual foundations of his widely transmitted European representations of China as a center of sophisticated civilization and history.[18] Other Catholics contested Ricci's approach to synthesizing Catholicism with Confucianism, especially with regard to the outcomes of this synthesis in ritual. What was particularly controversial was the question of Chinese ancestor veneration. Matteo Ricci and the Jesuits around him believed that the veneration of ancestors was not necessarily in conflict with Catholic teachings as long as it was practiced and understood as simply part of Chinese cultural life.[19] Critics also contested his use of other Chinese words for God that did not clarify the boundaries separating Christianity and Chinese religion. Critics argued that one word in particular—namely, Heaven (天, tiān)—should be abandoned in favor of Lord of Heaven (天主, tiānzhǔ).

As in the case of the Jesuits in Japan under Valignano, the Jesuits' Portuguese patrons were less concerned about intra-Church controversies than they were about the new outcomes of Ricci's cultural access: European diplomatic relations in Beijing's Forbidden City. In stark contrast with the powerful daimyo Hideyoshi's late sixteenth-century clash with the Jesuits and his abrupt ending of Nagasaki's lease to Portuguese administrators, Hideyoshi's Chinese contemporary—the Ming's Wanli Emperor (r. 1572–1620)—cultivated an enduring relationship with both Portuguese merchants in Macau and their mapmaking Jesuit clients in Beijing. In the case of the Portuguese in Macau, upon getting involved in the trans-Pacific silver trade via Spanish Manila, the Portuguese flooded the Chinese market with Mexican and Peruvian silver some one hundred years after the Ming moved away from paper currency towards silver as a monetary standard. That is, the Portuguese in Macau were perfectly positioned to satisfy Ming economic demands. Following a century of low domestic silver production, Ming China's import of American silver via the Portuguese beginning in the 1530s enabled a century of Chinese commercial growth until the Ming's fall to the Qing in 1644.[20] Simultaneous with this growth was the further development of a scientific courtly culture, one that saw Persian- and Chinese-language cartography dating back to the Yuan era incorporate a growing Jesuit-compiled Latin-language cartographical tradition drawing on Portugal and Spain's century of global exploits.[21] One of the most important outcomes was a process of cultural transfer that saw bilingual Chinese-Latin maps, produced in China in collaboration with Chinese scholars, brought back to Europe. It was Ricci's students who ushered in this era of translation and transmission, including the transmission of Ricci's work, during the early 1600s.

Matteo Ricci's Scientist-Theologian Successors and the Transfer of Maps to Europe

One of the chief legacies of Ricci and his successors in Beijing was the production of maps and books of geography. Ricci's most famous work, *A Map of the Myriad Countries of the World* (坤輿萬國全圖), was produced in 1602 under the Wanli Emperor's patronage and in collaboration with several Chinese colleagues including the newly Catholic Hangzhounese official Li Zhizao—also known by his baptized name Leon.[22] Ricci's colleagues, fellow Italian Diego de Pantoja (龐迪我, Páng dí wǒ) and Spaniard Sabatino de Ursis (熊三拔, Xióng Sānbá), worked in both Nanjing and Beijing and collaborated with Ricci in the production of the *Record of Foreign Lands* (職方外紀).

The Chinese atlas, *A Map of the Myriad Countries of the World*, some eight scrolls in length, was of monumental significance in both Chinese and European history, as it was China's first global atlas that added a variety of information and details to the geographies shown in Ricci's world map.[23] The maps and descriptions comprising the atlas were edited, revised, and compiled by Venetian Republic–born Giulio Aleni (艾儒略, Ai Rulüe) and published by Hangzhounese official "Michael" Yang Tingyun in 1623. By 1631, the atlas was in Joseon Korea, having been introduced to the kingdom by a Korean diplomat in China named Jeong Duwon (d. 1581). Joao Rodrigues (陸若漢, Lùruòhàn), a Portuguese Jesuit and one-time Japanese-language interpreter for Toyotomi Hideyoshi and Tokugawa Ieyasu, met Jeong Duwon in Shandong while training one of its governor's troops in the use of cannons against the rising Qing. That governor, "Ignatius" Sun Yuanhua (d. 1632), was himself a convert to Christianity in a period when both Japanese and Chinese proximity to Jesuit scientist-theologians correlated with the integration of European firearms with the older Chinese gunpowder technology.

By the late Ming period, Ricci's successors remained active in Chinese diplomatic and courtly scientific circles and began to bring back to Europe some of the writings the Jesuits produced in China. The career of Nicolas Trigault (金尼閣, Jīn Nígé) of Douai (present-day France) was particularly influential. Trigault was appointed procurator of the China mission to Europe in 1612 by Nicolo Longobardo (龍華民, Lónghuá Mín), who had been Ricci's successor as Superior General of the Jesuits' mission in China since 1610. Longobardo himself arrived in 1597 in Shaozhou and remained in China into his nineties in the 1650s. Trigault, whom Longobardo appointed as procurator, was responsible as a go-between connecting the Jesuits' China mission with Rome and transmitting Jesuit-Chinese works back to Europe.

Trigault first arrived in Nanjing in 1611 and eventually died in Hangzhou in 1628. As procurator of the mission in China, he headed for Europe via Macau in 1613 in order to report to Rome on the Jesuits' accomplishments and, on behalf of the late Ricci (d. 1610), find scientific experts for the Jesuits' work in China. By 1614, Trigault was in Rome and completed an influential work on behalf of the Jesuits: an edition and Latin translation of Ricci's Italian *On the Christian Mission among the Chinese by the Society of Jesus*. The text was published in Augsburg, Germany, in 1615 and in French in 1616.[24] Among the people Trigault met in Europe was Johann Schrek, with whom Trigault procured a telescope to bring back to China. When Trigault led a mission back to Macau in 1619, Schrek was part of the group, as was Johann Adam Schall von Bell (湯若望, Tāng Ruòwàng) and Giacomo Rho (羅雅谷, Luó Yǎgǔ). While in Macau, Trigault completed his *Aid to the Eyes and Ears of Western Literati*, a text that built on Ricci's work on Chinese romanization. By 1630, the Jesuit mission in Macau sent Trigault and Rho together to Beijing to work on reform of the Chinese calendar.[25]

Trigault's work in Beijing in the 1630s began about a decade before the fall of the Ming, when Jesuits working in China successfully managed to emphasize their role as scientists in order to navigate the shift in political authority. One of the outcomes of their ability to straddle competing loyalties to the late Ming and early Qing was the continued production of their collaborative Ming-sponsored scientific works in Chinese and their transfer back to Europe in translation. The careers of two Jesuits in particular, Michal Piotr Boym and Martino Martini, offer a window into these continuities and the culturally symbiotic nature of the Jesuits' scientific works in China.

The Polish Jesuit Michal Boym (卜彌格, Bǔ Mígé) established a Jesuit mission in Hainan and wrote works on Chinese geography, including detailed analyses of Chinese flora and fauna. He also completed Chinese-Latin and Chinese-French dictionaries. Upon the arrival of the Manchu Qing armies, Boym fled to Tonkin on the southern coast in 1647. One of the legacies of his career was the surprising conversion to Catholicism of the last claimant to the Ming throne, the Yongli Emperor (r. 1646–1662) of the Southern Ming (1644–1662), in a period when the Great Ming (1368–1644) had already lost Nanjing and Beijing to the Qing dynasty (1644–1912). With the capitals lost to the Qing, surviving Ming members sought help from Western powers.

More specifically, in 1649, the vice-provincial of the Jesuit China mission in Guangzhou, Alvaro Semedo (曾德昭, Céng Dézhāo), sent Boym to the Southern Ming's capital that was ruled by the Yongli Emperor. There, the Southern Ming Emperor converted to Catholicism and sought help from European powers against the Qing. Within a few years, however, the Qing arrived in Southern Ming domains, forcing the Jesuits to flee or transfer their allegiances. Martino Martini was one of the Jesuits who managed to navigate this shift in political power while living in Southern Ming domains, and his story demonstrates the continuing political import of the Jesuits as political and cultural go-betweens and courtly scientists well into the early modern era.

While the Qing were marching across China, Martino Martini (衛匡國, Wèi Kuāngguó) was working in Zhenjiang close to Nanjing under the Southern Ming's Longwu Emperor (r. 1645–1646), who preceded the Yongli Emperor. According to Martini's own account, in preparation for the arrival of Qing soldiers, he hung a large red poster above the door of his home that read, "Here lives a doctor of the divine Law who has come from the Great West."[26] Martini placed a series of scientific devices below the poster, including telescopes and books with elaborate bindings, giving the impression to the soldiers that they had stumbled upon someone of major political significance. According to Martini, the commander of the forces invited him to transfer allegiance and allowed him to remain in charge of the Hangzhou church. Martini's colleague Johann Adam Schall von Bell (1592–1666) likewise managed to transfer allegiances from the Ming to the Qing, ultimately working in the Bureau of Astronomy. This legendary story of how Martini, like many of his colleagues, survived the arrival of the Qing in the 1640s fits into a larger pattern of Jesuit scientists of the Ming era continuing their work during the Qing (1644–1912) as diplomats, scientist-theologians, and ultimately cultural go-betweens ushering in Europe's growing fascination with and imagination of China and the wider Sinocentric world of East Asia. Back in Europe, the axis around which this imagination turned was the rising Dutch print culture of the 1600s that became the nexus of East Asia's past Iberian exchange and rising Dutch encounter.

DUTCH PRINTERS: MAPPING CHINA AND IMAGINING THE JESUITS' CONFUCIUS IN AMSTERDAM

The print culture that developed in late seventeenth-century Amsterdam and Antwerp, two centers of the Dutch East India Company's (VOC) commerce, served as a catalyst for the crystallization of an enduring European image of China in its late Ming form. The growing European imagination that grew out of these images drew originally on the Jesuits' experiences in Macau, Hangzhou, and Beijing, and increasingly the experiences of Dutch merchants along the VOC trade routes to Edo-era (1603–1868) Nagasaki. In the form of rare high-priced atlases, the maps printed in Amsterdam and Antwerp became luxury objects alongside a variety of VOC-imported foreign commodities like sugar and, as discussed in the next two chapters, porcelain and tea. Taken together, these objects became part of a growing portfolio of items constitutive of a growing European picture of Portugal's and the VOC's intertwined worlds in Asia. What made the first and most influential annotated European atlases of China possible was the combination of Jesuits traveling through the Netherlands in the early Qing era and coterminous VOC-era Dutch printers interested in publishing the Jesuits' annotated maps for wider circulation. Martino Martini, the previously mentioned Jesuit whose scientific credentials famously impressed a Qing military force, was one of those Jesuits.

By the time Martino Martini headed from China to Rome via the Netherlands in 1651 in order to report on the Jesuits' Asia mission, the heyday of Dutch cartography was in full force in correlation with the Dutch East India Company's (VOC) meteoric rise.[27] VOC commercial gains since the company's establishment in 1602 occurred on the heels of Portuguese political losses throughout Asia, particularly in Japan. With the rise of the Tokugawa shogunate in 1603 and the protectionist Sakoku ("closed country") Edict of 1635, the Portuguese and Spanish permanently lost any chance of regaining any political or commercial foothold in Japan's harbors. The VOC, established just thirty years before the Sakoku Edict, negotiated an exclusive role as the only European power allowed to trade in Japan, specifically in Nagasaki where the Portuguese first gained a foothold in the 1580s.[28] By 1641, six years after the edict, the VOC captured Melaka from the Portuguese, leaving the Portuguese in East Asia with their small but enduringly lucrative settlement in Chinese Macau. By the end of the sixteenth century, the VOC had established trading outposts connecting the Indian Ocean with the South China Sea, from Hormuz and Jakarta to Taipei and Nagasaki. Accounts and maps from the Portuguese were beginning to circulate in southern Europe and, together with the scientific works and maps of the Jesuits, propelled the rise of Dutch printing. An influx of Chinese and Japanese material culture from this VOC trading world likewise accelerated the eruption of a kind of Chinamania in northern and western Europe throughout the mid- and late-1600s. This fervor for all things Chinese further pushed forward Dutch printing. Many of these Dutch publishers' first clients were the Jesuit astronomers and cartographers of the late Ming and early Qing eras, who increasingly traveled through cities like Amsterdam aboard VOC vessels.

Martini was one of these Jesuits active along the old Portuguese trade networks who had his works printed in VOC centers, leading to his pre-eminent legacy throughout Europe as an authority on China. Martini's works included *Novus Atlas Sinensis* (*New Atlas of China*), which became the tenth volume of bookshop owner and publisher Joan Blaeu's *Atlas Maior* (*Great Atlas*).[29] The multivolume atlas was published in parts between 1662 and 1672 and was one of the most expensive production projects of the seventeenth century, with translations following in French, Dutch, German, and Spanish.

Atlases and Globes in Joan Blaeu's Bookshop in the Netherlands
Joan Blaeu was the inheritor of the family printing business founded by his father William Blaeu. William originally conceived of a bookshop along Amsterdam's Damrak canal that would sell not only books but also globes and maps. His son Joan Blaeu's *Atlas Maior*, which included Martini's maps, was the final version of a set of earlier atlases that Joan originally published with his father.[30] The first version, which included more than two hundred maps, was published in 1635 and appeared in German, Latin, Dutch, and French. This version, in turn, drew on an earlier tradition of atlases dating back to Gerard Mercator (d. 1594).

In the old Flemish city of Leuven, Mercator had a hand in engraving and printing, publishing, and geography. In 1595, Mercator's maps were published as *Atlas sive Cosmographicae Meditationes de Fabrica Mundi et Fabricati Figura* (*Atlas or Cosmographical Meditations on the Creation of the World and on the Form of Created Matter*). While Mercator and his colleagues had ancient models to draw on, especially Ptolemy's ancient set of maps (*Geografia*), Mercator coined the term *atlas* to describe a set of maps in accordance with the persona of Atlas of Greek mythology, that is, the titan who was condemned to holding up the world on his shoulders. Like Ptolemy, Mercator had in mind the integration of maps into a kind of visual cosmology. By the time William Blaeu (d. 1683) was publishing almost one hundred years later, the term *atlas* came to mean more simply a collection of maps, but with a growing set of annotated geographical features.

What was unique and different about Martini's maps, which were integrated into the final version of Blaeu's multivolume set of atlases (*Atlas Maior*), was the kind of data visualization—especially land surveys—that his maps offered, which was in deeper dialogue with Chinese maps than was the case in his predecessors' works. Martini's work drew heavily on land surveys found in Chinese works, including Luo Hongxian's (d. 1564) Chinese-language *Enlarged Terrestrial Map*.[31] This Ming-era map was based partly on a Yuan (Mongol) map by Zhu Siben (d. 1337), compiled between 1311 and 1320.

The dissemination of Martini's atlas through Blaeu's work formed the basis of a new European imagination of and fascination with China some five hundred years after Marco Polo traveled eastward from Venice. Among the key dimensions of this new imagination was the breadth and depth of its detail and accuracy, together with the clarity of what exactly constituted "China" and where specifically it was located. More specifically, the Jesuits' reports facilitated the convergence of two earlier images of China: inland China, known in Marco Polo's writings and in the translated Persian accounts as "Cathay," and coastal China, known in the Portuguese, Spanish, and Arabic accounts as "China." Prior to the Jesuits, European writers debated the boundaries of Cathay and China, unaware that Cathay was a term commonly used in Persian and other Central Asian languages as a reference for China. Matteo Ricci himself suspected that everything written about Cathay in Persian and in the works of Marco Polo referred to the inland areas of the same China discussed by the Portuguese in Southeast Asia. Martini confirmed the connection in Leiden, where he met a specialist of Arabic manuscripts named Jacobus Golius (d. 1667).

Golius was an early Orientalist who was familiar with China from the accounts of the Portuguese and Arabic writers in Southeast Asia, where China was used in Malay to refer to the kingdom northward beyond Guangzhou. While Arabic-language texts likewise spoke of China (*Sin*), both Arabic and Persian texts had a long history of describing a second land further inland beyond the Central Asia steppe: Cathay. Marco Polo similarly wrote about Cathay, as did the Jesuit Bento de Gois (1562–1607) who learned Persian and traveled throughout northern India and Central Asia. In Martini's meeting with Golius in Leiden, the two confirmed what Ricci previously suspected: that Central Asian texts about Cathay were describing the same Tang-era, Song-era, and Yuan-era Chinese kingdom referred to as China in Southeast Asian accounts.

By the mid-1700s, through the continued interest of Dutch publishers, the Jesuits who remained active in China facilitated not only a growing European familiarity with China's inland and coastal geography but also an imagination of China's two most influential early thinkers: Confucius and Mencius.

Chinese Philosophy's First Wave in Europe: Confucius and Mencius

In the decades leading up to Leibniz's (d. 1716) influential Enlightenment-era interests in Chinese wisdom and specifically Confucianism, the Blaeu family publishers and their successors were at work making Confucian writings available to northern European audiences for the first time. By the time Thomas Paine (d. 1809) was writing, European philosophers frequently invoked Confucius alongside Aristotle in the claim that rationalist ethics had ancient forebears across time and geography. For the Jesuits in the 1500s and 1600s, the enterprise of translating Confucian works for Europe had slightly different goals. The first was to represent Chinese beliefs and customs as having a monotheistic basis in order justify to the Catholic Church the Jesuits' cultural accommodationist approach to theological education in Asia. The second was to facilitate Chinese language learning among new Jesuit recruits using Confucian writings. Education in Chinese language and ethics among the Chinese literati themselves was oriented around the Four Books of Confucius, which made the Confucian corpus an essential companion for the Jesuits' mission.[32] As in the case of the Jesuits' atlases, the Jesuits' Confucian translations reached European audiences through Dutch and Flemish printers, including the previously discussed Blaeu family.

The same William and Joan Blaeu (d. 1673) who published Martino Martini's (d. 1661) atlases were again on the scene when it came to printing the Jesuits' translations of Confucian writings. The VOC shipping network connected northern Europe with centers along the old Portuguese routes where the Jesuits were active, and the Jesuits themselves rode these ships throughout the 1600s during their trips to and from Asia. Prospero Intorcetta (殷鐸澤, Yīn Duózé) was one of these Jesuits, traveling to China during his first trip with Philippe Couplet (柏應理, Bǎi yīng lǐ) in 1659. Under Couplet's guidance, and in collaboration with fellow Chinese-speaking Jesuits Christian Wolfgang Herdtrich of the Austrian Empire and Francois de Rougement of the Netherlands, Intorcetta completed a Latin-language translation of some of the Chinese classics. In 1671, when Intorcetta returned to Europe, the original plan was to publish with Blaeu, but the texts ended up being brought to Rome from Amsterdam upon the request of the German Jesuit and scientist Athanasius Kircher.[33] There they remained for several years before any complete translation would be printed in 1687 in Paris.

These works offered the earliest translations of the Confucian corpus in European languages, and their content reflected their original use among the Jesuits as language-learning tools. In their earliest forms, they included Chinese characters together with Latin transliterations, Latin glosses, and Latin commentary. This format can be seen in Intorcetta's *Sinarum scientia politico-moralis*, half of which was originally printed in 1667 in Guangzhou, while the other half was first printed in 1669 in Goa. *Sapienta Sinica*, originally published in Jiangxi province in 1662, likewise included Chinese characters, Latin transliterations, glosses, and commentary.

The completion of works on Mencius in 1710 by Flemish Jesuit François Noel (衛方濟, Wèi fāng jì), which were the first Jesuit works on Mencius, represented the culmination of the Jesuits' foundational work on Chinese wisdom in the decades leading up to Enlightenment-era writing on the topic.[34] Noel's works on Mencius in Latin came some twenty-five years after *Confucius, Philosopher of the Chinese* was completed by Couplet, da Costa, and Intorcetta, and more than a century after Ruggieri worked with Confucian texts in Salerno upon his return from China in the 1580s. With the transmission of these Jesuit-authored Latin works on Confucius and Mencius throughout Europe via the Netherlands by the same seventeenth-century Dutch publishers who published the Jesuits' annotated maps of China and Japan, Europe was primed for a full-fledged Sinophilic intellectual current during the eighteenth-century Age of Enlightenment that quickly transformed into the Sinology component of nineteenth-century Oriental studies.

Imagining China during the Enlightenment
Born in 1737 in England, Thomas Paine included Confucius in a list of moral teachers in world history alongside Jesus and the Hellenistic philosophers.

Paine was posthumously remembered as one of the central thinkers of the so-called Age of Enlightenment or Age of Reason, which makes his emphasis on Chinese philosophy striking. Why would a figure associated with the Enlightenment, a period of thought remembered as having undermined the religious authority of the Church, have placed so much emphasis on a figure associated with a Chinese spiritual tradition that historically intersected with Daoism and Buddhism?

The answer can partly be found in how Enlightenment-era thinkers extracted ethical principles from ancient figures of wisdom without necessarily adopting all of the spiritual practices and doctrinal beliefs associated with their followers. For Thomas Paine, this meant believing in representations of Jesus in the broad sense of his ethics and virtues without accepting the entirety of Christian doctrine. Of Jesus, Paine wrote: "He was a virtuous and an amiable man. The morality that he preached and practiced was of the most benevolent kind; and though similar systems of morality had been preached by Confucius, and by some of the Greek philosophers, many years before, by the Quakers since, and by many good men in all ages, it has not been exceeded by any."[35] In this context, Paine represents Confucius and Jesus as wise philosophers in a sense. There were parallels in the case of Voltaire (d. 1778).

In Voltaire's work, one finds representations of both China's imperial history and the story of Confucius. In the former case, Voltaire wrote a play in 1755 on the Chinese clash with the Mongols, which represented Genghis Khan as the villain. The play, called *The Orphan of China* (*L'Orphelin de la Chine*), was based on a Chinese play titled *The Great Revenge of the Orphan of Zhao* by Ji Junxiang (d. ca. 1279). Voltaire was introduced to it by the Jesuits, and by 1755, his version was being performed by Paris's premiere acting troupe: La Comédie Française. The Parisian acting troupe was established in 1680 by royal decree and was the product of a merger between Paris's only two acting troupes: Guénégaud Théâtre and Hôtel de Bourgogne. Throughout the eighteenth century, attendance at the Comédie Française shows was an important pastime of the French nobility. The French, thus, became one of the first and most prominent groups of Europeans after the Dutch who were on the receiving end of Jesuit-transmitted representations of Chinese political and intellectual history. Beyond rearticulating these originally Jesuit-formulated images through his playwriting work, Voltaire wrote other works that curated these images of China according to a metanarrative about Confucianism's merits and China's overall cultural advancement.

The currency of Chinese intellectual culture once identified by the Jesuits in the sixteenth century, in other words, was being identified by influential European philosophers and playwrights in the eighteenth century. In Voltaire's grand narrative of world history, titled *An Essay on Universal History: The Manners and Spirit of Nations* (*Essai sur les mœurs et l'esprit des nations*), Voltaire represents China as historically advanced in its ethical philosophies, especially Confucianism. Confucius "unveiled the light of reason to mankind," he claimed, and the example of a government run by Confucian literati represented the unachieved possibilities in Europe where philosophers ought likewise to serve as political administrators.[36] In the context of his interest in the possibilities and limits of rational thinking, Voltaire was impressed by how Chinese history makes "no mention of a college of priests," explaining that their ethical philosophies "brought morality to perfection."[37]

One of the most notable aspects of Voltaire's praise for Confucius and Chinese political culture, which parallels the contemporary commentary of the economist and physician François Quesney (d. 1774), is how it highlights Confucianism to the exclusion of China's equally important traditions of Buddhism and Daoism. On one level, in what points to the Jesuits' role in this phenomenon, Voltaire's writings echo the Jesuits' own Ming-era educational curriculum. On another level, in what points to the enduring legacy of Ming-era Chinese literati centuries after the fall of the dynasty, the Jesuits' Confucius-oriented Chinese cultural curriculum owed itself partly to Ming-era Chinese intellectual trends that sought to dissociate Confucianism from Buddhist influences.

More specifically, the representation of Confucius as a kind of proto-Enlightenment rationalist philosopher was laid out by the reception of Confucius in the Ming period within the so-called Donglin Academy of scholars in Wuxi (Jiangsu), where Ming Chinese intellectual choices had an effect on the Jesuits' own transmission of Confucianism westward. Built originally under the Song dynasty in 1111, the Donglin Academy was restored by the Ming dynasty's Wanli Emperor (r. 1572–1620) and reflected the growing role of the literati in Chinese political life.[38] Leading Song-era and Ming-era literati of the Donglin movement identified Confucian ethics as a source of new moral principles that could guide politics. Between 1592 and 1594, Donglin scholars gathered for discussions on a variety of topics including the moral compass of politics and society. Two of its key figures were Ku Hsien-Ch'eng (Gu Xiancheng) (d. 1612), a Grand Secretary, and Kau P'an

Lung (Gao Panlong) (d. 1626). Both believed that among the Three Teachings (Confucianism, Buddhism, Daoism), it was Confucianism that ought to be championed and prioritized by the literati, who in turn should serve as an intellectual elect guiding political leadership. These scholars were explicitly critical of Song-era and Ming-era trends of incorporating Chan (Zen) Buddhism into Confucian thought, which simultaneously occurred in Japan, and were in favor of recovering the writings on human nature written by Mencius, one of the key interpreters of Confucius.

In their turn towards Confucianism to the exclusion of Buddhism and Daoism, what was at stake was the possibility of political reform led by the Ming according to the moral principles of Confucius. For these Neo-Confucian scholars, these moral standards included both the relationship bonds—namely, ruler and subject, parent and child, husband and wife—as well as the constant virtues—namely, benevolence, righteousness, propriety, wisdom, trustworthiness. For Ku Hsien-Ch'eng, one example of a Confucian principle being problematically fit into a Buddhist precept was the practice of releasing animals captured for food, which represented the virtue of Confucian filial piety being extended to include animals in accordance with the Buddhist precept of nonkilling. A critique of this line of thinking would argue that the identification of vegetarianism as a Confucian practice, where captured animals are part of the human hierarchy of social relationships, is actually an attempt to dress a Confucian virtue—namely, filial piety—in Buddhist ritual clothing in order to serve Buddhist ethics and not Confucian ethics.

Their Neo-Confucian approach drew on the thought of Wang Yangming (d. 1529), whose interpretation of Confucianism has been called Yangmingism in Western historiography. Where Donglin scholars distinguished themselves from Yangming's disciples was in more strictly pushing out Buddhist and Daoist influences that they believed appeared in the writings of his students.[39] Feng Tsung-Wu (d. 1627), for example, was a student of Hsu Fu-yuan, who was in turn a student of Wang Yangming's colleague Chan Jo-Shui (d. 1560). For Feng Tsung-Wu, "We Confucians have our own effort (gong fu), and the Buddhists have their own effort."[40]

Jesuit activity in translating these works correlated with the contemporary activity of the Donglin Academy, though the exact relationship remains subject of debate. Like the Donglin literati, the Jesuits wrote favorably of Confucianism but were critical of Buddhism. According to one perspective, this Jesuit adoption of Confucius to the exclusion of Buddhism may have been a kind of appropriation of a local Ming critique of Buddhism that was broader than the Donglin Academy's critique.[41] Independent of the exact connection between the Donglin and the Jesuits, the outcome was the same: the form of Chinese intellectual culture transmitted by the Jesuits to Enlightenment Europe was a specifically Ming-era Neo-Confucian intellectual culture that made China—in European eyes—neither the land of Gautama's Buddhist followers, as it was in some Persian texts, nor the land of Lao-Tze's Daoist followers. It was, rather, the well mapped and intellectually familiar land of two timeless philosophers: Confucius (孔夫子, Kǒng fūzǐ) and Mencius (孟子, Mèngzǐ). With the arrival of the Dutch, this European fascination with China reached new depths in the realm of design, aesthetics, and technological innovation.

FIGURE 5.1. Queen Isabella of Portugal, spouse of Habsburg Emperor Charles V, was the de facto ruler of the Iberian peninsula during the many years of her husband's absence in the early 1500s. The queen lived through a time of tremendous change in Spain and Portugal that was illustrative of Iberia's transformation during the Age of Exploration. Edicts banning the practice of Islam and Judaism in the peninsula in the late 1400s meant the rise of two new Roman Catholic groups: the formerly Muslim *moriscos* and formerly Jewish *conversos*, many of whom continued to practice Islam and Judaism privately. Interestingly, both moriscos and conversos were part of Spanish society during Isabella's reign and were among the Iberians who traveled to the Americas in the age of Columbus. The rise of Catholic indigenous peoples and African descendant populations in the Americas meant the proliferation of new administrative and popular categories of Spanish subjects based on heritage. More specifically, alongside the administrative language of Roman Catholic moriscos and conversos was an expanding vocabulary that identified new groups of different races (*razas*) alongside the Iberian categories of moriscos and conversos: *mestizos* of both European and indigenous heritage, urban *mulatos* of European and West African heritage, *zambos* of indigenous and African heritage, and the like. That moriscos of Muslim heritage would slowly disappear into the alterity of mixed marriages and exile was the product of specific policies of the early 1500s. These policies were oriented around pushing Iberia's recent Islamic cultural dimensions further into the past. In contrast with an enduring political discomfort with the presence of questionably Roman Catholic moriscos, Iberian ruling circles embraced the newly evangelized future of Hispanized indigenous-heritage mestizo clients in the Americas. That Queen Isabella lived through these changes could be seen in how she famously pushed for leniency on bans against the last moriscos' *zambras* dances, which were popular among for-hire wedding festivities and that survive within modern flamenco. Queen Isabella simultaneously facilitated the long-term independence of Portugal and Spain within the Habsburg empire, which in turn allowed her son Philip II—namesake of the Philippines—to turn the Americas into one of his priority projects as king of a unified Spain and Portugal. Philip notably pushed for stringent bans on the travel of moriscos and conversos to the Americas and likewise oversaw the expansion of Spanish administration from the Americas to the South China Sea. One of those administrators was Miguel López de Legazpi, a Spaniard of Basque origins who spent much of his career as the governor of the Spanish Americas. In his elderly years, he undertook an expedition to Manila several decades after Magellan first charted a route from Spain to Acapulco and Manila via the Patagonian Straits, also known as the Strait of Magellan. One of the Muslim rulers active in the region was a relative of the Sultan of Brunei who met Magellan several decades earlier. In the aftermath of de Legazpi's capture of Manila, Spanish administrators sponsored the Manila-Acapulco galleons between 1565 and 1815 that connected Chinese and Filipino material cultures with the Iberian and Mesoamerican cultures of the Americas. This past mix of Iberian, Roman Catholic, Muslim, and Filipino cultural legacies can be seen in two modern phenomena: On the one hand, the galleons are still celebrated on Galleon Day (El Día del Galeón) in the Philippines, which celebrates the journey of Augustinian Fray Andrés de Urdaneta on the galleon *San Pedro* from Manila to Acapulco in 1565. On the other hand, Manila features a bust of one of the last Muslim rulers of Manila, who originally resisted Spanish conquest before surrendering. Notably, Islam remains prominent in the Philippines closer to Brunei, while Manila is a center of Roman Catholicism. The Manila-Acapulco galleons made annual and biannual roundtrips that allowed Spanish access to the Sinocentric commercial market of the South China Sea. Merchants brought luxury goods such as spices and porcelain from Manila in exchange for American silver, which together with Japanese silver was a source of Chinese currency.

Source: Museo del Prado/Wikimedia Commons. Public domain. https://commons.wikimedia .org/wiki/File:La_emperatriz_Isabel_de_Portugal,_por_Tiziano.jpg

FIGURE 5.2.   Chinese Macau, off the coast of southeastern China, became a central transit point for all Portuguese traffic in Southeast and Northeast Asia. The city connected Portuguese commercial ventures in Lisbon and Goa with those in Melaka, Manila, Nagasaki, the Americas, and inland China. The intersection of trade networks meant that the city became a cultural crossroads that drew on the customs, cuisine, and social networks of the various merchant groups who traded with one another: Portuguese, Malayan, Japanese, Chinese, Goan, and the like. The key languages of the city historically were Cantonese and Portuguese. Among the ways that the city remained connected to Portugal was through the marriage of local Macanese residents with foreign Portuguese arrivals and the two-way exchange of cultural customs, fashion, and taste. Roman Catholicism and its institutions, including the Roman Catholic Church, were part of what tied Macau to other nodes of Portuguese and Spanish life throughout Asia. The Our Lady of Penha Chapel (Capela de Nossa Senhora da Penha), established in 1622 in the parish of São Lourenço, is one of the most prominent churches in Macau (above) with an architectural style that reflects its almost half millennium history. São Lourenço is one of five parishes in the former Municipality of Macau, which is one of two municipalities with administrative functions that China abolished in December of 2001, two years after Portugal transferred sovereignty of Macau to Beijing.

Source: Jssfrk/Wikimedia Commons. Public domain. https://commons.wikimedia.org/wiki/File:Capela_de_Nossa_Senhora_da_Penha_2011a.JPG

FIGURE 6.1.   Flemish painter Peter Paul Rubens completed a drawing of French Jesuit Nicolas Trigault (d. 1628), one of Matteo Ricci's successors among the Jesuit scientist-theologians working in China and Japan, while Trigault was passing through the Netherlands during a trip between Asia and Rome. The Jesuit use of Chinese and Japanese robes was contested by Portuguese Jesuit Francisco Cabral (d. 1609), who was critical of the linguistic, intellectual, and cultural accommodationist approach to teaching and learning that the Jesuits, and specifically Jesuit cofounder Francis Xavier, took in Japan and China beginning in the mid-sixteenth century.

Source: The Metropolitan Museum of Art. Public domain. https://www.metmuseum.org/art/collection/search/337844

FIGURE 6.2.   Jesuit Matteo Ricci completed the renowned Chinese world map *Kunyu Wanguo Quantu* (Map of the Myriad Countries) under the patronage of the Ming-era Wanli Emperor in 1602. Building on a variety of earlier cartographical traditions, from Arabic- and Chinese-language cartography to Latin-language cartography, the map became the basis for a variety of Japanese world maps. The ability of the Jesuits to live and work in China and collaborate with Chinese scientists and cartographers facilitated the specifically French Jesuits' completion of the first systematic geographic survey of the Chinese Empire. By the 1700s, French cartographer D'Anville drew on the French Jesuits' works to produce the world's most advanced maps of the region (above). Du Halde's "Description geographique de la Chine" was compiled based on the first systematic geographic survey of the entire Chinese Empire by a team of French Jesuits (c. 1700). The work of Jesuits in China was not limited to astronomy, cartography, and calendrical sciences and included a variety of other works from botany to mechanical devices. A Chinese-language work on European hydraulics, for example, was completed by Italian Jesuit and scientist Sabatino de Ursis in 1617.

Source: "China in Maps" special collection, Hong Kong University of Science and Technology Library/Wikimedia Commons. Public domain. https://en.wikipedia.org/wiki/Jean-Baptiste _Bourguignon_d%27Anville#/media/File:CEM-44-La-Chine-la-Tartarie-Chinoise-et-le -Thibet-1734-2568.jpg.

FIGURE 6.3.   During the golden age of Dutch cartography and printing, coinciding with the rise of the Dutch East India Company, Jesuits who worked under Portuguese and Chinese patronage became a key source for knowledge about the geography, climate, flora, and fauna of Asia. The Blaeu family publishers incorporated this information, together with the Jesuits maps, in their seventeenth-century multivolume atlases. The atlases included world maps (above) and more regional maps and were part of the Dutch golden age of printing. The counterparts of the atlases were globes. The Blaeu family's most famous globes of 1602 represented both the terrestrial world of the earth and the celestial world of the cosmos. These maps were expensive ventures that circulated in a variety of translations around Europe.

Source: Biblioteca Nacional de España. Public domain. https://commons.wikimedia.org/wiki/File:Nova_et_Accuratissima_Terrarum_Orbis_Tabula_(J.Blaeu,_1664).jpg

FIGURE 7.1.   Jan Pieterszoon Coen was the architect of a Dutch inter-Asian commercial strategy for securing Japanese silver, which the Portuguese previously secured in their negotiations with the *bakufu* around Nagasaki. In a letter sent in 1619 to the seventeen heads of the VOC (Seventeen Gentlemen), Pieterszoon writes, "We can extract silver from Japan with Chinese goods," and to make this exchange possible, "sandalwood, pepper, and rials we can barter for Chinese goods and Chinese gold." His plan included Gujarat, the coast of Sumatra, the coast of Coromandel, and Banten. In an illustration of northern European businesspeople's original interest in inter-Asian commerce as a priority over European-Asian commerce, he wrote that "all of it can be done without any money from the Netherlands and with ships alone." It was within this inter-Asian system of exchange that the VOC first traded in porcelain and cultivated European consumption of it. Dutch consumers in the seventeenth century developed a taste for specific Chinese designs, particularly wide dishes and deep bowls with blue-and-white decorations. By the 1700s, local Dutch artisans began to perfect a local variety of Chinese blue-and-whites in the city of Delft: Delftware. By the Industrial Revolution, the use of factories and new machine technologies allowed their mass production, which in turn facilitated their export back to Asia in the aftermath of new trade deals following the British-led Opium Wars.

Source: Westfries Museum/Wikimedia Commons. Public domain. https://commons.wikimedia .org/wiki/File:Jan_Pietersz_Coen_by_Jacob_Waben.jpg

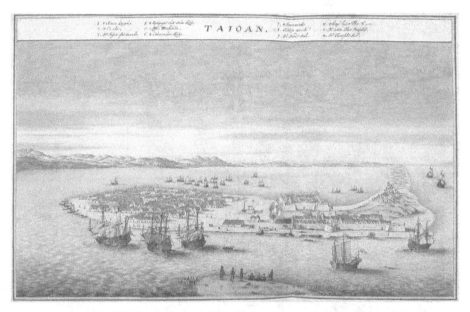

FIGURE 7.2. The VOC's warehouse in Hirado, a reconstruction of which stands in Japan, was the base of Dutch commercial shipping in 1609 until permission was granted for a new base outside Nagasaki in 1641. The hundreds of VOC bases of commercial operations from Northeast and Southeast Asia to the Indian Ocean ranged from small offices and warehouses to large factories. Several seventeenth-century artists depicted one of the VOC's most important centers of operations, namely Fort Zeelandia along the southwest coast of Taiwan (above). The site, located today in the bay of coastal Tainan city in Taiwan, was a central transit point for Dutch ships bringing Chinese and Japanese porcelain southward to Dutch Batavia, where they would then be taken across the VOC's Indian Ocean bases to the Netherlands.

FIGURE 7.3. Dutch painter Johannes Vermeer's seventeenth-century "Milkmaid" was one of many works of the era that captured the growing royal and domestic taste for VOC-imported Chinese porcelain and Dutch-made pseudo-porcelain. In this example, Dutch-made Delftware skirting tiles depicting Cupid run along the lower right of the painting. The tiles' signature blue and white colors echo Ming blue-and-whites that are similarly seen in the works of Willem Kalf. Paintings from the era frequently included maps of the Netherlands and other parts of the world in an illustration of European fascination with the growing sophistication of cartography, printing, globes, and travel.

Source: Rijksmuseum/Wikimedia Commons. Public domain. https://commons.wikimedia.org/wiki/File:Johannes_Vermeer_-_Het_melkmeisje_-_Google_Art_Project.jpg

FIGURE 8.1.   One of the first influential figures in Europe to popularize the consumption of tea was Portuguese monarch Catherine of Braganza (above), spouse of King Charles II and Queen of England, Scotland, and Ireland (r. 1662–1685). Upon moving to the British Isles, Catherine brought not only her taste for tea but also her fondness of porcelain. Before Turkish-Arabic coffee and Chinese black tea dominated the seventeenth-century northern European taste for exotic caffeinated beverages with complex flavor profiles, they competed with a third beverage from the Spanish Americas: chocolate. Depicted in a portrait by Raimundo de Madrazo y Garreta, savory chocolate without milk resembled black coffee in taste and texture. Once the English East India Company was able to bring the secrets of Chinese tea cultivation southward to the plantations of British India in the nineteenth century, tea's lower prices together with growing royal taste for the newly branded Anglo-Indian imperial beverage meant that Chinese black tea would finally eclipse coffee and chocolate altogether until the late twentieth century. Raimundo de Madrazo y Garreta likewise featured tea in his works. The paintings were evocative of scenes within Japanese paintings of tea consumption featuring nearly identical tea pots. Japan dominated the export market for porcelain in the years before the British and Dutch produced their own varieties of pseudo-porcelain tea sets.

Source: Ann Longmore-Etheridge/Flickr. Public domain. https://www.flickr.com/photos/60861613@N00/4027178542/

FIGURE 8.2.   Tea bricks, or compressed tea, are blocks of whole or finely ground black tea, green tea, or post-fermented tea leaves with stems that have been packed and pressed into block form. Tea in brick form was widely exchanged across Central Asia as far west as Russia, and it even became a form of edible currency. This was the most commonly produced form of tea in ancient China prior to the Ming dynasty, when pieces of tea were broken off of tea bricks in order to be brewed as a concoction similar to Turkish coffee. The Ming era saw a shift towards the production and consumption of loose-leaf tea, which in some cases was also compressed (above), but that was brewed as an infusion without consuming the whole or ground tea leaves themselves. British tea brewing practices were based on this later Ming-era infusion. The use of the term *tea* in English, as opposed to *cha* in Russian, points to contrasting geographies of origin and varieties of Chinese spoken in these geographies. While Russian tea was imported via China's northwestern frontiers, British tea was imported from southeastern Chinese ports, especially Canton (Guangzhou). Thirteen *hongs* were built in the city to manage commercial relations with European powers, where there was an insatiable taste for Chinese tea. A nineteenth-century Chinese painting depicts the activities of the most influential players at the time: Denmark, Spain, the United States, Sweden, Britain, and the Netherlands. By the end of the nineteenth century, with the British transfer of Chinese tea cultivation secrets to British South Asia, Chinese tea was slowly rebranded as British tea by the British East India Company and the British Crown.

FIGURE 8.3.   The Opium Wars had a staggering effect on China's political culture and were the subject of a variety of European and Chinese paintings. China's territorial losses represented the biggest rupture with the past, accelerating debates among Qing-era administrators about the need for political and military reform. The key administrator involved in negotiating the Treaty of Nanking was Prince Kung (above), whose experience with European powers in China shaped his most influential first project: the establishment of a new multilingual diplomatic bureau known as the Zongli Yamen. The bureau represented the Qing government's foreign office, and it was staffed with a team of administrators able to read and write various European languages. The office handled the requests of foreign ministers to China. In the realm of military reform, Yuan Shikai rose to prominence years later as a high-ranking Qing general. At the height of nationalist rebellion, Shikai chose not to follow imperial orders and negotiated with Sun Yat-Sen and other nationalists to end imperial rule. Many of these nationalists studied Japan's political and industrial modernization during trips to Meiji-era Tokyo. Upon the fall of the imperial dynasty, Yuan Shikai and Sun Yat-Sen rose to prominence as the first two presidents of the republic. Many of the reforms they instituted were built on those of earlier figures like Prince Kung who were involved in the peace treaties following the Opium Wars.

Source: Wikimedia Commons. Public domain. https://commons.wikimedia.org/wiki/File:Prince_Gong.jpg

FIGURE 9.1.　Arai Hakuseki, administrator and scholar of both Dutch science (*rangaku*) and Chinese Neo-Confucian political and social ethics (*kangaku*), rose to prominence in Japanese administrative circles in the late 1600s. In continuity with Tokugawa shogun Ieyasu's interest in providing the Dutch exceptional European access to Japanese markets, Hakuseki played a prominent role in facilitating Edo-era Japan's preindustrial assimilation of Dutch medicine and technology into Japanese official and private education. His writings from the early 1700s, which included translations of Dutch works, were closely studied and further developed by Sugita Genpaku in the late 1700s and early 1800s. Genpaku was the author of the seminal *Various Stories about the Dutch*, which included diagrams of a variety of Dutch mechanical devices like the microscope. By the mid-1800s, against the backdrop of armed European and American advances on Japanese territory, Japanese political reformers called into question the value of Japan's seemingly excessive reliance on Chinese learning and political models and extended the long-standing local study of European medicine and technology to also include European political culture and social customs. This encounter of China, Japan, and the Dutch in the realm of science and intellectual culture was depicted (above) in the late 1700s by a painter named Shiba Kokan, whose representation of Japanese and Dutch figures on one side of a table (right) seems to foreshadow the changes that were ahead.

Source: Wikimedia Commons. Public domain. https://commons.wikimedia.org/wiki/File:Shiba_Kokan_A_meeting_of_Japan_China_and_the_West_late_18th_century.jpg

FIGURE 9.2.   Tokugawa Yoshinobu (above) was the last Japanese shogun. The son of prominent daimyo and political reformer Tokugawa Nariaki, Yoshinobu stepped down in 1868 despite a decade-long career as a political reformer. With the help of a French military delegation, Yoshinobu helped modernize the military. He also afforded the emperor in Kyoto greater political power in accordance with various domain-level daimyos' and samurai-turned-politicians' criticism of the shogunate's centralized authority. These reforms paved the way for the rise of the industrialized Japanese Empire. Many of the samurai who opposed the shogun came from domains with independent connections to European armed forces, which meant that they already modernized their own military forces in the early 1800s and were in a position to pressure the shogun to step down. Yoshinobu remained an active member of Japanese civil society after his resignation.

Source: Wikimedia Commons. Public domain. https://commons.wikimedia.org/wiki/File:1867_Osaka_Yoshinobu_Tokugawa.jpg

FIGURE 9.3.   Ito Hirobumi was one of many samurai of the late Tokugawa era who became a proponent of political and socioeconomic reforms during the Meiji era. Samurai participated in the late Edo-era proliferation of official and private education, which varied in curricula and included subjects like Dutch medicine, Japanese ancient and medieval historiography, and Chinese political and social ethics. This education began to draw on European political and administrative culture in the final years of the shogunate. In 1863, Hirobumi was one of the so-called Choshu Five who traveled to Europe to study at the University of London. In 1870, two years after Tokugawa Yoshinobu stepped down, Hirobumi traveled to the United States to study the American currency system, and by 1882 he was in Europe studying European constitutions. Hirobumi was one of the writers of the Meiji-era Japanese constitution and Japan's first prime minister. His career also coincided with the transformation of the military. In hopes of building a sphere of influence in Asia, French officials played a central role in modernizing the Japanese military. At the time, France's own military reforms dating back to the career of Napoleon were a century in development, and the country was in the process of securing its control over all of North Africa, other parts of Africa, and Vietnam. Hirobumi is pictured on the modern 1,000 yen note as he appeared in the latter decades of his career, wearing not a samurai's robe but a British-style suit.

FIGURE EPILOGUE.I.   By organizing meetings in advocacy of reforms like universal suffrage (above), women's movements in Japan and across Asia have emerged as one of a variety of reform movements that have reshaped the socioeconomic landscape of Asia. With the emergence of Asia's tiger and so-called "tiger cub" economies, these reform movements have simultaneously converged with and diverged from the West. The leadership of women in finance and technology-oriented economies in cities like Singapore points to the many ways that Asian countries have begun to offer their own lessons for Western reform and innovation. In recent years, lessons for the West from cities like Tokyo have expanded into the world of art, design, and aesthetics.

Source: Bain Collection, Library of Congress/Wikimedia Commons. Public domain. https://commons.wikimedia.org/wiki/File:Woman%27s_Rights_Meeting_Tokyo.jpg

CHAPTER 7

Porcelain across the Dutch Empire

The seventeenth century saw a major shift in European competition for trade access to China, with the Dutch and British East India companies slowly eclipsing the mighty empires of Portugal and Spain. As late as the 1600s, the shift was still slow and unpredictable as both the Portuguese and the Dutch continued to reach major milestones in their paths to political access in the South China Sea. On the Portuguese side, the settlement in Macau in 1557 marked just the start of an enduring and unmatched level of European diplomatic and cultural access to China through Portugal's Jesuit clients. Matteo Ricci, the most influential Jesuit scholar and scientist active in Macau, was invited to the Wanli Emperor's court in Beijing in 1601, becoming the first in a series of Ming- and Qing-era Jesuits to work under imperial patronage.[1]

On the Dutch side, 1602 marked the start of a monumental shift in northern European commerce in Asia. That year, the Dutch government granted a monopoly in the trade of Asian spices to a single holder: the United East India company, better known as the Dutch East India Company (VOC). What distinguished the VOC from its Iberian predecessors was a unique obstacle in the construction of its trade portfolio. Despite the establishment of the Dutch West India Company in South America, where the Iberians procured American silver and gold, the Dutch were never able to access the silver bullion required to pay for the silk and spice commodities available in Southeast Asia. In the early years of VOC history, VOC administrators realized that their dependence on inter-European exchange with the Iberians to access American silver was not a scalable venture. The alternative was to rely exclusively on inter-Asian commerce, including the demand for Japanese silver in Ming China and the simultaneous demand for Chinese porcelain in Edo Japan, Southeast Asian markets, and Safavid Iran.

Like the Portuguese, VOC administrators conceived of a new role for themselves as inter-Asian merchants operating between Japan and late Ming China. Their first challenge was to push out the Portuguese from East Asia through the art of monopoly—that is, the same strategy the Portuguese used previously to keep the Spanish from advancing westward from Manila.[2] The second challenge, particularly in Japan, was to ingratiate themselves to their Chinese and Japanese administrative interlocutors as the Portuguese had done previously and demonstrate their own political and commercial value.

During Japan's Muromachi period (1336–1573), corresponding with the European Age of Exploration, Japanese daimyos were notably not dependent on foreign powers for commerce with other East Asian centers, and the situation remained the same with the arrival of the Portuguese and later the Dutch. A famous example of the far reach of Japanese political networks long after the arrival of the Portuguese and Dutch is the career of Yamada Nagasama (d. 1633). Born in Numazu, Nagasama became an influential merchant in the Japanese settlement of the Ayutthaya Kingdom in Thailand, even being hired as a political official in Thai service.[3] Vietnam was a second major center of Japanese trade in Southeast Asia. Most of the so-called red-seal ships of the early Tokugawa era, which were armed Japanese vessels with official imperial permits guaranteeing protection, went to Vietnam. What the Portuguese offered, then, was the cultivation of greater commercial exchange in select harbors like Nagasaki at a time when rival daimyos sought to bolster the political and commercial strength of their domains. With the rising Tokugawa clan's expulsion of the Portuguese following the losses of the Portuguese-aligned bloc of newly Catholic daimyos, and with the newly centralized Tokugawa government's issuing of the "closed country" Sakoku Edict of 1635 favoring official government-controlled trade over private trade, VOC administrators were able to secure an opening as the successors of the Portuguese in Nagasaki. While the Portuguese previously brought Japanese silver to China in exchange for a variety of Chinese commodities, especially Chinese silk, the Dutch capitalized on the rising global demand for two other Chinese commodities: porcelain and tea, which Amsterdam in the seventeenth century developed an insatiable appetite for during the same years when Dutch printers were publishing Jesuit-authored maps and accounts of China and Japan.

SILVER FOR PORCELAIN: THE DUTCH EAST INDIA COMPANY'S MING-ERA INTER-ASIAN TRADE

The VOC came into existence at the end of the Ming period, which meant that its involvement in Japanese and Chinese commerce came on the heels of the Portuguese. What facilitated Dutch commercial access to Japanese silver was daimyo Toyotomi Hideyoshi (d. 1598) and daimyo-turned-shogun Tokugawa Ieyasu's (d. 1616) previously discussed fallout with Portugal's Jesuit clients, with their Dominican and Franciscan counterparts based in Spanish Manila, and with the bloc of newly Catholic daimyos allied with the Portuguese. These events in the final decades of the sixteenth century were coterminous with the career of Jan Pieterszoon Coen (1587–1629), a Dutch officer who served as the fourth Governor-General of the VOC from 1619 to 1623.

Pieterszoon was the architect of a Dutch inter-Asian commercial strategy for securing Japanese silver, which the Portuguese previously secured in their negotiations with the bakufu around Nagasaki. In a letter sent in 1619 to the seventeen heads of the VOC (Seventeen Gentlemen), he writes, "We can extract silver from Japan with Chinese goods," and to make this exchange possible, "sandalwood, pepper, and rials we can barter for Chinese goods and Chinese gold."[4] His plan incorporated Gujarat, the coast of Sumatra, the coast of Coromandel, and Bantam. Most importantly, he argued, "All of it can be done without any money from the Netherlands and with ships alone."

It was within this inter-Asian system of exchange that the VOC first traded in porcelain and cultivated European consumption of it. Dutch consumers in the seventeenth century developed a taste for specific Chinese designs, particularly the wide dishes and deep bowls of the blue-and-white variety (qingbai). The Dutch called it Kraak (Kraakporselein), potentially in reference to the carrack ships used by the earlier Portuguese to transfer porcelain shipments. Pieterszoon took special interest in porcelain. Writing in 1616 to the seventeen heads of the VOC, he noted that "the porcelains are made far inland in China," in reference to Jingdezhen, which was far from the coast.[5] He wrote that the varieties sold to the Dutch merchants "are put out to contract and made afterwards with money paid in advance," pointing to a bulk purchase by order that was mentioned previously by Ali Akbar Khitayi in Istanbul some one hundred years earlier.[6] Under the Song and Yuan before the Ming, this pattern of porcelain exchange was already well developed between China and the Middle East. Under the late Ming, this exchange took a more global turn as it extended to Europe, first in the Venetian Republic via Mediterranean exchange with Mamluk Egypt and then Portugal via their Indian Ocean shipping routes.

In 1461, almost forty years before Vasco da Gama brought porcelain back to Portugal for King Manuel I, the sultan of Mamluk Egypt presented the Venetian doge Pasquale Malpiero with a diplomatic gift of more than twenty blue-and-white porcelain wares. The Mamluk Sultanate similarly presented Lorenzo de Medici with blue-and-white porcelains in 1487. By the early 1500s, after Vasco da Gama returned from Asia with blue-and-whites, King Manuel I himself began to offer gifts of blue-and-white porcelains to royal families around Europe.[7] By the 1520s, the German printmaker and painter Albrecht Dürer was writing about gifts of blue-and-white porcelains he received on two occasions in Antwerp, one of the main cities connected to the markets in Lisbon and rising Amsterdam.[8]

It would take another one hundred years after Dürer received gifts of porcelain in Amsterdam for Pieterszoon to begin planning a VOC-dominated import of porcelain from Jingdezhen. By 1639, within twenty years of his plans, Dutch porcelain dealers in Amsterdam were sending drawings for special orders from China, asking for ewers with two handles. The key to the VOC import of porcelain was the establishment of two trading bases: Taiwan, which offered access to China's port cities independent of Portugal's settlement in Macau, and Japan, where factories at Dejima (Nagasaki) and Hirado provided an alternative source of porcelain production.

From the Pescadores to Taiwan

In the early decades of VOC activity around the South China Sea, neither the Portuguese in Melaka and Macau nor the Fujianese officials of Ming China's southeastern coast opened their ports to the Dutch. The Sultanate of Banten (1527–1813), which controlled the bordering regions of southern Sumatra and western Java, extended settlement privileges to the VOC around the same time that the Tokugawa shogunate allowed the VOC trading privileges in Japan. By 1619, following a breakdown in relations, the Dutch captured Jayakarta (Jakarta) by armed force. It would be another twenty years before the Dutch took over Portuguese Melaka militarily in 1641. In the interim, the Pescadores and Taiwan were the VOC's two sites of interest in their mission to enter the world of Chinese commerce. What made the venture of establishing port in the South China Sea complex was fact that VOC commanders, unlike the Portuguese, were willing to experiment— albeit unsuccessfully—with engaging Ming China militarily.

The Penghu (澎湖, Pēnghú) archipelago, called the Pescadores by the Portuguese, were just outside Taiwan and had a long history of serving as an intermediary maritime center connecting Indian Ocean and Southeast Asian commerce with Northeast Asian harbors. During the Song dynasty, the Pescadores were Chinese fishing grounds and became a center for trade among so-called junk sailing vessels (Javanese: *jong*) during the Mongol Yuan era.[9] Under the late Yuan and early Ming, the Pescadores became a center of commerce beyond Chinese government purview, where a potpourri of groups whom the Ming called *wokou* (pirates) traders were active: rogue masterless Japanese samurai (*ronin*), Chinese and Korean fugitives, and a variety of mariners connected with or who associated themselves with pirates from Japan. The Ming established a military presence in the Pescadores in 1603 in the interest of driving out these groups.

In 1622, the same year that the Dutch failed to capture Macau from the Portuguese, the VOC fleet arrived and built a fort in the Pescadores through the labor of local Fujianese workers whom they recruited for the task. Coen, now Governor-General (r. 1618–1623, 1627–1629) of the Dutch East Indies based in Dutch-held Batavia (ca. 1619–1942) and Dutch-held Melaka (1641–1825), himself ordered the Dutch occupation of the Pescadores, sending Commander Cornelis Reijersen (Reyersen) to the islands after learning that the Spanish were attempting to establish a base in Taiwan.[10]

Upon arrival in the Pescadores, VOC Commander Reijersen undertook a series of operations that resembled piracy in Ming eyes. To direct traffic to the Pescadores, Reijersen blockaded both Chinese junk traffic to Spanish Manila and traffic from Portuguese Macau to Japan. The Dutch, in other words, took a page from an earlier Portuguese playbook, but with weapons. Decades earlier, to establish a monopoly in the interest of Macau's Portuguese port, Portuguese merchants lured Chinese trade in Spanish Manila to Macau by paying inflated prices for the same goods in China and reselling at high prices in Manila along the Macau-Manila smuggling route. What made the Macau-Manila route illicit for Iberian merchants was the fact that it was banned during the union of the financially independent Portuguese and Spanish Empires (1580–1640), which theoretically protected their respective financial interests across the Portuguese Goa-Melaka-Macau route and Spanish Seville-Acapulco-Manila route.

From a Ming perspective, the aggressive manner that Reijersen's armed VOC force established a base in the Pescadores contrasted with Portuguese negotiations for settlement privileges in Chinese Macau. Simultaneous with these piracy-like activities were intermittent and unsuccessful negotiations, including the visit of four Dutch delegates to Ming China in 1623. By 1624, following Dutch raids on the Chinese coast, the Ming sent ships to expel the Dutch from the Pescadores, leading the VOC to set their eyes further away from Ming activities: Taiwan.

Prior to the Dutch arrival, Taiwan was a key intermediary point serving Chinese-Japanese trade relations, and the Chinese who lived there during the early Ming period came primarily from the Hakka and Fujian regions. The port that the Dutch established in Taiwan, Zeelandia, became a long-term trading base. After Batavia in Java, Taiwan in the middle decades of the 1600s became the VOC's key East Asian base for building their trade operations across the company's hundreds of offices and warehouses in Northeast and Southeast Asia.[11] In the hierarchy of VOC governance in the Dutch East Indies, the governor of Zeelandia—Reijersen's successor Maarten Sonck— answered to the governor of Batavia, who in turn answered to the Seventeen Gentlemen (*Heren Zeventien*) back in the Netherlands.

The port of Zeelandia was strategically located on Taiwan's southwest coast in the district of Tayouan (Dayuan)—that is, the present-day Anping District of Tainan, Taiwan. What Zeelandia offered the VOC was a central station for building a profitable and global Chinese porcelain business, the construction of which was a drawn-out endeavor that took several decades. In the early years of the VOC's inter-Asian trade activities, silk and spices remained the most significant motivation for European merchants to explore trade possibilities with China. Under governors Maarten Sonck (r. 1624–1625) and later successor Pieter Nuyts (r. 1627–1629), the Dutch were able to grow their trade in silk and sugar, which was considered a spice in this era. By 1630, Zeelandia had grown into a major transit port connecting Taiwan with Dutch Batavia in Java, with the VOC inter-Asian portfolio having simultaneously grown far beyond silk. In Japan, where there was a strong market for Chinese, Southeast Asian, and Indian Ocean silk commodities, the Dutch were able to procure Japanese silver with the Tokugawa shogunate's approval following restrictions on private trade in 1635. From 1636 to 1667, the VOC was able to purchase more than twenty million taels of silver, most of which they brought to Zeelandia. About half of that was brought from Zeelandia to China, where it was used to purchase gold. Sugar was shipped to northwest India, where it continued to Iran.

As mentioned, by the mid-1600s, the key addition to the VOC portfolio was Ming porcelain. Dutch merchants originally purchased porcelain from Chinese merchants outside China and sold it in Edo-era Japan, where there was high demand, in exchange for Japanese silver. Centers like the Malay Sultanate of Patani (est. ca. 1457), north of Portuguese Melaka (1511–1641) and south of Ayutthaya, constituted one of the earliest sources of Chinese porcelain for Dutch merchants headed to Japan in the early 1600s. The first shipment of porcelain moving in the other direction towards the Netherlands arrived early in 1610, which was early in the history of Dutch inter-Asian trade yet far from the profitable venture of transporting Japanese porcelain around the world a century later. That year, some 9,227 pieces of porcelain arrived in the Netherlands, which was almost certainly Chinese porcelain given how nascent the Japanese porcelain industry was in the early seventeenth century.[12]

With the rise of Zeelandia as a new center of operations in East Asia together with new commercial relations with coastal Ming officials discussed in the next section, and with the simultaneous growth in northern Europe of the previously discussed royal and popular Dutch fascination with atlases, objects, and narrative accounts of China, the volume of porcelain exports to the Netherlands dramatically increased in the three decades after the first porcelain shipment. By 1638, some 475,000 pieces made in Jingdezhen were sent to Europe via Zeelandia. By the end of the seventeenth century, the scope of the export of porcelain was enormous, with more than fifteen million porcelain articles transported in Dutch ships to ports throughout the South China Sea, Indian Ocean, and the Dutch North Sea coast. What turned the VOC's Chinese porcelain business from an unremarkable component of their inter-Asian portfolio to a massively profitable one was the simultaneous rise of genuine porcelain production in Japan and the VOC's establishment of export factories near centers of production.

Dutch connections with Japan, which date back to the first ten years of the VOC, became a pivotal dimension of the company's ability to navigate the Ming-Qing transition of the 1640s while operating from Taiwan. During the transition, the Dutch ran into supply problems partly connected with

the breakdown of Chinese coastal authority. In Zeelandia, the Dutch operated in the shadow of the independent authority of Zheng Zhilong, once an
independent shipper who became a Ming official. Zhilong, who was forty
years old when the Qing captured Beijing, had become familiar with European merchants during his many years as an independent shipper operating
between Fujian, Macau, Taiwan, and Japan. Born in Fujian in 1604, Zhilong
was baptized as Nicholas Gaspard during a brief period as a youth in Macau,
where his uncle lived. Zhilong even spoke Portuguese, which naturally facilitated communication with the various Portuguese, Spanish, and Dutch
merchants active in the seventeenth-century South China Sea.[13] Beginning
with his early days sending trade shipments to Japan on behalf of his uncle
in Macau, Zhilong became a powerful independent contractor of sorts by
the 1620s, rising to become one of the most influential figures in the South
China Sea at the head of a massive armada of several hundred junk ships.
By 1628, after previously collaborating with the Dutch in Zeelandia and even
sacking a Ming fleet in collaboration with a pirate ring known collectively
as the Shibazhi, Zhilong was hired by the Ming and fought against both
the Dutch and various independent forces off the coast of Fujian.

With the fall of the Ming and rise of the Qing, Zhilong initially worked
for the Southern Ming until his defection in 1646 to the Qing, with whom
he quickly fell afoul. The Dutch, increasingly desperate to revive trade connections with China and simultaneously hoping for more direct trade with
private mainland Chinese merchants, finally sent Frederick Schedel from
Batavia to Guangzhou in 1653 to meet with the new Qing and Qing-allied
forces. An agreement with the governor of Guangzhou originally allowed
the Dutch settlement rights and a factory, but the agreement was quickly
withdrawn. Though official trade relations with the government in Beijing
were finally restored about fifteen years after the start of major Ming-Qing
hostilities, the connections the Dutch already cultivated in Japan coupled
with the growth of a local porcelain industry ended up providing the basis
for the VOC's late seventeenth-century global porcelain business and, in
turn, the transformation of European taste and material culture.

EXPANSION IN JAPAN

The story of the VOC's connection with Japan dates back even before the
establishment of the VOC, when an earlier company from Rotterdam sent
an expedition of five ships to the Spice Islands. The Rotterdam mission's

goal was to reach the Strait of Magellan through an English route traversed previously by Francis Drake (d. 1596), the Elizabethan-era explorer and one-time Vice Admiral for the English naval forces. Two of the Rotterdam ships that sailed Drake's route westward successfully reached Asia, namely the *Liefde* (Love) and the *Hoop* (Hope). The *Liefde* continued all the way to Japan and landed on the Kyushu islands. Jan Josten van Lodenstein (d. 1623) of Delft and Englishman William Adams (d. 1620) of Gillingham were two of the surviving members, both of whom were given an audience with Tokugawa Ieyasu (d. 1616).

Tokugawa Ieyasu was Hideyoshi's previously discussed ally whose ascendency as shogun marked the start of the Edo period and the expulsion of the Portuguese and Jesuits from Nagasaki. In what foreshadowed the special relationship that the VOC was able to cultivate with the ruling Tokugawa clan, Van Lodenstein and Adams served as the new shogun's advisers shortly after surviving their trip on the *Liefde*. The story of how these originally Rotterdam-based crew members, who were active as merchants in Hirado, ended up working as go-betweens connecting Japan with the VOC relates to the story of the VOC's own subsequent interest in Hirado as a base for the trade of porcelain.

Warehouse in Hirado

In 1605, having heard of the arrival of the newly established VOC, two other *Liefde* crewmates in Hirado—namely, Jakob Quaeckernaeck (d. 1606) and Melchior van Sanvoort (d. 1641)—were given permission to establish contact with the VOC in the Malay Sultanate of Patani (est. ca. 1457) between Ayutthaya and Portuguese Melaka (1511–1641). The Patani Sultanate allowed the VOC and the rising English East India Company (est. 1600) to operate trading warehouses on the Malay Peninsula in the early 1600s before the Dutch took over Jayakarta (Batavia) in Java from the Sultanate of Bantam.

The rulers of Hirado were interested in the potentially lucrative trading opportunities offered by Quaeckernaeck and Van Sanvoort's contact with the Dutch in 1605. By 1608, following their trip to the Patani Sultanate, the VOC sent diplomatic gifts to the Japanese shogun that included six porcelain bowls. The outcome of VOC-Japanese contact was that in 1609, the VOC was given permission to establish a kind of factory or, more accurately, a trading warehouse in Hirado. Quaeckernaeck ended up remaining in Patani, where he rendezvoused with his relative from Rotterdam Cornell Matlief de

Jonge (d. 1632), the legendary VOC admiral and rival of the Portuguese in Southeast Asia. Quaeckernaeck died while participating in Matlief's siege of Portuguese Melaka in 1606, which only fell into Dutch hands decades later in 1641.

Following the construction of a VOC factory in Hirado, Jacques Specx became the first chief merchant in Japan, with a short tenure from 1610 to 1613 and an additional year in 1615. During the early years of the Dutch presence in Hirado and VOC Hirado-Batavia exchange, porcelain was listed in Batavia's *dagh* registers (daily journals) as the third of the eight foreign articles that were in demand in Japan.[14] By the 1640s, when the Dutch were permitted to build new warehouses in the artificial island of Dejima in Nagasaki Bay, a robust industry was in formation of creating pottery made to order from the Netherlands. Much of this industry passed through Taiwan. It was this industry that became increasingly central to the VOC inter-Asian portfolio during the Ming-Qing transition period, when Jingdezhen-sourced porcelains became difficult to access and when Chinese commodities were generally less available to VOC merchants in the South China Sea.

Jingdezhen, situated inland about halfway between Shanghai and Guangzhou, was one of two major sources of porcelains traded by the VOC in the early seventeenth century. The other source was the coastal province Fujian, which Ali Akbar Khitayi writing in Istanbul in the previous century mentioned as one of the heartlands of porcelain production. By the 1640s, with the fall of the Ming, the Dutch turned increasingly to porcelains produced in Fujian. The kilns in Fujian, however, did not produce the shapes and decorations that the European market was familiar with, as Fujianese ceramics were intended for Southeast Asian markets. Even the Fujianese source, moreover, was a limited one, as the previously discussed negotiations between the VOC and Qing governing circles limited VOC-Qing trade to tributary exchange, and the Qing additionally limited official exports to Europe of commodities like Chinese porcelain between 1656 and 1684. By the end of the Ming period, in other words, Japanese-made porcelains were rising to become the principal source of blue-and-white porcelains with Ming Chinese designs to satisfy the rapidly growing demand for the Chinese porcelain market in Europe. Interestingly, what facilitated the logistics of the VOC's ability to sustain their porcelain import boom in the Netherlands while the company made the Qing-era transition from Chinese-made to Japanese-made porcelain was the fact the VOC had access to replicas in an expected source: their newly established warehouses in Safavid Iran.

Batavia's Dilemma: Between Iranian Replicas and Japanese Originals

By 1622, one hundred and twelve years after the Portuguese captured the port of Hormuz, and some two hundred years after Ming forces under admiral Zheng He visited Hormuz, a joint Safavid and English East India Company (est. 1600) armed force pushed out the Portuguese, paving the way for greater British activity throughout the Indian Ocean. Unsurprisingly, the Dutch were not far from the scene and managed to secure commercial access to Iran's ports. Shah Abbas (r. 1571–1629), who commissioned the joint force to take over the island of Hormuz from the Portuguese, simultaneously in 1623 allowed the VOC to establish a trading center in Bandar Abbas, which Shah Abbas sought to cultivate as a new commercial center. This occurred just fourteen years after the Dutch established a factory in Hirado, making the transition from Chinese imports of the early seventeenth century to Japanese imports in latter half of the century the story of an Iranian manufacturing interlude.

More specifically, 1652 to 1684 saw the massive export of pseudo-porcelain to the various VOC centers throughout Asia, including Surat on the Indian coast as well as the VOC headquarters in Batavia. From an early period, however, there were questions about the quality. On one side was the perspective of Raphael Du Mans, the French traveler and member of the Franciscan-related Capuchin order. In his memoirs, titled *L'estat de la Perse en 1660*, he related that the wares that came from Kirman, where the best was made, were difficult to distinguish from Chinese wares. Sir Jean-Baptiste Chardin, the French jeweler and one-time jewelry agent for Shah Abbas II, made similar comments. On the other side were VOC agents in Surat who complained about the shipments. A letter from 1656 requesting three hundred pieces qualifies the request with the warning that if the shipment cannot be of sound quality, "Please do not send them because then they may be obtained here [in Surat] from what is carried here by the Moors . . . and we don't want to be served with refuse [from Bandar Abbas] as last year," referencing the albeit pricier availability of porcelain within coastal India's merchant networks trading throughout the Indian Ocean.[15]

Likewise, in 1663, a Dutch letter from Surat indicates that a shipment of porcelain was so disappointing that it may as well have been Persian. The explanation for the disparity in perceived quality is clear: while the Japanese after the 1650s were able to acquire both the ingredients and skills necessary to produce genuine kaolin-based porcelain, Safavid potters' centuries-old innovative pseudo-porcelain slipware technique—using a white slip over clay earthenware—was impressively similar to porcelain but was lacking in certain ways. Specifically, one the one hand, Iranian pseudo-porcelain featured a pleasing portfolio of Chinese and West Asian designs including phoenixes, dragons, peonies, and lotus flowers, all of which reflected a sophisticated synthesis of Chinese, Abbasid, Ilkhanid, and Timurid styles. On the other hand, there were a least three things that distinguished genuine porcelain: the ring of the vessel when struck, its resistance to damage, and how uniquely stainless and impermeable it was compared to more porous materials. By the end of the seventeenth century, the only solution to the VOC's supply problems was to double down on their Japanese source. What worked in the company's favor was the fact that Japanese artisans had perfected the art of producing porcelain and had simultaneously continued to cultivate both archaic blue-and-white Ming-era designs and new polychrome designs.

The manufacture of porcelain in Japan in the 1620s was originally a domestic affair, catering especially to the import market for Chinese-made Ming blue-and-whites. Japanese artisans also produced pseudo-porcelain overglazed enamelware similar to the Safavid pseudo-porcelain earthenware, which helped answer the high local demand for porcelain during the transition from the Ming to the Qing eras. From the VOC's perspective, the beneficial outcome of Japan's cultivation of a pseudo-porcelain industry alongside genuine porcelain was the fact that the former industry produced a variety of designs that would be used in the growing domestic porcelain industry, which would in turn expand Dutch tastes for East Asian porcelain designs beyond the classic Ming blue-and-whites. The Japanese porcelain industry generally came to be known as Aritaware, which takes its name from the kilns of Arita. While Japanese-made blue-and-white porcelains originally dominated exports to European and Southeast Asian markets via the ports of Imari and Nagasaki, polychrome porcelains drawing on the earlier pseudo-porcelain industry grew in demand in Europe.

In sum, by the end of the 1600s, with the interruption of the VOC's supply from Jingdezhen and the development of a local Japanese porcelain industry, the transfer to the Netherlands of Ming blue-and-white porcelains gave way to both Japanese Ming-style blue-and-whites and new polychrome styles following a brief Iranian pseudo-porcelain interlude. By the eighteenth century, with the rise in the Netherlands and later England of local pseudo-porcelain industries, the northern European world of metalware, stoneware, and earthenware finally saw the ubiquitous proliferation of durable white ceramics, where white backgrounds signaled the vessel's genuine porcelain construction or pseudo-porcelain construction with an expectation of porcelain-like durability. What constituted northern Europe's ceramics revolution, in other words, were the two elements that spread from China to West Asia during the Tang, Song, and Ming dynasties—the rise of these imported porcelains in the palaces and households of the Netherlands and later England as well as the development of this local pseudo-porcelain industry, which in the case of Europe was documented in the photo-realism of Dutch still-life painting.

EUROPE'S PORCELAIN REVOLUTION

Vermeer and the Art of Painting China

One of the most influential painters in Dutch history built his career in the very city that produced Europe's most celebrated Ming-emulating industry of pseudo-porcelain wares: Johannes Vermeer (d. 1675) of Delft, where local potters produced Delftware ceramics. Vermeer's paintings included still-life works and coincided with the Portuguese and VOC import of Ming blue-and-whites. The outcome of this chronology is that seventeenth-century Dutch painting offers a strikingly photographic window into two phenomena: the transfer to Europe of objects from Ming China and Edo Japan and, in what reflects a new industrial Chinoiserie, the proliferation and commodification of this taste with the invention of pseudo-porcelain tin-based Delftware and its mass production during the Industrial Revolution.

For contemporary observers in the Netherlands, the abundance of international luxury imports was something to discuss in the seventeenth century. A Dutch poet and politician wrote, "Everything heaven sends or grows out of the earth . . . comes to us by sea imported," while a British traveler in 1699 noted, "Perhaps [the Netherlands] may yield to none . . . in riches and the vast extent of its trade and commerce."[16] Dutch paintings told this story in almost photographic detail across works laden with each artist's interpretation of the increasingly global world on display along the walls, shelves, and, in the case of Vermeer's "Milkmaid," floorboards of households and palaces throughout the Netherlands.

Vermeer's "Milkmaid," one of the painter's most celebrated works, offers a subtle window into the slow and steady influx of both Chinese and Chinese-inspired blue-and-white ceramics into the public and private spaces of the Netherlands. The oil painting was completed sometime between 1657 and 1661 and features both an older form of stoneware and the new so-called Delftware, made of tin.[17] The stoneware is found at the center of the painting, which features a domestic worker carefully pouring milk from a simple earth-colored stoneware jug into a vessel of similar material. In the background, the base of the wall is lined with a series of tiles that function as floorboard-like skirting tiles in British architecture, protecting the lower portion of the wall and offering an aesthetic transition between the wall and the ground. The tiles in this case are Delftware tiles. On the one hand, their blue and white color offers a striking contrast with the browns and beiges used for the hanging basket, stoneware jar and dish, and bread loaves. On the other hand, the tiles are difficult to miss because of the rich blues that dominate the lower half of the painting, from the tablecloth to the subject's apron. The Delft tiles offer a subtle counterpart to the deep blues of the tablecloth and apron and simultaneously suggest the global tastes of both Vermeer and the house's owner. Delft tiles were still new in the mid-1600s. The oldest surviving factory, De Porceleyne Fles, dates back to 1653, when both the process and aesthetic of pseudo-porcelain Delftware production remained intrinsically tied to contemporary taste for imported Ming and Ming-like blue-and-whites from Qing China and Edo Japan. The fact that a hanging map was one of two items Vermeer originally painted in "The Milkmaid"—later painted over in the final copy—further suggests that Vermeer, despite never traveling abroad, was well attuned to the expanding global connections of the VOC-era Netherlands and was himself a consumer of the exotic East Asian imports in circulation. Likewise, the hanging maps in his "Woman with a Lute" and "Artist in His Studio"—not painted over in these cases—reflect his enduring interest in capturing through art some of the global tastes of the time. As one of several painters who shaped Dutch still life, Vermeer was not alone in this interest.

Willem Kalf was one of the best-known painters of the era whose work, like Vermeer's, offers an aesthetically pleasing documentary record of the kinds of global commodities that shaped Dutch and northern European taste, from Chinese porcelains to Turkish carpets and Sevillian oranges. In his "Still Life with a Chinese Porcelain Jar," Kalf prominently integrated blue-and-white porcelain with pseudo-porcelain. What stands out is Kalf's emphasis on the shine and translucency of porcelain in contrast with stoneware, an aesthetic quality that explains comparisons between porcelain and pearls among Arabic-language writers almost a millennium earlier. Kalf notably used a jar with a less common color combination of white designs on a blue background, as opposed to the more ubiquitous blue-on-white design. Vermeer's Delft tiles featured blue designs on white backgrounds, including a representation of Cupid in blue that repeats across the length of the skirting tiles. With Kalf's choice of a Chinese jar with the less common white-on-blue color combination, the result is a striking and contrasting balance of the work's cool ultramarine pigment and the warm pigments used for both the fruit and the tall and similarly exotic Venetian fluted glass. Many of the pieces featured in his works are Wanli wares from the Ming Wanli Emperor's (r. 1573–1620) reign, one of which even features Daoist figures. The pieces featured in his works, in other words, are original Chinese porcelain vessels distinct from the tin- and clay-based blue-and-white pseudo-porcelains that began to be produced in the Netherlands for the local blue-and-white consumer market.[18]

Delftware's Answer to the Market for Fine China

The rise of a profitable and local pseudo-porcelain earthenware industry in Delft, where Vermeer built his career, represented simultaneously the possibilities of innovation in local manufacturing and the promises of innovation in industrial technology. Genuine porcelain on a par with the fifteen-hundred-year-old Chinese porcelain industry was just a few decades away from being created using genuine kaolin clay, feldspar, and the once mysterious techniques necessary for producing sound batches consistently. Until then, Delft and other centers of pottery construction and design in the 1600s—Haarlem, Rotterdam, Amsterdam, Middleburgh—would continue perfecting their own method for producing pseudo-porcelains out of tin and clay. The process begins with the placement of ground clay materials in vats until the consistency is smoother. The clay is then put into brick vats and divided into pieces to be shaped by hand or wheel. The pieces are then dipped into molten tin enamel to create a milky-looking surface, and designs are then painted onto them before being fired. An additional layer of white tin glaze is used around the area where the decorations are, followed by a clear ceramic glaze around the rest of the vessel. As the method was perfected, artisans began to use white tin glaze around the entire vessel before decorating it, then adding a layer of clear glaze to create a strong resemblance to genuine imported Chinese porcelain.

From the perspective of technological innovation and northern European cultural currency, the peak of Delftware's popularity around eighteenth-century Europe coincided with a development that foreshadowed a coming change in northern European–Chinese relations during the Industrial Revolution. Delft's pseudo-porcelain Ming-like blue-and-white ceramics, despite their popularity around Europe, began to be eclipsed by a competing British industry with a particular technological edge. English artisans, drawing on Dutch innovation, were able to produce a massive amount of these pseudo-porcelain products in a short period of time at a low cost, and were simultaneously able to transport them in large volume across long distances by rail.

Throughout the eighteenth century, in a process that eclipsed Delftware and that was part of the background of the Industrial Revolution, English ceramics industries became intertwined with the rise of factory systems and mass production. Pottery was originally a craft industry for centuries, but in the late eighteenth century, a certain potter named Josiah Wedgewood was on the verge of revolutionizing the industry by creating a production system oriented around the division of labor and an advanced transportation system. These developments occurred after 1775, when Wedgewood had just finished inventing a new way of processing jasper using cobalt oxide to give it an attractive blue color. Wedgewood jasperware, the result of his experiments, was originally a form of blue-and-white pseudo-porcelain that used a layer of blue coating over white jasper. In the interest of both protecting trade secrets and increasing production output, Wedgewood hired workers who would specialize in individual parts of the production, even building separate entrances for each section of the factory. In the interest of protecting the pottery industry generally and increasing output in light of the competitive entrepreneurial atmosphere, Wedgewood simultaneously created a potters' association to lobby for improvements in transportation, including both roads and a canal. By 1760, the Trent-Mersey canal was opened and facilitated the long-term success of Staffordshire as the center of pottery production in England. By the late eighteenth century, the French government took a leading role in trying to clone British industrial methods in a decades-long competition over manufacturing, culminating in the early nineteenth-century eclipse of Delft as the center of ceramics production. Meissen, Sevres, Chelsea, and Staffordshire constituted the bulk of a robust competition in industry and manufacturing that was increasingly oriented around innovations in shipping, hydraulic engineering, land drainage.

In late Qing China and Edo Japan, nineteenth-century reformers noted the transformation of European industry through technological innovation. Technological advances in ceramics manufacturing and production went hand in hand with advances in a variety of industries that were brought to British and Dutch ports in Asia, including medicine and weapons technology. While the former generated interest in Northeast Asia from an earlier period of Dutch-Japanese relations, it was the latter and its use in British so-called gunboat diplomacy during the Opium Wars that introduced a certain urgency in nineteenth-century Japan and China to begin looking towards northern Europe for models of industrial reform. While the exact contours of industrial reform were part of a prolonged debate that dominated late nineteenth-century Chinese and Japanese politics, the outcome in both cases was the same: with the British Empire having overtaken the Dutch in Asia, and with British military advances having facilitated the transfer of Hong Kong to the British, both Chinese and Japanese administrators and intellectuals at the end of the Qing and Edo periods discussed the trajectory of northern Europe in a manner illustrative of a major shift in northern European—Northeast Asian cultural relations. Specifically, the cultural capital that China sustained around the world since the Age of Exploration was contested within its own borders and in neighboring Japan by, among other forces, a certain alternative: the promises of political empowerment and renewal in Northeast Asia through the emulation of European industrialization. Interestingly, the spark that ignited these debates came from yet another Chinese commodity that became fashionable and desirable in Europe in the eighteenth and nineteenth centuries, a commodity that the British Empire was willing to go to war with China over: Chinese black tea.

CHAPTER 8

Tea across the British Empire

Echoing the outcomes of sixteenth-century Iberian commerce across East Asia, the entrenchment of Dutch and British merchants in a world of Sinocentric trade in the following century meant extensive Chinese cultural transfer westward. In the case of the Dutch in Macau and Nagasaki, the technologically inimitable Chinese porcelain industry that transformed West Asian ceramics a millennium earlier finally began to revolutionize northern European material culture.[1] Among the favorite uses for genuine imported porcelains and locally made pseudo-porcelain was for northern Europe's newest pastime: the consumption of Dutch- and British-imported Chinese black tea.

What was new about the British transfer of Chinese black tea to London, and its displacement locally of Arabic coffee in the old coffeehouses, was the way British tea in London became something that Dutch pseudo-porcelain in Delft and Amsterdam never did: a European colonial commodity removed from the Chinese underpinnings that made imported porcelain fashionable among the Dutch. By the late nineteenth century, the English East India Company had reinvented Chinese black tea as the sugary, milk-laden imperial British habit of a self-styled civilizing and industrious elite living between London, British South Asia, and newly British-held Hong Kong. That British tea displaced coffee even in the heartlands of the coffee-drinking Middle East and North Africa speaks to a massive shift in northern

European cultural capital around the world. In Northeast Asia, the decades that saw the Middle East follow European trends of consuming British tea in place of Arabic coffee were the same decades that saw late Edo-era (1603–1868) Japanese reformers take unfettered turns towards Dutch science and British technology as part of an overall reform in learning and political administration. After a half millennium of European merchant networks since the Age of Exploration serving as agents of Chinese and Japanese cultural transfer westward to a rising Europe, Europe's industrial revolution—and especially its military outcomes during the British-led Opium Wars—inspired a new global imagination of European modernization and progress that would transform China and Japan's own political outlooks.

CHINESE TEA'S TREK FROM MING CHINA TO IMPERIAL LONDON

Tea's Origins: From Meal to Beverage

The European pastime of sipping warm brewed black tea—hot water infused with loose tea leaves poured into porcelain and pseudo-porcelain cups—was a product of the late Ming period. It was specifically a product of Ming-era cultural transfer made possible by the Portuguese, the Dutch East India Company, and most importantly, the English East India Company. Prior to the Ming, tea was more commonly one of two drinks: a frothy decoction of finely powdered tea whisked in individual cups with warm water, and a less frothy decoction of pulverized roasted tea leaves boiled in water. In both cases, whether finely powdered tea or pulverized roasted tea leaves, tea was originally chipped off or scraped from a brick of compressed tea. The infused loose-leaf teas, in contrast, were an innovation of the Ming era.[2] Also from the Ming era came the most widely consumed version of this loose leaf tea: black tea, which was the product of a sophisticated Chinese cultivation technique that the English East India Company tried desperately and successfully to bring to South Asia. In the early days of preparing Chinese tea for export to Europe, the cultivation and transportation process included fermenting tea, baking it as a preservative measure, and from there packaging it for the long maritime journey from Ming China to Europe.

Both in Europe and in China, and likewise in the Middle East, the consumption of Chinese tea began as something very different: medicinal food. The oldest form of ancient tea consumption in China and Thailand was as an invigorating ground ingredient added to foods. As a brewed beverage, there is evidence that the Dai people of the southern Himalayas were the first to brew tea some two thousand years ago, and it was through an ancient trade route northward that tea was brought to China.[3] Tea was originally procured from naturally occurring bushes prior to the rise of cultivation techniques. The ancient method of preserving and transporting tea, which was the one Europeans were first exposed to during the Ming period, included a key step between fermenting and baking tea: the leaves were pushed into bamboo, and what emerged was a cylindrical brick. When Genghis Khan imported tea to the city of Karakorum in present-day Mongolia in the 1200s, and when the Russian import market emerged in the 1600s, shipments of tea came in brick form as part of new bilateral trade along China's northwest frontiers: bricks of fermented and baked tea for Central Asian horses, and with the rise of Russia, tea for Russian-exported Central Asian fur.

Buddhist and Daoist monks were among the earliest to consume tea as a brewed beverage. Its stimulating properties served as an aid for meditation and concentration, just as coffee in the fifteenth century became a favorite beverage among Muslim mystics (Sufis) for the same reason. By the fourth century C.E., as the consumption of tea spread together with the spread of Buddhism, tea was still prepared by breaking off pieces of roasted tea bricks and brewing them in boiling water to create a frothy warm beverage. By the fifth century C.E., tea consumption was increasingly associated with the growing porcelain industry in Zhejiang, and there was simultaneously a definitive shift from acquiring tea from unharvested wild sources to cultivating tea using botanical and agricultural techniques that the British East India Company had tremendous difficulty replicating as late as the 1800s. Both developments were noted and assessed by the Tang-era writer Lu Yu (fl. after 733), remembered by later generations as a kind of literary father of tea. Lu Yu was raised by a Chan (Zen) monk in contemporary Hubei Province after being orphaned as a child. In his adulthood, he completed a multivolume work that drew on the knowledge he acquired in his youth: *The Classic of Tea*. The work, which is a comparatively short work of about seven thousand characters in length, represented the culmination of his research on and experience with tea. Its ten chapters cover topics including tea's origins, the tools and processes of its production, wares, its infusion methods, modalities of tea consumption, anecdotes of tea before the Tang, geographical regions where tea is found, and illustrations. Lu Yu noted, for example, the widespread custom of mixing tea with various savory and sweet additives, from ginger to fruit. Lu Yu believed that tea should be consumed in its pure unadulterated form. Tea for him and the rest of its Tang-era consumers was still a frothy powdery drink. It would take more than six hundred years, specifically the Ming period, for the custom of brewing loose-leaf tea to become the primary way of drinking tea in China. In the meantime, within the Tang ruling administration of Lu Yu's lifetime, both the cultivation and consumption of tea were becoming imperial affairs.

Simultaneous with the proliferation of tea drinking under the Tang dynasty was the ruling administration's involvement in the developing tea industry. The Tang dynasty was the first dynasty to establish vast tea gardens in southern and southwestern China, and the changing pattern of the governance of tea cultivation reflected a rising political debate about the exact role of various administrative bodies in the overall cultivation, exchange, and taxation of tea. In 817, some 300,000 catties of tea were transferred from the royal treasury to the Department of Public Revenue, which overlapped with the Salt and Iron Commission in the administration and taxation of salt pools and tea gardens.[4] In 821, various tea gardens belonging to the royal household were transferred to local authorities who nonetheless paid tribute to the emperor in tea. By 835, administrators Wang Yai and Cheng Chu attempted to confine all tea production to state-controlled plantations governed by the newly established Tea Commission (*chueh ch'a shih*). The commission's stipulations—ordering locals to destroy stocks of prepared tea and to transplant tea-shrubs to government plantations—caused unrest and cut the administrators' tenure short, leaving the plan unlikely to have been carried out on a mass scale. By the end of the dynasty, while state revenues from tea taxation remained small, the consumption of tea was a widespread pastime that reached deeply into Tang courtly culture and provincial culture.

The Song era saw new levels of refinement in the social customs oriented around tea consumption. Previously, during the Tang era, tea preparation involved breaking off pieces of coarse tea leaves in brick form to be brewed in a pot and served in porcelain cups. Under the Song, these bricks of tea were also composed of powdered tea rather than only coarse tea leaves, which made it possible to scrape off powdered tea directly into an individual consumer's tea bowl and whip the final concoction into a frothy green drink. It was this type of tea preparation that gave rise to Japanese *matcha* (抹茶, Chinese: *mŏchá*) and the Chan (Zen) tea ceremony. The earliest Chan (Zen) monastic tract, a Chinese text from 1103 titled *Rules of Purity for the Chan Monastery (Chanyuan Qinggui)*, outlines the etiquette of the tea ceremony.[5] By the end of the century, the Japanese Zen master Eisai brought the ceremony to Japan. In what illustrates the significance of Chinese material culture in these developments, the reigning Song Emperor Huizong (r. 1101–1125) commissioned the design of a variety of porcelain wares specifically for the consumption of tea. It was during this period when the famous Song black-glazed cups with tan-colored "rabbit hair glaze" lines throughout the interior came into popular use to complement the new powdered tea's frothy green color.[6] The monochromatic blue-glazed vessels are also from this period. Some nine hundred years before the modern fixation on the quality of latte foam, Huizong's reign saw the rise of competitions over who could perfectly froth *matcha* foam.

The late Song era also saw the rise of Japanese *sencha* (煎茶, Chinese: *jiānchá*), loose-leaf tea that was neither compressed into bricks nor pulverized and boiled in a decoction. Loose-leaf tea was the complete leaf, dried and infused with water. Under the Mongol Yuan, continuity in tea-consumption habits foreshadowed Ming-specific trends that spread around the world. Under Buyantu Khan (r. 1285–1325), Mongol court physician Hu Sihui compiled a compendium of Mongol culinary practices based on his experiences as a court dietician. The text, titled *Dietary Principles* (*Yinshan Zheng Yao*) and completed in 1332, notes a variety of tea preparation styles popular among the Yuan ruling circles.[7] Two of those included the use of yak butter, while another called for the infusion of complete loose-leaf tea in hot water in what reflects the continued development of this latter approach. Under the Mongols, a new method of roasting loose-leaf tea was developed that left the tea less burnt than traditional brick tea while still roasting it enough to avoid the bitterness associated with loose uncooked teas. The method, called *chaoqing* or "roasting out the green," involved pressing the leaves against the side of a wok-like cooking vessel by hand. By the Ming era, this method was perfected.

Ming-Era Black Tea Exports around the World

It was under the Ming when compressed bricks of roasted tea leaves, powdered tea (*matcha*), and loose-leaf tea (*sencha*) all became global Chinese exports. It was also under the Ming when loose-leaf tea overtook all other forms of tea in terms of elite and popular consumption. Along coastal ports, two centuries prior to the arrival of Portuguese merchants, exports of tea facilitated Muromachi Japan's (r. 1336–1573) rising tea culture that dominated the customs of both military diplomacy and Chan (Zen) rituals. Across the northern frontiers, where an ascendant Grand Duchy of Moscow (1283–1547) expanded into the Turco-Mongol steppe in the sixteenth century, the early Ming era saw the revival of an originally Song-era exchange of Chinese tea for frontier horses and fur. From a European perspective, the outcome was that while the Portuguese were the first Europeans to import tea beginning in the sixteenth century, the rise of a national tea-drinking pastime took off fastest in Russia via a late-Ming-era royal gift of Chinese brick tea to Russian ruling circles. As mentioned, prior to the rise of coastal exports to Europe via Portuguese and Dutch inter-Asian exchange during the so-called Age of Exploration, the Ming cultivated a tea-for-horses trade along the northwest frontier that developed into a tea-for-fur trade with Russia.

In all of these cases of Ming-era overland and maritime tea exports, the local production and foreign export of tea became part of a growing debate among Ming administrators about taxation domestically and commercial exchange abroad. Domestically, the Hongwu Emperor (r. 1368–1398) decreed in 1391 that all Chinese tea given as tribute to the Ming dynasty must be in loose-leaf form as opposed to brick tea. Abroad, there was originally little debate about the importance of exporting Ming tea beyond the northern and western frontiers in exchange for horses imported as tribute. The Ming court was in deep need of horses, which were central to military defense. Historically, Chinese dynasties were able to procure horses from as far away as Arabia, offering lavish gifts such as the esteemed four-clawed dragon robe to the ruler of Mecca in 1518 in this commercial context.[8] Arabia was far, however, and Middle Eastern interest in Chinese commodities was oriented around low-volume luxury imports like Chinese silk and porcelain that competed in the Middle East with local textiles and pseudo-porcelain slipware. In fact, tea as a high-volume import in the Middle East only began to sideline Arabic coffee in the nineteenth century under British commercial and cultural influence, which meant that this later import of tea came from British South Asia. Ming-era states along the northwest frontier, meanwhile, also bred horses, were closer, and had already developed a taste for brick tea. Where there was political debate about this frontier exchange of tea for horses was in the role of private trade.

In the context of this growing tea-horses trade along the northwest frontier, Ming administrators increasingly debated larger questions about the legality of private export and import trade outside the bounds of official government-controlled tribute trade. Under the late Song dynasty, the imperial Horse-Trading Office (*Ch'a-ma ssu*) was established, setting aside three times per year for trade along the northern borders in present-day Gansu and Qinghai provinces. The Hongwu Emperor's administration revived the system, but by the end of his reign in 1398, the export of tea was increasingly in private merchants' hands. The problem the Ming government faced throughout the fifteenth century was that the more the tea export trade was in private hands, the less frontier states were dependent on the Ming government and the Horse Trading Office for tea, which made it harder for the Ming to procure horses in exchange for government-provided tea. In the years leading up to the Zhengde Emperor's reign (r. 1505–1521) a century later, administrators increasingly formalized a system of working with local merchants to have them transport tea all the way to the frontier city of Shansi, and in exchange for their effort, they were allowed to conduct private trade without risk of penalty. Yang I-ch'in, a Yunnanese administrator appointed Left Vice Censor-in-Chief in 1502, played a key role in formalizing this arrangement, even though he was an enduring advocate of total imperial control over the tea-horses trade.[9] Prior to his appointment, he spent years in Shansi observing the administration of horse imports, and he came to believe that government control over tea-horses exchange would stabilize horse prices and the volume of horse imports. However, in a six-thousand-character memorial he completed in 1505, the first year of the Zhengde Emperor's reign, he acknowledged that there was no way around Ming cooperation with local merchants. Frontier tribes had access to tea from illicit exporters who knew that the private tea trade was more profitable than offering it to the government in exchange for silver payments. In correlation with this fact, horse imports from the frontier were at the low volume of approximately five thousand horses per year during the early years of Yang's administration. Official tribute missions were also expensive, and private merchants were making those trips anyway. Smuggling, meanwhile, ran the risk of steep penalties. The outcome was that despite the modern historiographical stereotype of an economically closed post-Yuan Ming-era China that contrasted with open Portuguese and Dutch states, the Ming allowed private trade in varying degrees both on the coast and on the frontier throughout the fourteenth and fifteenth centuries, with the need for military horses being one of the early motivations.[10] China's tea trade with Russia, in fact, was part of this private trade.

As mentioned, the rise of both Ming-controlled and private Chinese-Russian exchange during the Ming and the Duchy of Moscow (1283–1547) was a product of mutual Russian and Chinese import needs. Before the late 1500s, the Duchy of Moscow and the Ming dynasty simultaneously traded with the powerful nomadic steppe states that separated them. By the early 1600s, the expanded Tsardom of Russia (1547–1721) was in control of much of the previously Mongol-held steppe, paving the way for direct Russian import of Chinese commodities like brick tea. It was in 1638 when the first shipment of Chinese tea was sent westward, specifically with Tsar Alexis's ambassadors Vasilii Starkov and Stepan Neverov. The ambassadors were on a diplomatic mission to a Mongol khan whose territory remained unconquered by either Russia or Ming China. The khan was displeased with the low value of the gifts the ambassadors brought. After being asked or compelled to give the khan most of what was in their possession, the ambassadors were sent back to Russia with a variety of gifts: animals including two hundred sables, two beavers, two snow leopards, and some two hundred packets of tea. Starkov initially attempted to exchange the tea for additional sables given that the leaves were "unknown" in Russia.[11] During their reception with the khan, Starkov himself drank tea, and while he was certainly familiar with medicinal herbal infusions that resembled tea, he was unfamiliar with this particular beverage. Starkov described tea as a beverage consisting "of leaves, I know not whether from a tree, or an herb."[12] The outcome of the ambassadors' transfer westward of Ming tea was that it sparked the interest of Russian ruling circles, who by 1679 signed a trade agreement with the new Qing government stipulating the exchange of fur for tea. According to the agreement, a caravan of some three hundred camels with Russian fur would leave Russia to cross into China, stopping at various trading posts. Eight months later, the caravan would bring back some six hundred pounds of both loose-leaf and brick tea.

Within a century, that original Ming-era transfer of Chinese tea to Russia began to transform the landscape of Russian culinary habits and social customs, which were increasingly oriented around the private and public consumption of tea from a samovar. In 1778 specifically, Ivan Fyodorovich and Nazar Fyodorovich, sons of Russian businessman Fyodor Ivanovich Lisitsyn, registered Russia's first samovar-making factory. The samovar, which resembles a Mongolian hot pot, became the preferred tool for serving tea in Russia. Zvarka, a dense tea concentrate, was placed on top of the samovar, while a lower compartment held hot water kept warm by an internal tube with burning charcoal. Glasses were placed in metal holders, known as a podstakannik. In each glass, the preparer poured concentrated tea and added hot water depending on the desired strength. Echoing the Tang-era tastes for sweetening brick tea with fruits, Russian tea came with *syrnicki*, pancakes served with jam. By the nineteenth century, with a growth in direct Russian-Chinese trade precipitating a fall in tea prices, the scene of tea drinkers with their samovars had become so embedded in Russian culture that samovars were ubiquitous in paintings. In the same century, the samovar was making its way across Russia's southern border to the coffee-drinking capital of the world: the late Ottoman Empire. By the end of the nineteenth century, despite five centuries of coffee dominating elite and popular Ottoman culinary traditions, the Black Sea city of Rize was poised to become the center of a new tea-drinking culture that would make the Republic of Turkey the world's largest consumer of tea annually per capita in the modern era. Its neighbors, from Iraq and Syria to the Levant and Egypt, simultaneously began to consume the beverage under British influence following the very different story of Ming-era Chinese tea's transfer westward along the maritime routes to early modern Europe.

FROM PORTUGUESE ODDITY TO BRITISH MONOPOLY

Tea within the Portuguese and VOC Commercial Networks

The Portuguese first reported on the arrival of tea in Europe in 1559. Jesuit and Dominican writers throughout East Asia were among the earliest seafaring Europeans to express interest in tea upon their arrival in Chinese and Japanese ports. Dominican friar Gaspar da Cruz (d. 1570) of Portugal returned from China in 1560, writing in admiration of a custom he witnessed in households where visitors were served a drink "called *cha*" (*que chama cha*) in "a porcelain vessel" (*uma porcellana*) that was "somewhat red" (*tamalavez vermelha*), very medicinal, and steeped from bitter herbs.[13] Da Cruz was evidently writing about loose-leaf tea in China, while Valignano a short while later witnessed the rise of powdered tea in Japan. Valignano wrote that the Japanese are universally in the habit (*acostumbran universalmente en todo Japon*) of drinking a beverage made of hot water and some powder from an herb (*unos polvos de una hyerva*) that they call *chaa* (*que llaman chaa*). Valignano was particularly interested in the tearooms in residences. "Because hot water is called *yu* in Japan, and this herb *chaa*, they call the place for this *chanoyu*, which is the most valued and respected thing in Japan" where people "show love (*mostrar amor*) to their guests (*huespedes*)."[14] Luis Frois, a Jesuit who met Ashikaga Yoshiteru in 1564, believed that the Japanese tearoom was an ideal space for holding mass because of its cleanliness.

The Dutch caught word of both tea and coffee partly from a Dutch merchant named Jan Hugo van Linschoten (fl. 1563–1611) who was traveling with a Portuguese fleet to Japan. *The Voyage of John Huyghen Van Linschoten to the East Indies* (*Linschoten's Travels*) was published in 1598. Given the wide geographical expanse of his travels, van Lischoten was in the unique position to write about a variety of beverages including both coffee and tea. Van Lischoten wrote that the Japanese entertain guests with tea (*chaa*) prepared in hot water and served in cups that are valued not for their newness but for their age and high-quality workmanship.[15] Interestingly, he notes that "the Turks" have almost the same manner of drinking coffee, known as *chaoua* (Arabic Turkish: *qahwa*). Van Lischoten describes how they prepare the coffee beverage from a certain fruit, in reference to the coffee cherry containing the bean, and that they roast and eventually drink it in hot water every morning for strength.[16] Van Linschoten's identification of one method with the other— that is, Chinese tea and Turkish coffee preparation—points to the fact that he was witnessing the preparation specifically of powdered *matcha* tea. As mentioned, in contrast with the infusion of hot water with tea leaves, *matcha* is dissolved in hot water as a decoction similar to the pulverized leaves and powders chipped or scraped off of brick tea.

From van Linschoten's late sixteenth century comments on both tea and coffee, it comes as no surprise that the pastime of tea drinking arrived haltingly in Europe because of the parallel absorption of coffee from the Middle East from, specifically, Mocha (Yemen) via Istanbul. Tea's consumption as a beverage of entertainment was somewhat limited to European elites and royalty in the mid-1600s, while its use as a medicinal drink was more widespread. In The Hague, tea drinking was a fashionable luxury in 1640. Constantijn Huygens, the Dutch Golden Age composer and poet, addressed fellow members of the Muiderkring literary circle in Latin as "illustrious drinkers of tea" (*illustres Te-potores*) in a letter that is both an ode to his colleagues and to "divine tea."[17] In London, its most famous consumer— namely, the Portuguese royal Catarina de Bragança (r. 1662–1685), wife of Charles II—was not even English. In Germany, tea appeared on apothecary price lists in 1657.[18] By 1648, it was in Paris, and was used by select doctors and clergy who debated its value. After physician Philibert Morisset wrote an essay titled *Ergo Thea Chinesium, Menti Confert* claiming tea had a positive impact on the mind, fellow physician Guy Patin condemned it and called tea "the impertinent novelty of the century." By then, another exotic foreign beverage was already in vogue in Paris: coffee.

As mentioned, coffee's introduction to Europe in the sixteenth century was almost simultaneous with tea but slightly earlier, and its source was the nearby Ottoman Empire across the Adriatic and Mediterranean. The drink's immediate popularity may have been facilitated by its resemblance to another beverage that was in vogue in the same century: chocolate. In the sixteenth century, Spain had begun to import chocolate from Central America. Chocolate as a beverage, consumed originally in Mexico as a concoction of chocolate, water, cornmeal, and chili peppers, became a popular drink amongst the aristocracy of Habsburg Spain during the reign of Charles V (r. 1519–1556). The beverage, which soon spread to France and Austria, was consumed with a variety of flavoring spices such as jasmine and vanilla. By the mid-1600s, when the first chocolate houses opened in London, the price of chocolate remained high and the recipe of a sweet milk-based chocolate beverage was not yet universal.

The outcome of these developments was that European chocolate drinkers may have been primed in the mid-1600s for an interruption in Chinese tea's popularity and a turn first towards coffee in an economic and cultural context where coffee was available at a lower price and from a geographically close source: the Ottoman Levant of the eastern Mediterranean, source of Europe's rapidly growing Turquerie tastes that paralleled both contemporary Chinoiserie coming from the Indian Ocean and Mesoamerican cultural imports from across the Atlantic Ocean.

Coffee's relevance to the story of European tea imports appears in the background of how the Dutch East India Company (VOC) came to split their beverage portfolio between newly cultivated coffee in Java and Chinese tea, a development that contrasts with the English East India Company's (EIC) more exclusive turn towards tea imports. One of the earliest and most famous references to coffee comes not from the travel accounts of Dutch merchants in the Netherlands but from the police records of the Venetian Republic. Venice was a key node in the cultural transfer of Ottoman taste westward via the Venetian Republic's trans-imperial Venetian and Ottoman merchants. In 1575, an Ottoman textile merchant named Huseyin Celebi was killed in the city, and both Venetian and Ottoman records documented his demise. The reference to coffee comes from the inventory of his possessions, which included a *finian* in the Venetian records—that is, a *fincan* or Turkish coffee cup.[19] The Ottoman merchants of Venice based at the *fondaco dei turchi* prepared coffee for themselves, as did Venetian merchants who were part of the Venetian nation in Istanbul. The first coffeehouse in Venice opened in 1683, while it was already fashionable in neighboring Padua among the University of Padua's professors, students, and visitors.

By 1669, against the backdrop of the commercial decline of Venice and expanding Ottoman-French trade relations, a coffee-drinking Ottoman ambassador sent by Sultan Mehmet IV (r. 1642–1693) arrived in Paris to meet King Louis XIV. During his months residing in Paris, the Ottoman dignitary and his entourage in his temporary residence in Paris became the favorite subjects of local press coverage. Part of the lore of the ambassador's stay was the elaborate coffee service introduced to entertain Parisian guests, complete with porcelain cups and gold embroidered damask napkins.[20] By 1672, against the backdrop of a strong Armenian presence in Venetian-Ottoman and French-Ottoman trade relations, an Armenian merchant named Pascal sold coffee at the Saint-Germain-des-Prés fair, and by the end of the century, coffee was popularly available and consumed in London as part of a wave that soon spread to the British American colonies in the 1700s.

The significance of this simultaneous arrival of Turkish coffee and Chinese tea in seventeenth-century Europe was that it shaped the direction of VOC trade. In the early days of tea and coffee's simultaneous consumption in Europe, long before the drop in tea prices around the world, it was coffee that was the easily accessible lower priced popular drink of both elites and masses in Europe, while tea from distant China remained more of a specialty item with particular appeal in royal circles. The VOC responded accordingly, betting on a new coffee venture while the EIC, in later years, made the more profitable turn towards tea.

Coffee and Tea in the Competition between the VOC and EIC

By the late seventeenth century, the VOC responded to this dimension of northern Europe taste not only by dominating tea imports, but also by bypassing Europe's Ottoman coffee source through the cultivation of coffee in Dutch-held Javanese lands. More specifically, several decades after bringing the first bales of green tea from Batavia to Amsterdam, the VOC made a calculated decision to bring coffee plants to Java in 1688 in order to avoid dependence on either Ottoman Mocha (Yemen) along the Indian Ocean or Ottoman Istanbul along the Mediterranean.

The VOC's coffee gamble worked, at least in the short run. By 1726, 90 percent of coffee imports in Europe came from Java, while 10 percent came from Mocha.[21] Just five years earlier, the ratio was the opposite, pointing to the rapid success of the VOC coffee venture in Java. VOC tea imports from

Batavia continued to build momentum, but there was competition across the South China Sea. The English EIC had begun to dock at Canton during the decade 1710–1720 for direct access to the Chinese tea market, while the VOC remained focused on the Batavia junk trade. The VOC waited until 1728 to establish a regular route to Canton, allowing the EIC to begin its long-duration lead over the VOC. By the 1740s, tea constituted some 20 percent of EIC sales.

History will never know how the VOC would have proceeded in the following century, because by 1795, following a series of wars between the Dutch and the British (1752–1774) as well as management disagreements between the VOC board in the Netherlands and VOC governing administrators in the Dutch East Indies, the VOC was nearly bankrupt. By 1799, its royal charter expired. Back in the Netherlands, the Dutch Republic (1581–1795) had been replaced by the French-supported short-lived Batavian Republic (1795–1806), which was transformed into the French-controlled Kingdom of the Netherlands (1806–1810) before being annexed entirely into the Napoleonic French Empire. Back in the Dutch East Indies, meanwhile, the British invaded Java, where Stamford Raffles served as lieutenant governor from 1811 to 1815. Raffles was the famous founder of a British colony in Singapore in 1819 some fifty years after the British established trading posts in Penang. With the VOC edged out of the tea business and Chinese commerce, the EIC made the monumental move of dominating the global tea trade in the nineteenth century.

What distinguished tea's legacy in British commerce from its legacy in Dutch commerce were two stories. The outcome of both pointed to a massive shift in the geopolitical balance between the British Empire and Qing China in terms of their military power and cultural capital across Northeast Asia. The first story is how the EIC transformed Chinese tea into a royal British colonial commodity produced and sold within the empire to the exclusion of tea made in China. The second story is how this British zeal for a monopoly over global tea exchange escalated into an all-out conquest of Chinese ports that was unprecedented in European-Chinese relations. Both stories offer an illustrative window into one of the most important developments in the history of European-Chinese exchange, a development examined at the end of this chapter and in the next: the nineteenth-century reassessment in Qing China and Edo Japan of European cultural currency in light of clear advances in European military industrial technology and the urgency of political reform.

The Lead-Up to British Gunboat Diplomacy in Northeast Asia:
An Englishman's First Cup of Chinese Tea in Japan

Despite having been founded two years before the Dutch East India Company (VOC), the English East India Company (EIC) never achieved the geographical reach of its Dutch counterpart in Northeast Asia. Since the capture of a Portuguese carrack during the Anglo-Spanish war of the late sixteenth century, British merchants had been eager to enter the Northeast Asian commercial world where late Ming China and Muromachi Japan loomed large. The EIC only briefly operated in post-Muromachi Edo-era Japan between 1613 and 1623, focusing its efforts instead on eclipsing the Portuguese maritime empire's South Asian presence in Portuguese India (Estado da Índia). Formal relations between the Netherlands and Japan, by contrast, were deep and enduring after their first establishment in 1609. The VOC traded in Nagasaki for the next two centuries. Still, the few years when the EIC had an office in Japan were influential. Those years introduced the English to what an Englishman in Japan called in English *chawe*, which the previously mentioned Jesuit and Dominican travelers called *cha* decades earlier.

During his tenure as an agent for the EIC in Japan from 1613 to 1618, Richard Wickham requested the "best sort of chaw" in a letter to a certain William Eaton, the company's agent in "Meaco"—that is, Miyako (Kyoto).[22] In a later exchange a few years later, Eaton wrote to Wickham saying that he hoped Wickham would remember Eaton favorably for that request of "chaw." More than a decade later, in the final years of the Ming period, the British traveler and merchant Peter Mandy recorded in his *Itinerarium Mundy* that the "chaa" of Fujian was "only water with a kind of herb boiled in it. It must be drank warm."[23] By 1657, coffee vendor Thomas Garway was experimenting with the sale of tea alongside Arabic coffee in his coffeehouse in England, which was an enterprise that appeared in Italy only a few years earlier via Ottoman-Italian commercial exchange.

By the 1700s, the coffeehouses that sprung up throughout England were selling coffee as well as VOC- and EIC-imported Chinese tea, including both green and black varieties.[24] It would be another century before tea would become the imperial drink of British royalty and administrators produced within the empire and for the empire. Until then, throughout the latter 1700s, the EIC's ability to satisfy the growing taste for Chinese black and green tea depended on direct access to Chinese ports around Canton, which EIC negotiations increasingly and successfully facilitated in contrast with the Dutch's intermittent lack of access to Canton in the late seventeenth century.

The many trips the British made to Canton throughout the eighteenth century occurred as part of the so-called Canton System, which dated back to 1757. For the previous two centuries, the Qing dynasty limited European trade to four ports: Ningbo, Quanzhou (Arabic: Zaytun), Xiamen, and Canton. After 1757, only Canton was open to European trade, while Spain was given exclusive privileges in Xiamen for Philippines commerce. Silver was the key currency and commodity of value in Canton, which meant that British trade through Canton facilitated a massive transfer of commonly Spanish-sourced silver into Qing China. According to the journals of Major Samuel Shaw, the first American consul at Canton, British ships anchored a few miles outside Macau in order to be registered by Chinese and Portuguese authorities.[25] After then sailing through the Pearl River and anchoring at Whampoa, cargoes were then transferred to smaller Chinese junks for the final twelve-mile stretch, where they would then be offloaded at warehouses controlled by merchant families (hongs) that were given a Qing-controlled monopoly over foreign trade in exchange for various obligations to the Qing government.

The monopoly China had over its own tea in the early nineteenth century posed an obvious problem for the colonizing aspirations of the EIC, which was a notably armed corporation with its own military and security forces. Though the British Empire granted the EIC a royal monopoly over tea trade in Asia to the exclusion of other English companies, a government-granted monopoly was limited in practice given the market monopoly Qing China held over its own commodity. For both the EIC and the various private traders operating in the South China Sea, this problem had two possible solutions, both being as far-fetched and possibly disastrous for British profits and security as they were attractive in their potential financial returns. The first solution was the mass cultivation of tea outside of China in British-held South Asian domains, which seemed technologically impossible given how well guarded Chinese tea cultivation secrets were. The second was a more militarily aggressive approach to negotiations with Qing China that would force the Qing to export tea. The EIC, armed with its own security forces and with often fluctuating support from the British Crown, pursued both avenues.

Chinese Tea Cultivation in British South Asia and
the Turn towards Gunboat Diplomacy

The cultivation of Chinese tea in India followed changes in British policies towards royal monopolies. In a move that allowed private British merchants greater access to trade opportunities in South Asia, the British government abolished the EIC's government-decreed monopolies on Asian commodities in 1813 except for Chinese imports, the most lucrative being tea. In 1833, the government then abolished the EIC's tea monopoly altogether. By that time, efforts were underway among private English merchants to cultivate Chinese tea south of China closer to British-held Mughal regions.

Robert Bruce, a Scottish adventurer and one of the many non-EIC merchants trading in the region, happened upon a tea-drinking tribe in Assam in 1823 during his travels around the Himalayas. Assamese nobleman and later British-appointed tax officer Maniram Dewan facilitated an introduction to the tribe chief, and within ten years, Bruce's brother had several Assamese tea leaves sent for botanical analysis to Calcutta, where the leaves were confirmed to be a variety of unknown non-Chinese tea.[26] The always-enterprising English East India Company intervened and, in collaboration with botanists like Robert Fortune, managed to covertly steal some tea leaves from China and hire Fujianese tea growers to bring their tea cultivation trade secrets to Assam. The long-term outcomes were the development of Chinese tea in Darjeeling, the cultivation of hybrid varieties of Sino-Indian tea in new plantations in Assam, and the total bypassing of China in the tea trade. At the same time, despite the diminishing dependence on China for Chinese tea, British merchants were still interested in forcing their way into China's markets. In the lead-up to more aggressive tactics of engaging Qing China militarily, the short-term solution to accessing greater volumes of Chinese tea was to smuggle opium from British South Asian territories into Qing China.

In the late eighteenth century, with diminishing Chinese demand for European commodities, the EIC marketed opium as a medicinal product to China in order to meet the massive demand for tea in Europe. Opium was grown in British South Asia, including frontier regions close to Afghanistan, and sold to private traders who brought it to China. When the Qing government banned the narcotic and confiscated some twenty thousand chests of opium traded on the black market, the British cartels involved pressured the British government into demanding the lost costs from Beijing. When the Qing refused, the British unleashed something that would occupy the heart of Chinese and Japanese debates about political reform throughout the nineteenth, twentieth, and twenty-first centuries: state of the art military technology epitomized by the notorious *Nemesis*, the first British steam- and sail-powered ocean-going iron warship and the most notorious player in the First Opium War (1839–1843) between Qing China and the British Empire.[27]

The armed gains throughout the Pearl River made by the crew of *Nemesis* and the rest of the British royal navy brought the Canton System to a spectacular end in 1842. From the perspective of China's early military dominance against the Portuguese and Dutch, it was a shocking end. As part of the peace agreement to end the war, Hong Kong would be transferred from the Qing to the British Crown. Five ports were likewise forced open to foreign trade: Canton (Guangzhou), Amoy, Foochow, Ningpo and Shanghai. The Treaty of Nanjing was negotiated and signed by Qing imperial commissioner Qiying and British representative Henry Pottinger aboard the British warship HMS *Cornwallis* in the once mighty eastern capital Nanjing in 1842.

In October 1843, Qiying and Pottinger negotiated the follow-up Treaty of Bogue, which stipulated that British warships be allowed to station at each of the ports. According to the letter of the document, in what reflected a continuing use of diplomatic deferential protocols towards China despite its military weakness, the British requested that the Qing's "imperial favor" extend to allow the British to "maintain control over" its expatriates at the ports through the presence of these warships. Fifteen years later, the British government took over direct control of the EIC-held territories in South Asia, making the British Crown a colonial force with direct governing control over a swath of strategic territories and ports—the British Raj—that far surpassed what the VOC and Portuguese forces ever controlled in Asia. By the end of the nineteenth century, with a massive supply of Sino-Indian black tea that allowed the British to drop tea prices below that of coffee, England eclipsed Portugal, the Netherlands, and Russia as Europe's premier tea-drinking nation that simultaneously bought and sold tea within its own imperial domains.

On one level, the story of Sino-Indian British tea is the story of an ancient Chinese pastime with elaborate social rituals and delicate porcelain cups becoming a colonial British pastime. On another level, it is the story of one European power, the English East India Company, far surpassing its Portuguese and Dutch predecessors in the history of militarily escalating the European pursuit of Chinese commodities and reaching unprecedented outcomes. While the Portuguese and Dutch claimed Chinese client states in Southeast Asia but treaded carefully in their diplomacy with China, the British were the first to escalate their pursuit of Chinese commodities to a forced military occupation of one of Qing China's most important commercial territories and several ports. From this perspective, the story of tea is also the story of European industrial military technology, and both the Chinese and Japanese political reformers were taking note on the eve of their own late nineteenth-century Western-inspired industrialization reforms.

CHINESE CULTURAL CURRENCY CONTESTED: DEBATES ABOUT WESTERNIZATION IN LATE QING CHINA

By the time the British government transferred Hong Kong to Beijing in 1997 as a semiautonomous region, a unique culinary institution had proliferated across the island: *cha chaan teng*, which literally means "tea restaurant." *Cha chaan teng* establishments offered fast economically priced dishes and beverages in a social environment that became a fixture of local neighborhoods, particularly since World War II. What distinguished them from establishments in mainland China was the eclecticism of their most well-known offerings: pineapple bun, egg tart, milk tea made with evaporated milk, and a combination of milk tea and coffee known as Yuenyueng.[28] Egg tart in Hong Kong is a close relative of the Portuguese *pasteis de Belem* found in Macau, and its preparation similarly calls for the use of unsweetened evaporated milk.[29]

How did sugary milk tea and ingredients like evaporated milk become so ubiquitous in the culinary landscape of Hong Kong by the time of the British handover to China? The obvious answer was that Hong Kong's cultural landscape, like that of coastal China, reflected a century and half of British political and cultural influence. The twentieth century saw British habits like sugary milk-tea consumption, a European offshoot of an unsweetened savory Chinese-derived pastime, transfer to China's ports alongside a variety of British cultural markers like the English language. Hong Kong's *cha chaan teng* establishments, with their multilingual conversations and global culinary choices, represented just one arena where this twentieth-century combination of Chinese past and British present took shape. One of the most notable aspects of this cultural exchange is the extent that it was not limited to British Hong Kong or neighboring Portuguese Macau in the twentieth century, but rather shaped the entirety of late Qing China's political landscape beginning in the late nineteenth century.

In dialogue with contemporary British developments, the second half of
the nineteenth century saw an eruption of debates among political administrators and literati about the possibilities of reform or renewal in light of
unprecedented losses of imperial sovereignty. The profile and activities of
this era's protagonists illustrate how much British cultural transfer in China
was neither specific to ports with British military presence nor simply a
function of British administrative authority over local governance, which
was a pervasive phenomenon in neighboring British South Asia. In the long-
duration history of these debates, two of the most significant outcomes
were the technological overhaul of the military and the rise of industrial
manufacturing.

Military and Industrial Modernization in Late Qing China
Late Qing China saw both technological and intellectual reforms that were
part of a major epistemic shift in nineteenth-century Chinese politics and
society. This shift was epitomized in the writings of Qing scholar-officials
who, like their neighbors in Edo Japan, debated how to face the urgency of
European military advances on China's territorial integrity.

Since their earliest trips from Europe to the Spice Islands across the
Indian Ocean and South China Sea, western and northern European traders
and intellectuals studied the geographies, commercial systems, foodways, and
technological secrets of the Sinocentric East Asian world in pursuit of silk,
spices, knowledge, porcelain, and tea. In this pursuit, these merchants were
continuing the legacy of earlier Middle Eastern, South Asian, and eventually
Venetian and Genoese merchants, who procured these items together with
Chinese paper and gunpowder throughout the medieval period—that is,
during China's Tang, Song, and Yuan dynasties.

The nineteenth century, in contrast, saw a very different phenomenon.
The late Qing era saw Chinese scholar-officials pursue a kind of political and administrative reform that was unprecedented in its degree in the
previous millennium—namely, European-inspired reform that challenged
the Ming- and Qing-era Confucian underpinnings of Chinese political
theory and social practices. On the one hand, there was a long history of
cultural transfer eastward into China. Indeed, official Chinese tributary
commerce and imperial administration had a long and ancient history of
absorbing administrative techniques and material culture from powers based
further west, including the ancient Sogdians of pre-Islamic Samarkand and

the medieval Arabic and Persian-speaking merchants of Abbasid Iraq and Ilkhanid Central Asia. On the other hand, the degree that late Qing-era intellectuals and scholar-officials began to debate a massive political and infrastructural transformation of China along the lines of Europe was unprecedented, particularly as the same western and northern Europeans whose military technology brought about this urgency for reform were previously seen as pirates. What made this epistemic shift a debate was the fact that there were scholar-officials who were not on board with proposed models of Westernization in circulation, and even those who were in favor managed to subsume conceptions of European reform into a revision of Confucian political theory itself. What follows is a closer look at both the critics and advocates of Westernizing reforms, together with their shared legacy, in the decades leading up to the declaration of a Chinese republic in 1912.

Among the key figures who resisted Westernizing reforms were literati like Wang K'ai-yun, Yu Yueh, Wang Ping-hiseh, and Liu Ping-chang, who argued that Western institutional and intellectual imports—from telegraph lines to mines and railways—interrupted the cosmic order of the physical and metaphysical worlds epitomized by concepts like *feng shui*.[30] According to this argument, feng shui played a role in people's prosperity and phenomena like the growth of crops, and it would be disturbed by the shortcomings of Western industrial technology and its outcomes of unsustainability, its unsuitability for Chinese geography, and its negative ramifications for social justice.

From the perspective of European debates about the social and environmental problems that developed in twentieth-century industrial-era European cities and their late twentieth-century deindustrialized successors, the Chinese argument against wholesale adoption of European industrial reforms had some merit. At the same time, it was a losing one. The momentum of Qing losses and the empire's inability to control and administer foreigners chipped away at more traditional interpretations of Neo-Confucian political and social ethics. By the 1860s, Qing-era literati increasingly embraced various forms of political pragmatism and its institutional outcomes, including changes in judicial law and the economy. The turning point in this shift was the Anglo-French siege of Beijing.

The rise of a strong reformist and pragmatist trend among scholar-officials during the 1860s followed China's crippling defeat in its own capital by Anglo-French forces in 1860. That year, a combined Anglo-French military force entered the Qing capital Beijing. The siege of Beijing was the culmination of the Second Opium War (1856–1860), which was the result of an eruption of British-Chinese hostilities during the twenty years following the Treaty of Nanjing. The siege reached as far as the Forbidden City, where Matteo Ricci was invited some three hundred years earlier under the very different circumstances of imperial patronage of European clients. As was the case during the First Opium War, the Second Opium War represented the culmination of long-standing international disagreements about opium imports and British military presence in China. The French entered the second war under the pretext of seeking justice for the execution of French missionary Auguste Chapdelaine of the Paris Foreign Missions Society.[31] The Russian empire, which did not send military aid to the Anglo-French force, was able to diplomatically maneuver the inclusion of an envoy during the negotiations. As the emperor himself had fled for Rehe province, the Xianfeng Emperor's brother Kung was in charge of negotiation in Beijing.[32] The outcome was the ratification of the Treaty of Tianjin and its supplement, which included several territorial changes and trade agreements: the transfer of Kowloon island adjacent Hong Kong island to the British, the transfer of parts of northeastern China to Russia, the legalization of the opium trade, the opening of foreign embassies in Beijing including an American and Russian embassy, the opening of a variety of additional ports including Nanjing to foreign trade, the opening of the Yangtze River to all foreign vessels and, famously from the perspective of American history, the right of the British to carry indentured Chinese to the United States.

In the decade ahead, scholar-officials adopted a pro-reform approach to Chinese learning that refashioned Neo-Confucian arguments for Western modernization and change. For Wang T'ao, for example, there was a kind of cosmic silver lining to China's political situation. According to his own theoretical interpretation of contemporary events, heaven caused Western powers to converge on China so that China could become wealthy and powerful by exploiting Western innovations.[33] The administrative turn from a conservative defense of Chinese political culture towards an ideological pragmatism was epitomized in the emperor's brother Kung himself.

Kung's attitude towards political reform saw an about-face following European entry in Beijing. Kung and an adviser named Wen-hsiang (Wenxiang), who was involved in the Beijing negotiations, advocated more loose-rein tactics oriented around keeping the peace with European imperial powers and drawing on their expertise. As part of these reforms, Kung and Wen-hsiang founded the new Qing foreign office, called the *Zongli Yamen*, which offered a medium of communication between the Qing government and the new European embassies.[34] The *Zongli Yamen* was the first major institutional addition to the growing Qing bureaucracy since the Yongzheng Emperor (1722–1735) established the Grand Council, of which Wen-hsiang was a part in the 1850s. Wen-hsiang was one of the architects of the so-called "self-strengthening movement" and played a key role in cultivating the Qing's cooperative policy towards European powers throughout the 1860s and 1870s. Wen-hsiang also established the Interpreters' College (*Tongwenguan*) in 1863 in collaboration with Prince Kung, stipulating that select Manchu youth learn foreign languages including French, English, German, and Russian.

By the 1870s, Li Hung-chang (Li Hongzhang) rose to prominence as one of a variety of scholar-officials advocating for military and economic reform along Western lines in order to preserve the empire's sovereignty and prevent further internal rebellions.[35] With coastal and inland shipping taken over by foreign powers, Li Hung-chang established the China Merchants' Steam Navigation Company in 1872. In 1877, he founded the Kaiping mines to fuel the ships. Three years later, he built China's first railway to bring coal to the docks where the ships were stationed. By 1881, he established the first telegraph lines. By 1882, he established the Shanghai Textile Mill, China's first cotton mill. Li Hung-chang's entire project was to recover Chinese economic control by bringing Chinese individuals into positions of industrial leadership, and he was not alone in this aspiration.[36] Ting Jih-Ch'ang (Ding Richang), a contemporary reformer, resisted the British attempt to operate telegraph lines in China, insisting that modern enterprises be controlled by China.

In sum, in the long run, independent of the theoretical underpinnings of this accommodation of Western administrative and technological practices, late Qing scholar-officials pushed ahead with these Westernizing reform projects and, increasingly, were themselves products of it.

End of an Era: Yuan Shikai, Sun Yat-Sen, and the Declaration of a Republic

Many of the Western reforms that were instituted in late nineteenth-century Qing China occurred in the realm of technology and infrastructural innovations. By the very end of the century, among a generation of Qing-era generals and intellectuals who acquired a deep knowledge of Western political models and who were watching neighboring Japan's Meiji-era (est. 1868) political transformation, two other political developments were taking shape. Both developments drew directly on European models. The first was a new interest among Qing ruling circles in establishing a constitutional monarchy. The second was a project among various revolutionaries to establish not a constitutional monarchy but an ethno-nationalist republic, one that would be defined in terms of an increasingly popular dichotomous distinction between the Manchu and those of Han lineage. By 1911, an advocate of the former model—namely the Manchu official and military commander Yuan Shikai—made the surprise decision of facilitating the fall of the monarchy altogether and the rise of this ethno-nationalist republic under the provisional leadership of revolutionary Sun Yat-Sen.

Yuan Shikai was a Qing military and government official who was an ally of Li Hung-chang, the previously discussed Qing official who pushed for industrial and military modernization. A political reformer himself, Shikai was originally in favor of transforming Qing rule into a constitutional monarchy in the years before he helped negotiate the fall of the dynasty. In 1895, following Qing losses to Japan's modernized military, Yuan rose to prominence as commander of the formidable Beiyang Army, a semi-independent military force that would eventually form the core of the Qing's modern thirty-six-division New Army.[37] Decades later, following the collapse of the Qing dynasty in 1912, it would fragment into several militias, but under his authority at the turn of the century, it held together under Shikai's patron-client relationship with several protégés whom he appointed as divisional commanders and senior officers.

Shikai's authority over the Beiyang Army was what allowed him to emerge as one of the most powerful figures in the final years of the Qing, and he was only able to command this authority because of the overall devolution of central military authority decades earlier. Indeed, late Qing China saw a variety of semiprofessional militias operating loosely under Qing authority. One was the Xiang army, organized by Confucian scholar and military general Zeng Guofan.[38] The purpose of the Xiang army was to quell the Taiping Rebellion (1850–1864), one of the first anti-Qing uprisings to appeal to a variety of farmers, miners, and workers with promises of greater egalitarianism. Much of this Xiang army was subsumed into the later Huai army, under former Xiang army commander and political reformer Li Hung-chang. Zhou Shengchuan, one of the units' commanders, encouraged Li Hung-chang to acquire modern foreign weaponry and even criticized

Western advisers like Shanghai-based general Charles Gordon for not going far enough in recommending the Qing's acquisition of Western industrial technology as part of Qing military growth. By the 1880s, Li Hung-chang's newly established navy and parts of his Huai army were subsumed into the new Beiyang Army, which was the primary military force involved in the Sino-Japanese War. By 1901, Yuan Shikai had taken over the army.

During much of Shikai's career, most of Qing titular imperial power resided in the position of the emperor's mother—namely Empress Cixi, consort of the previously discussed Xianfeng Emperor who fled the 1860 siege of Beijing before his brother Prince Kung (Gong) took over negotiations.[39] Upon the Xianfeng Emperor's death, his son with Empress Cixi was crowned the Tongzhi Emperor for a brief eleven years before his death in 1875 at the young age of nineteen. The Xianfeng Emperor's brother Yixuan played a central role in the power struggle that brought the Tongzhi Emperor and his mother Empress Cixi to power, which meant that upon the Tongzhi Emperor's death in 1875 without an heir, Yixuan's own son—cousin of the late Tongzhi Emperor—became a candidate for the throne by being adopted by Empress Cixi into the Xianfeng Emperor's line. This son of Yixuan was crowned the Guangxu Emperor (1871–1908). By 1908, upon the death of both Empress Cixi and the Guangxu Emperor, and with the enthronement of the Guangxu Emperor's son Puyi as the last emperor of the Qing, Yixuan's other son and the Guangxu Emperor's brother Kaifeng took power for three years (1908–1911) before the Qing faced a political impasse: the spread of anti-Qing uprisings and the uncertainty of Yuan Shikai's attitude towards them.

When an armed revolution began to spread from Hubei province in 1908 following disagreements over railroad nationalization, the prince regent Kaifeng called on Yuan Shikai to suppress it. From the perspective of Kaifeng, who governed China during the ascendancy of the child-sovereign and last emperor Puyi, only Yuan Shikai and his Beiyang Army had the military might to quell the rebellion in Hubei. However, the Qing dynasty's interest in calling upon Yuan Shikai and his corps was a gamble, one that Kaifeng was willing to take on behalf of the Qing dynasty. What made it risky was that Yuan Shikai's military authority had already demonstrated its independence of the Qing imperial household during the Boxer Rebellion, which erupted against foreign presence on Chinese soil. When Empress Cixi supported the Chinese Boxers, Yuan Shikai helped quell the rebellion instead of following the empress's lead. Li Hung-chang, likewise illustrative of the decentralization of authority, negotiated with foreign powers in Shanghai at that time.

Ten years later, with the rise of the Wuchang Rebellion in 1911 during the reign of Empress Cixi's successor Kaifeng, Yuan Shikai did not adhere closely to Kaifeng's orders and instead pursued a more rogue approach: Shikai went against the imperial household and negotiated with the rebels.

The results of Shikai's departure from Kaifeng's orders were staggering for Chinese imperial history. Kaifeng, the prince regent of the five-year old Emperor Puyi, resigned. Puyi would be the last emperor, as 1911 marked the rise of a new group of post-Qing revolutionary politicians who looked increasingly and syncretically westward for models of reform in governance. Among them was Sun Yat-Sen, who was in New York in 1911 looking for international support for Chinese revolutionaries at the time of Kaifeng's resignation.

Sun Yat-Sen, one of the founding figures of modern Han Chinese nationalism, was born just six years after the British-led siege of Beijing. In the final years of the Qing, Sun Yat-Sen was one of a variety of figures who conceived of an original revolutionary political philosophy that was as syncretic in its integration of Chinese and European political philosophies as his own educational background. Sun Yat-Sen's reformist ideals developed against the backdrop of both the Westernizing reforms adopted by the scholar-officials of the previous generation and the Western education he received in British Hong Kong and the Kingdom of Hawai'i.

In 1883, after seven years of living with his brother in Hawai'i since the age of ten, Sun Yat-Sen was a seventeen-year-old student enrolled in Hong Kong's Diocesan Boys School. The school was founded by the Anglican Church, and its headmaster, George Piercy, was previously the headmaster of the Government Central School.[40] Sun Yat-Sen would spend the next several years as a student at the Government Central School, the headmaster of which was once responsible for supervising all schools in Hong Kong before the establishment of the Inspector of Schools office in 1879. During Sun Yat-Sen's time there, British officials moved the school and changed its name to Queen's College. The official who presided over the bricklaying ceremony that Sun Yat-Sen attended was none other than the British governor of Hong Kong himself, Sir George Bowen. The young revolutionary then studied medicine at Guangzhou Boji Hospital under the physician and missionary John Glasgow Kerr before being licensed as a doctor by the Hong Kong College of Medicine for Chinese, the forerunner to the University of Hong Kong.

Sun Yat-Sen's education and training as a physician in Hong Kong, in other words, put him in the heart of the Sino-British encounter that shaped late Qing political and social reform movements. For Sun Yat-Sen, and for many reformers critical of Qing modernization efforts, the pace of this transformation was not fast enough. The First Sino-Japanese War in 1895 demonstrated that Japan, which saw a major modernization campaign during the late Edo decades and early Meiji years (1868–1912), had surpassed China in the speed of its military and industrial transformation. Even the once tributary Korean kingdom was on the verge of total political separation from the Qing. Questions about how far to take Qing China's political reform were at the heart of Sun Yat-Sen's political activities in the years leading up to 1912. On one side were reformers like Liang Ch'i-Ch'ao, who argued that the answer to the Qing's woes was support for initiatives such as the Guangwu Emperor–led Hundred Days Reform (June–September 1898). In theory, its outcomes of industrialization and the establishment of a constitutional monarchy would help quicken the pace of innovation required to push back the collapse of China's role as East Asia's political center. On the other side were figures like Sun Yat-Sen and a variety of other nationalists, who argued in favor of abolishing the Qing monarchy and establishing some sort of elective republic defined in terms of what the philologist and revolutionary Zhang Binglin (d. 1936) called "Han lineage" or race (*Hanzu*). According to the practical applications of Zhang Binglin's ethnolinguistic theories, speakers of Sinitic languages were native Han peoples, which made the Manchu of the northeast foreigners. In later decades, in order to accommodate the reality that the borders of the Qing empire included a much wider variety of people than speakers of languages like Shanghainese and Cantonese, post-Qing political theories experimented with the definition of "Chinese nation" (*Zhonghua Minzu*) to include those beyond the *Hanzu* category. During the late Qing era in the lead up to 1911 when these nationalists were active, however, the language of a Han-Manchu dichotomy built momentum. With the decision of Yuan Shikai to abandon the Qing dynasty in 1912, Sun Yat-Sen stepped in as the first provisional president of the Republic of China (est. 1912), with Yuan Shikai as its first formal president.

Global China in the Twenty-First Century

Had Yuan Shikai remained loyal to the Qing household and pushed the constitutional monarchy system that he previously advocated onto the Qing family, and had he remained a military figure with a clear successor rather than pursue pretensions of political leadership, China may have moved in a very different direction over the next century of military chaos. Still, at least one of the outcomes would have remained the same. The days of a Sinocentric East Asian political, economic, and intellectual world, with a half millennium of cultural transfer westward to Europe, had come to a temporary halt. Chiang Kai-Shek and Mao Zedong were eighteen and twenty-four years old respectively during the fall of the Qing dynasty, a generation younger than the forty-five-year-old Sun Yat-Sen and the fifty-three-year-old Yuan Shikai. For the remainder of the twentieth century, in continuity with Yat-Sen's and Shikai's own reformist views, models of modernization would look increasingly and syncretically to Europe and Japan for intellectual inspiration. The era of China's global cultural transfer had come to an end, at least for the remainder of the twentieth century.

Only at the start of the twenty-first century has the world begun to observe a new story of cultural transfer from China westward. Among Western writers and policymakers, debates about the future of Western cultural currency have grown contentious. Do state-of-the-art advances in automated manufacturing and big data in cities like Shenzhen represent models of efficiency worth emulating, or do they offer a window into a high-tech dystopian future that challenges the essence of what it means to be part of a Western political and social world? In the end, as design and manufacturing innovations from Shanghai to Shenzhen continue to impact American start-ups and as British coffeeshops increasingly accommodate Europe's second wave of Chinese-imported tea consumption, the Western world's new political and cultural encounters with China tell us at least one thing—namely, that the story of China in the twenty-first century is as much about shifts in the global economy as it is about a new era of Western innovation and taste that remains in dialogue with Asian cultural production.

CHAPTER 9

China's Eclipse and Japan's Modernization

B y the late nineteenth century, in the aftermath of the Opium Wars and the establishment of high-tech British manufacturing, northern Europe demonstrated that its political and technological advances had finally outshined China's centuries of innovation. What emphasized the extent that the Industrial Revolution pushed China's global era into an eclipse was what occurred in neighboring Japan in the Opium Wars' aftermath. Japan was closely intertwined with China's political and intellectual world since the Ming era, but by the 1840s, administrators and reformers had begun to discuss the possibility of transforming Japan along British models.

What introduced an unprecedented degree of urgency to adopt Western military models was the arrival of Commodore Perry off the waters of Tokyo, ready to invade Japan in 1853 shortly after the conclusion of the Second Opium War in China. Japan had a head start because of its long history of exchange with the Dutch. In accordance with the exceptions that the Tokugawa dynasty offered the Dutch following the Sakoku Edict, Japanese administrators already had hundreds of years of exposure to European models of political and social organization. This exposure, in turn, facilitated the ability for Japanese reformers to contest the Sinocentric Neo-Confucian underpinnings of Japan's older political and social order altogether. Upon the collapse of the Edo-era Tokugawa dynasty and the start of the Meiji period in 1868, Japan saw a political and social transformation that formed the basis of both the rising Japanese Empire and China's own long path to industrialization.

JAPAN, THE WEST, AND THE INDIAN OCEAN SILK TRADE DURING THE CAREER OF ARAI HAKUSEKI

In 1682, a young Japanese scholar and bureaucrat named Arai Hakuseki (d. 1725) found employment under the daimyo Hotta Masatoshi (d. 1684). The daimyos were local rulers above the wider samurai warrior circles who were under the authority of the shogun and who exercised territorial control over the vast lands of Japan held privately as estates. The daimyo Hotta Masatoshi who employed Arai Hakuseki was also the *tairo*, or chief councilor, to the shogun Tokugawa Tsunayoshi (r. 1680–1709).[1] Two years later Arai Hakuseki became tutor to Tokugawa Ienobu (r. 1709–1712) who was the heir apparent to the throne. By 1709, when Ienobu became shogun, Arai Hakuseki was the chief architect of Japanese policy. The flourishing of Arai Hakuseki's career took place less than one hundred years after the famous edicts restricting entry and exit from Japan, the beginning of the *sakoku* or so-called isolation period in 1635. More than a century after Hakuseki's final years, Commodore Perry arrived in Japan in 1853 during the lead-up to Japan's late Edo-era and early Meiji-era political and military transformation.

Among Arai Hakuseki's legacies during the early Edo era was the reform of Japan's bureaucracy, its currency, and the further tightening of governmental control over trade. One of the most interesting aspects of the early Edo era during Hakuseki's tenure is that despite the Sakoku Edict, Japan continued to be a central player in global metals and textiles markets. Slightly before Arai Hakuseki's time, one-third of the world's silver supply came from Japan through Chinese and Dutch (VOC) intermediaries. The Dutch were also involved in facilitating Edo Japan's import of Indian Ocean silk commodities via Bengal, a pattern that was in continuity with Muromachi-era trends of Japanese consumption.[2] Japanese commerce in the 1600s saw several coterminous developments that led to the Dutch taking on this role as one of the primary intermediaries for Japanese–Indian Ocean trade during the Edo period: the Portuguese withdrawal from trade with Japan in the early seventeenth century, the Japanese government issuing the Sakoku Edict that relegated all commerce to official channels to the exclusion of private trade, and the late-Ming dynasty's (1368–1644) restrictions on Japanese trade.[3] Through Dutch shipping, Japanese silver shipments were sent across the South China Sea and Indian Ocean to the harbors of Coromandel, Siam, Tongkin, Batavia, Surat, and Hormuz among others. The region of Bengal, in turn, became a central exporter of silk to Japan.[4] The import of large amounts of raw silk from Bengal to Japan in the 1640s and 1650s offers important context for the previously mentioned policy that Arai Hakuseki pursued: limiting the export of precious metals and growing Japan's textile trade.

Interestingly, the VOC's role in facilitating Edo-era Japanese consumption of Indian Ocean textiles echoed the earlier Portuguese inter-Asian trade and did not yet foreshadow the degree of European cultural transfer eastward seen during Japan's Meiji-era Western-style industrialization campaign. Indeed, the VOC's import of Indian Ocean silk commodities occurred against the backdrop of a pre-Edo-era elite and popular Japanese taste for Persian, Indo-Persian, and Southeast Asian textiles. As seen in the case of the Japantowns and the groups of Japanese merchants that the Portuguese encountered around the South China Sea during the late Muromachi era (1336–1573), Japanese merchants themselves traded along the routes traversed by the VOC.

In the decades just before the Sakoku Edict, textiles from Persia and the Indian Ocean world became highly prized commodities within Japanese military circles both for diplomatic ceremonies and as public and private clothing. Daimyo Toyotomi Hideyoshi (d. 1598) wore a *jinbaori*—a kind of overcoat or tabard worn over a samurai's armor—that was made from the fabric of a Safavid Persian silk carpet. The overcoat featured representations of dragons, hunting scenes, and other designs that were historically evocative of military might and royalty throughout Asia.[5] This example was part of a larger phenomenon in which daimyos wore clothing made of imported bright fabrics from various foreign lands illustrative of the daimyo's global connections. Examples of textiles coming directly from Safavid Iran point to how the VOC's vast maritime network of ports facilitated Japan's early connections with Middle Eastern and European innovation.

Among the diplomatic ceremonies where these textiles were used was the tea ceremony examined in the last chapter. The Edo era also saw the growing intersection of Indo-Persian textiles with the rituals and visual culture of the tea ceremony, which was oriented around the previously discussed Ming-era powdered *matcha* tea concoctions and *sencha* tea-leaf infusions. Prior to its association with Chan (Zen) Buddhism, the tea ceremony was connected with intellectual gatherings in Chinese literati culture and the military elite's rituals of diplomacy. Daimyo Maeda Toshitsune of the Kaga domain (present-day Ishikawa Prefecture), for example, was a practitioner of the tea ceremony known to have sent a vassal to procure textiles in Nagasaki in 1637.[6] The Maeda family had developed a large collection of Chinese, Indo-Persian, and Southeast Asian textiles by that time, and the patterns seen in their surviving collection demonstrate the historically global dimensions of Japanese political culture during the heyday of Asian commodities production and on the eve of European industrialization.

In this context, the ceremony's practitioners in both Japan and China had a long history of incorporating visually exotic décor, including Indian Ocean textiles, as part of its ceremonial. *Meibutsugire*, a term coined in the late sixteenth century and more formally theorized in the seventeenth century, was a Japanese reference to imported textile masterpieces that brought value to tea-related objects and vessels, including tea cozies. While Chinese textiles were categorized in Japan according to technique, non-Chinese textiles were categorized according to origin, from the striped and lattice-patterned *kando* of Southeast Asian origin to the *moru* of South Asian origin.[7] By the Edo era, textiles and objects with Persian and Indo-Persian patterns began to be used in the tea ceremony not only for tea cozies but also hung tapestries and ceremonial clothing.[8] Yamaga Soko (1622–1685), a Neo-Confucian scholar-official contemporary with Arai Hakuseki, wore a coat made from a seventeenth-century painted cotton textile produced in South Asia for a Southeast Asian market.[9]

The increasingly popular tea ceremony began to be practiced even by merchants, who found yet another context for the purchase and sale of textiles during the Edo era: public festivals. The use of these textiles in neighborhood float carts (*yamaboko*) during a variety of public street festivities translated into the July Gion Festival becoming an opportunity in late sixteenth- and seventeenth-century Kyoto for wealthy artisans and textile dealers to compete in the import of luxury Chinese, Persian, and Indian textiles.[10] By the eighteenth century, the use of Indian Ocean textiles in public festivals and processions simultaneously fueled an industry of locally made replicas.

These developments in the Edo-era import of Chinese and Indian Ocean textiles, facilitated by Chinese, Japanese, and VOC merchants in Nagasaki, shed light on the enduring presence of the Dutch in Japan despite the Sakoku

Edict. Far from serving as Edo-era Japan's only connection to the world prior to the opening of Japan's ports to Western powers in the nineteenth century, the VOC in the seventeenth and eighteenth centuries accelerated Japan's long-established encounters with the material cultures of Safavid Iran, the Indian sultanates of the Mughal and Deccan domains, and the sultanates and kingdoms of Southeast Asia.[11] As late as the early nineteenth century, in the decades preceding the late Edo-era and early Meiji-era modernization of Japan's military, the European presence in Japan remained one that was neither proto-colonial nor the primary source of foreign cultural transfer into the shogunate's capitals. Edo Japan at the start of the nineteenth century was characterized by its enduring Sinocentric intellectual culture and its eclectic material culture, much of which drew on the sultanates of the Indian Ocean.[12] Against this backdrop, where Dutch cultural transfer in Nagasaki did move from the margins of Edo Japan's overall cultural landscape to its center was in the case of medicine and technology, which in the nineteenth century became one of the central realms of Japan's early administrative turn towards political and social reform on the eve of the Opium Wars.

From Chinese to Dutch Learning during the Career of Sugita Genpaku

Following a career that saw reforms in the trade of metals and textiles, Arai Hakuseki retired in 1716 several years after the new shogun arrived. During his retirement, he applied his polymathic background as a Confucian philosopher and bureaucrat to his growing body of writings, which included works on geography, philosophy, and law. One of his most well-known works was a five-volume text on world geography titled *Varying Worlds Observed (Sairan Igen)*. An early work of its type in Japan, it drew on a variety of regional and foreign sources illustrative of Japan's continued global connections long after the Sakoku Edict.[13] Among these sources were conversations with Jesuit Giovanni Battista Sidotti, (d. 1714), who entered Japan illegally and was captured before being brought to the court and meeting Hakuseki.[14] The work also drew on the Chinese writings of Matteo Ricci (d. 1610), who worked in Beijing via Macau under Portuguese and Ming patronage. A final source of Hakuseki's world geography was the writings of the Dutch in Nagasaki, which collectively came to be known in Japan as "Dutch learning" (*rangaku*).

Among later Japanese writers interested in European thought, Arai Hakuseki's *Varying Worlds Observed (Sairan Igen)* became an important cornerstone of his posthumous legacy as the father of Dutch learning (*rangaku*) in

Japan. Hakuseki's particular connection with Dutch learning was the fact that he had at his disposal Dutch books, which were available in Nagasaki and that were increasingly translated into Japanese. In the era of shogun Tokugawa Ietsuna (1651–1680), who ruled during the early decades of Hakuseki's career, the head of the Dutch factory in Nagasaki—namely, Hendrik Indyk—presented the shogun with a Dutch work on animals translated into Japanese. One of the later shoguns Tokugawa Yoshimune (r. 1716–1745) obtained a copy of this work, and it became one of the reasons behind his support for more widespread administrative interest in Dutch.[15] Yoshimune was the shogun that came to power just as Arai Hakuseki was retiring. When Arai Hakuseki wrote *Varying Worlds Observed* (*Sairan Igen*), therefore, it became the symbol of the formation of Dutch learning in Japan despite the fact that Chinese sources still outnumbered Dutch sources. Hakuseki came to be associated with the gradual introduction of Dutch learning in Japan in part because of the way eighteenth- and nineteenth-century Japanese writers, including Yamamura Shoei, edited and enlarged Hakuseki's work as additional European sources on topics such as medicine were increasingly available and of widespread interest. Hakuseki's original work, however, drew most heavily on non-European sources, particularly Chinese works. By the time a later administrator named Sugita Genpaku was writing, however, the balance of Chinese and Dutch sources in works on geography and the natural sciences was shifting towards the increasingly available Dutch sources in translation.

Sugita Genpaku (d. 1817) was one of these later Neo-Confucian administrators most closely associated with the study of Dutch medicine and technology on the eve of the Opium Wars. Interestingly, the chronology of his long career allowed him to witness the uptick in administrative interest in Dutch learning during his lifetime, and he even commented on it with some surprise. In his own words, "It is really surprising that 'Dutch learning' (*rangaku*) has gained such great popularity lately. Far-sighted intellectuals study it with enthusiasm, while the ignorant praise it grandly in glowing terms. This pursuit of 'Dutch learning' was casually started by us—very few of us—about fifty years ago. We never expected that it would come into such a great vogue."[16]

Genpaku's comments illustrate two points. The first and more obvious point is that new generations of Japanese intellectuals were increasingly fascinated by the variety of medical and technological innovations not found in Chinese learning, which they studied simultaneously. The second and more nuanced point is that in Genpaku's eyes, there was no urgency for Japan to make the turn that it made just a few decades later towards a complete administrative overhaul of Japanese politics, society, and technology along Western models. That urgency, which came first in the realm of military technology, only came about several decades after his death with the rise of new and unprecedented facts on the ground: British military activity in Northeast Asia during the Opium Wars, including the forced opening of Chinese ports and the transfer of Hong Kong to the British Empire, followed by the arrival of Commodore Perry in Japan in 1853.

Genpaku died some twenty years before the First Opium War, which makes it unsurprising that he was unaware of the impending urgency for Japanese administrators to compete with the increasingly industrialized powers of Europe on their own military terms. During Commodore Perry's mission to force the opening of Japan's ports to Western trade in 1853, the USS *Susquehanna* was equipped with six giant Paixhans guns, which were the first naval guns designed to fire explosive shells. The Ottoman Empire witnessed the destructive power of Paixhans shell guns the very same year in an encounter with Russian warships during the Crimean War.[17] The French and the British, like the Ottomans, commonly employed wooden hulled warships. In anticipation of the impending advances in naval weaponry, both the French and the British experimented with a shift from wood to ironclad ships beginning in the 1850s. The French *Gloire*, designed in 1858 by Stanislas Dupuy de Lome, was a hybrid wooden hull clad warship with a 4.7-inch iron plate, iron fastenings, and an iron deck. The British subsequently managed to design a fully ironclad warship called the HMS *Warrior*.[18]

The timing of Commodore Perry's arrival in 1853 helps illustrate one of two reasons why Japan's late nineteenth-century military reform was able to advance so quickly between 1853 and 1890. The first reason is that Japan's rapid military modernization, which began in the late Edo period and continued in the Meiji era, was in fact the culmination of a process that was intimately intertwined with a particular aspect of Dutch learning's (*rangaku*) history in Japan—namely, the expansion of Dutch learning beyond medicine to include topics in technology and, in turn, the integration of these topics into the curricula of both official and private education among administrators and domain-level samurai. That process began as early as Arai Hakuseki's career.

More specifically, it was under Tokugawa Yoshimune (r. 1716–1745), the previously mentioned shogun in power just as Arai Hakuseki retired, that the bakufu legally relaxed restrictions on the translation and circulation of

Dutch books coming from Nagasaki. During this period, Edo (Tokyo), Osaka, and Kyoto were already growing to number among the largest cities in the world with rapidly growing literacy rates. The fully literate samurai were educated either in the central Confucian academy (*shoheiko*), a successor to Neo-Confucian scholar Hayashi Razan's (d. 1657) private Confucian academy, or domain schools (*hanko*) built on its model. By the end of the Edo period, up to a quarter of domain schools incorporated Western studies of military affairs, medicine, and shipbuilding in their curricula.[19] Western studies were also found in the private academies (*shikuku*) and closely related temple schools (*terakoya*), which were found both in cities and rural areas and that enrolled a wider populace of merchants and farmers. In accordance with the variety of students enrolled, Dutch learning was more frequently found in urban academies than in rural schools.

Against this backdrop, Dutch learning began to circulate widely and included a variety of genres beyond medicine. From the perspective of Japan's later industrialization, the most significant subjects were those comprising early modern industrial technology. Morishima Churyo's *Dutch Miscellany* (紅毛雑話, *Komo Zatsuwa*) of 1787, for example, discussed not only Dutch use of Western hospitals but also microscopes, hot air balloons, copper plates for printing, static electricity generators, and large shipping vessels.[20]

Several decades before the urgency of military reform emerged, one area of Dutch technology that was especially influential in the rise of Edo-era industrial technology was the steam engine. Given the history of Japanese exposure to Dutch technology, it should come as no surprise that Japanese engineers completed a domestically constructed steam warship in 1866 based on European drawings—namely the *chiyodagata*—even before the Meiji era.[21] Kawamoto Kōmin's *Odd Devices of the Far West* (遠西奇器述, *Ensei Kiki-Jutsu*), completed twenty years earlier in 1845, included detailed drawings and descriptions of steam engines and steamships.[22] Tanaka Hisashige, founder of what became the Toshiba Corporation, was the first to manufacture a combustible fuel-powered steam engine and locomotive after seeing a demonstration of a steam engine by the Russian ambassador Yevfimiy Vasilyevich Putyatin in Nagasaki in 1853.[23]

In sum, by the nineteenth century, Dutch learning was integrated into both the official and private education of administrators and samurai who were increasingly in consensus about the importance of drawing on European military technology in Japan, even as they disagreed about whether the shogunate should appease Western powers and reopen private trade with European merchants beyond the Dutch or, alternatively, use the increasingly modernized military might of the shogunate and daimyo-led domains against European and American powers. It was this latter question that informs the second reason why Japan was able to modernize its military might so quickly after 1853. Commodore Perry's arrival in 1853 was actually the culmination of a series of challenges to Japan's centralized authority in Edo (Tokyo), where the shogun was managing daimyo-led domains that were not in consensus about either the future of the shogunate's centralized authority over the daimyos or the shogun's apparent readiness to appease newly arriving Western powers by granting trading privileges and legal extraterritorial rights. The middle decades of the nineteenth century, thus, saw both the shogun and provincial daimyos reforming their respective military forces through advances in European technology that were available to them partly from these very same European powers themselves. That process, which culminated in the resignation of the Tokugawa shogun and the rise of a variety of Meiji-era administrators from domains that were previously in rebellion, was undergirded by a third intellectual movement beyond both the older Chinese Neo-Confucian mode of political and social ethics (*kangaku*) and the newer Dutch curriculum of medicine and technology (*rangaku*). This third intellectual movement was the learning of the Mito domain (*mitogaku*) oriented around ancient Japanese imperial historiography, which together with the study of the Japanese classics (*kokugaku*) gave nineteenth-century daimyos, samurai, and select scholar-officials an intellectual argument about the need for reviving Japan's ancient imperial glory and rejecting the Tokugawa shogunate's unimperial and increasingly Western-appeasing model of political administration. By the late Edo period, this intellectual argument and its militarized domain-level supporters became an argument for the restoration of the semi-defunct Kyoto emperor's political authority in conjunction with the authority of domain-level leadership. The outcome of this combination of Dutch technology's widespread assimilation in official and private education since the eighteenth century, the multifaceted shogun-level and domain-level Dutch-facilitated militarization process before and after 1853, and the intellectual turn in the mid-nineteenth century towards reviving ancient Japanese imperial historiography and literature was a staggering one: the resignation of the shogun and the rise of the Meiji-era Japanese Empire, which saw administrators turn against the Sinocentric

Neo-Confucian political models of Japan's past in favor of a syncretic Anglo-Japanese model of political, industrial, and social modernization.

REFORM AND FALL OF THE SHOGUNATE

Nariaki, Mitogaku, and the Debate about Political and Military Reform

Tokugawa Nariaki (r. 1829–1844), a bakufu official during the shogunates of Tokugawa Ienari (r. 1787–1837) and Tokugawa Ieyoshi (r. 1837–1853), was one of the few daimyos who was also a relative of the ruling Tokugawa clan in Edo (Tokyo). Among Nariaki's legacies was his early advocacy for the reform of the shogunate's military forces. Nariaki pursued this project even prior to Commodore Perry's arrival, and he began this work locally in his own domain, Mito. In Mito, Nariaki constructed a local shipbuilding and iron industry and, in accordance with Japan's special relationship with the Dutch, began to introduce Western military technology such as the casting of cannons.[24] Nariaki was a relative of the ruling clan and worked closely with the shogunate, which meant that the militarization of his domain was not inherently problematic. What would pose a problem, however, was if all the domains were to militarize, which would risk strengthening the daimyos at the expense of the bakufu's centralized authority.

Nariaki's interest in the militarization of Japan, beginning with his own domain in Mito, went hand in hand with his argument that the samurai should be relocated from the cities to the rural areas. Nariaki believed he was serving the interests both of Japan's central government and the daimyos by sounding the alarm about Western plans in Northeast Asia. He believed, in other words, that militarization of Japan would protect the shogunate's borders and facilitate the expulsion of Western powers. For critics including the young *roju* Abe Masahiro (r. 1843–1855), Nariaki's logic had some merit, but it risked decentralizing Japanese political and commercial authority and bringing Japan back to an era of uncontrolled foreign trade and internal war.[25]

The intellectual underpinnings of Nariaki's reformist plans included a broader administrative push beyond education in *kangaku*, the Sinocentric Neo-Confucian political and social-ethical system studied and taught by Edo-era Japanese administrators. Apart from *rangaku's* (Dutch learning) previously discussed inclusion of Western medicine and technology as well as *kokugaku's* (Japanese "country" learning) study of Japanese classics, there were other intellectual movements that facilitated a larger epistemic shift among administrators and samurai away from the early Edo era's Sinocentric Neo-Confucian intellectual world. *Mitogaku*, established by one of Nariaki's early predecessors among the Mito daimyos, is particularly notable for its place in the late Edo era's semi-nativist and almost proto-nationalist conceptions of political reform. Like *kokugaku*, *mitogaku* emphasized the study of Japanese classics and, most importantly, a revival of a specifically Japanese historiographical worldview oriented not around the Middle Kingdom's (China) ancient and medieval emperors and spiritual traditions but those of Japan itself. There are parallels with semi-nativist dimensions of the Persian *Book of Kings* in the early Islamic era, which saw the formation of a local Persian historiographical tradition oriented not around early Persian-speaking Muslims or Arab-Persian (*arabi-ajami*) cultural transfer but rather the ancient Persian royal tradition. Works of this sort by *mitogaku* scholars included the *Dai Nihonshi* (大日本史, *Great History of Japan*), which traced the history of Japanese imperial rule back to a legendary Emperor Jimmu (r. 660–585 B.C.) to the exclusion of the more common historiographical emphasis on Chinese imperial chronology when tracing Japan's history.

Dai Nihonshi was a multifaceted historiographical work that cultivated an image of Japan as an empire—that is, a state led by an emperor. This picture notably contrasted with the reality of the Tokugawa shogunate based in Edo (Tokyo), which was only theoretically led by an actually powerless emperor in Kyoto. In practice, the shoguns were both practically and even formally the rulers of Japan to an extent that made the shoguns of Edo (Tokyo) and not the emperors of Kyoto the object of European diplomatic efforts.[26] In the nineteenth century's early decades of political reform and critique, *Dai Nihonshi*'s imperial Japanese historiography and the *mitogaku* learning it came from offered an intellectual foundation for two reformist positions. The first was a call for restraint in the authority of the Tokugawa shogunate with reference to the checks and balances represented in the office of the emperor. The second was a critique of the diminished authority of the daimyos in contrast with the centralized authority of Tokugawa shogun, whom critics in Mito found to be particularly unrestrained and autocratic during the reign of Tokugawa Tsunayoshi (r. 1680–1709) in the previous century

While *mitogaku* and works like *Dai Nihonshi* served to contest a Sinocentric understanding of Japanese and broader Northeast Asian historiography, they were not critical of the fundamental political and social ethics of Neo-Confucian learning. Rather, *mitogaku* works served to reinterpret those

Neo-Confucian ethical principles in service of a Japan-centered conception of world history. Confucian dimensions of the *Dai Nihonshi*, for example, included the way the text ascribes an ethically or morally positive judgment to Japan's ancient and medieval history of emperor-led rule. This positive view of imperial leadership, including its presumptions about the unity and stability offered by an emperor-led political and social hierarchy, agrees with Sinocentric Confucian texts' explanation of the Middle Kingdom's (China) historical success as an emperor-led state. *Mitogaku* works, in other words, were somewhat syncretic in their Sino-Japanese political and intellectual dimensions, even foreshadowing the syncretic dimensions of later Meiji-era Western-modeled political and social reforms and their linguistically Sino-Japanese theoretical justifications. On the one hand, in what reflected the enduring Chinese intellectual impact in late Edo-era Japan's political reform movements, the Chinese-language Neo-Confucian ethical principles used in the *Dai Nihonshi* to glorify this Japanese imperial history were a product of the same Ming-era intellectual cultural transfer that grew Chan (Zen) Buddhist learning in Japan. On the other hand, the emphasis on Japanese emperors to the exclusion of Chinese emperors became intertwined with uniquely Japanese spiritual traditions that were neither Confucian nor Buddhist. More specifically, the *Dai Nihonshi* emphasized the connection of ancient Japanese deities with ancient Japanese emperors in what the text describes as the almost mystically divine-human origins of Japan's imperial dynasty.[27]

As mentioned, the completion of the *Dai Nihonshi* by *mitogaku* scholars of the early Edo period foreshadowed some of the intellectual developments that would occur under the late Edo period. During his tenure as Mito daimyo (r. 1829–1844), Nariaki's development of *mitogaku* saw this form of learning become further intertwined with *kokugaku*, the previously discussed nineteenth-century form of Japanese learning that simultaneously questioned Japan's intellectual dependence on Confucian and Buddhist texts while calling for a revival of Japanese classic texts oriented around Shinto—that is, traditional Japanese sacred beliefs and rituals.

In an analysis of Nariaki's political activities, one can argue that his simultaneous engagement with *mitogaku* (Mito-domain learning), Shinto-oriented *kokugaku* (Japanese "country" learning), and *rangaku* (Dutch learning) correlated with three of his political positions respectively. First, in accordance with the wisdom of *mitogaku*, he believed that there should be a return to an ancient golden age of Japanese politics when the emperor had a more prominent politically unifying role even as a shogun continued to provide military leadership. Second, drawing on *kokugaku*, he believed that Japan should strengthen the more local or semi-nativist non-Sinocentric dimensions of its intellectual or cultural spirit. Third, based on the lessons of *rangaku*, he believed that Japan should strengthen its military through Western technology to fight the encroachment of Western powers in Japanese affairs.

Notably, while Nariaki himself never advocated for the shogun to step down, all three positions were central to the 1850s and 1860s political movement that brought about the end of the Tokugawa shogunate in favor of a restoration of the emperor's rule—that is, the so-called Meiji Restoration in reference to the restoration of imperial power under Emperor Komei's (r. 1831–1867) son, the Meiji Emperor. Indeed, there were key differences between Nariaki's approach and the one that came into political vogue during the final years of the Edo period. The key difference was about how Japan should conduct its diplomatic relations with Western powers.

More specifically, between Commodore Perry's first episode of gunboat diplomacy in 1853 and the Meiji Restoration of 1868, the bakufu and various political reformists critical of the shogunate converged on their shared interest in a broad militarization of the country even as the shogun worried about empowering the local daimyos against himself. Where the shogunate and the reformers diverged most sharply was in the enduring debate about what a culturally renewed imperial Japan with updated Western military technology should do about Western powers. As Euro-American military pressure compelled Japan to open its ports to Western trade, should the shogunate put up armed resistance as Nariaki and many daimyos argued? Alternatively, as various administrators argued, should Japan instead temporarily embrace Western access to the ports and benefit from proximity to Western political know-how in order to strengthen the Japanese state, even if this position came with the problematic outcome of submitting Japan to Western political influence? While many daimyos and several increasingly prominent samurai—especially in the Satsuma domain—argued for the former position, a variety of scholar-officials pushed for the latter position, arguing that lifting the Sakoku Edict altogether and working more closely with Western powers in Japanese ports would bring Japanese vessels back into the world of international trade but with a new element: a modern navy.

One of the government officials who pushed for the latter position was former Hikone daimyo and later regent (*tairo*) Ii Naosuke, who offered a

spin-off of the Western appeasement position that was intended to accommodate Nariaki's pro-sovereignty anti-Western encroachment position. Naosuke argued that military development for the preservation of
Japan's sovereignty was critical, but it depended in the short term on closer
diplomatic relations with Western powers and not a preservation of the old
Sakoku Edict's restrictions on Japanese-Western trade relations. In other
words, Japan's special relationship with the Dutch and the lessons of *rangaku* learning were not enough to build the military. In his own words, "It
is impossible in the crisis we now face to ensure the safety and tranquility
of our country merely by an insistence on the national isolation laws as we
did in former times."[28]

For Nariaki, there was a contradiction in Naosuke's spin-off of the appeasement position. According to Nariaki's counterposition, the establishment of diplomatic relations with Western powers and the overall departure
from the Sakoku Edict towards open trade would lower the morale—that
is, the call to arms—essential to the long-term sovereignty of Japan. In the
final decades of the Tokugawa shogunate, Naosuke's appeasement position
built momentum as the shogunate in Edo (Tokyo) began to depart officially
from the Sakoku Edict and take what seemed to be the safer approach of
appeasing Western powers economically while drawing on their military
knowledge. To some extent, within ten years of the arrival of Commodore
Perry, the decision about ending *sakoku* was already made for the shogunate,
which made Nariaki's pre-1853 call to arms increasingly unviable. The immediate spark for the unraveling of the Sakoku Edict—that is, officially
opening Japanese ports to Western powers beyond the Dutch and the Japanese pursuit of commerce abroad—was the series of "unequal treaties" that
Japan signed after 1853. Facts on the ground in the 1850s and 1860s clashed
with the increasingly antiquated ideals of the Sakoku Edict and the politically centralized hierarchical social order intertwined with it.

For the bakufu, the original ideals of the Sakoku Edict included the political and social stability that came from centralizing the security and trade
apparatus in the government. This approach was intended to contrast with
the earlier Muromachi-era wars between daimyo-led domains, which had
grown into armed mercantile fiefdoms. Some of these domains, as discussed
previously, were allied with the Portuguese on the eve of Hideyoshi's and
Ieyasu's unification of Japan under Tokugawa rule.[29] The Edo era's centralized political and economic system, in other words, departed from the world

of decentralized daimyo-led states with clashing armies of rural samurai funded typically through feudal land arrangements and, in cases like pre-Tokugawa Nagasaki, international sources of financial revenue.

What opened the floodgates that unraveled Tokugawa Japan's idealized political and social structure was the signing of these "unequal treaties" after 1853, which extended the VOC's exceptional privileges in Nagasaki to a variety of Western powers throughout Japanese ports. The outcome, however, was not a return to the so-called Warring States period of the late Muromachi era, but rather a zero-sum conflict in the last years of the Edo period between two groups that emerged out of a variety of political reform movements: the shogunate in Tokyo, on the one hand, and the daimyos and samurai of key domains in rebellion including Satsuma. Notably, while disagreeing on how to deal with Western powers, both sides converged on the urgency of Western-style military reform in the final years of the Edo period. In the aftermath of this conflict, a variety of late Edo-era samurai in the latter group rose to prominence as political reformers in the Meiji era during the construction of the Japanese empire.

The Last Shogun during the Edo-Era's Final Years: The Convergence of Ruling and Revolutionary Circles on Western Reform

Moving into the final years of the Edo period in the 1860s, the Japanese political landscape saw a buildup in the momentum of critique—both within the government in Tokyo and outside of it in the most politically disconnected domains—against the shogunate's policies of appeasement. The names of ruling administrators in the previous decade, including senior councilors (roju) Abe Masahiro and Hotta Masayoshi, had become notoriously connected with the 1858 Treaty of Amity and Commerce (Harris Treaty), which opened six ports to the United States and granted extraterritorial rights to Western powers. In the last two years of the shogunate's rule, the last shogun who came to power was Nariaki's own son Tokugawa Yoshinobu, who worked as a high-level official in the years leading up to his appointment. Paradoxically, Tokugawa Yoshinobu's brief tenure as shogun was characterized by the exact same reformist policies that the shogunate's domain-level critics called for. First, in accordance with the previously discussed position of regent Naosuke on using Japanese-Western diplomatic relations to strengthen Japan's military might, the young shogun rapidly constructed a national army and navy with Western assistance. His military reforms, in other words, signaled his commitment to the reformist ideal of reviving Japanese sovereignty over its borders and ports. Second, the shogun himself facilitated a restoration of the Kyoto-based emperor's theoretical and practical authority in Japan, illustrating to the domains that the power of the shogun in Tokyo and that of the emperor in Kyoto no longer needed to be mutually exclusive. Why, then, did the shogunate fall? What follows is a closer look at the events leading up to the Meiji Restoration and the rise of the modern Japanese Empire. Notably, what these events illustrate is a convergence of governmental and domain-level political positions on the necessity of modernizing Japanese military power in anticipation of further losses of sovereignty.

Daimyos who grew to be most critical of the Tokugawa shogunate in its final years comprised the so-called *tozaima* daimyos—that is, daimyos from domains that were more politically disconnected from the Tokugawa clan such as those of Choshu and Satsuma. Nariaki, both a former Mito daimyo and Tokugawa family member, was not among these daimyos. As a political insider, he attempted to have his son become shogun in 1858 in what illustrated how his Japanese imperialist ideals went hand in hand with his commitment to the shogunate's continued existence in Tokyo. The Choshu daimyo and samurai, in contrast, increasingly worked outside the shogunate system by rebelling against the shogunate altogether in 1864.[30] The successive daimyos of Satsuma, meanwhile, originally took a middle position. After first collaborating with the shogunate and pushing back militarily against Choshu's all-out rebellion in 1864, the Satsuma daimyo then changed positions in 1868 and joined Choshu in bringing about the fall of the shogunate.

What seems paradoxical about the final years leading up to the fall of the shogunate was how both groups in the 1850s—that is, the ruling West-appeasing shogunate administrators in Tokyo, on the one hand, and the pro-emperor internal and external critics of the shogunate's policies of appeasement, on the other hand—shared an interest in studying and implementing Western military reform and preserving Japan's sovereignty over its ports. Given these shared goals, why did they not come to a working arrangement along the model of an emperor-bakufu alliance that would start pushing back against Western encroachment using newly learned Western military technology?

Although this model of an imperial-bakufu alliance would seem like a counterfactual missed opportunity from the perspective of the 1868 collapse of the shogunate, a jointly led imperial-bakufu government had a brief and elusive existence. There were two events that highlight this point in 1863 and 1866 respectively. In 1863, the Tokugawa shogun Iemochi traveled from Edo (Tokyo) to the imperial court of Emperor Komei (r. 1846–1867) in Kyoto, escorted by an entourage of some three thousand retainers. The last time a Tokugawa shogun had visited the imperial palace in Kyoto was more than 250 years earlier during the reign of Tokugawa Iemitsu (r. 1623–1651), who was the shogun associated with the original Sakoku Edict of 1635. Under Iemitsu, the shogunate appointed a liaison known as the *kyoto shoshidai* to work with the emperor and court nobility, whose high public prestige contrasted with their limited administrative power in shogun- and daimyo-dominated Japanese political affairs throughout the Tokugawa period (1603–1868).[31] The earlier visit under Iemitsu served to demonstrate the shogun's power and his independence of the imperial court, and it was followed by the settlement of Edo (Tokyo) as the new center of Japanese power. In Tokugawa Iemochi's more recent visit to Kyoto in 1863, the primary goal of the trip was a reconciliation with the imperial court at a time when a growing number of daimyos were turning away from Edo towards the alternative center of authority that Kyoto represented. Before the shogun could leave, however, he was called upon to join a public imperial visit and massive procession (*gyoko*) to the ancient Kami Shrine, one of Kyoto's sacred centers for the veneration of ancient Japanese spirits. Imperial progresses of this sort were massive and public affairs with several thousand in the emperor's entourage. The ceremonial deference and ritual humility shown by the shogun further signaled in a public context a potential blurring between the emperor's formerly defunct theoretical authority and his growing practical authority within the shogunate system. In what highlights the uniqueness of this event and what it signaled of the late Edo era revival in imperial authority, the last imperial progress of the sort took place when Emperor Go-Mizunoo organized an imperial visit to Kyoto's Nijo Castle, where the shogun of the time was staying. The castle, where Tokugawa Iemochi was himself staying during this recent trip in 1863, was originally built during the reign of Tokugawa shogunate founder Ieyasu (r. 1543–1616) as a symbol of the new shogunate's prestige and military power vis-à-vis the daimyos and the emperor. The imperial visit of the emperor and shogun to the Kami Shrine more than two hundred years later in 1863, in other words, signaled a changing tide in emperor-shogun relations, where the emperor's political prestige was matched by actual political power by virtue of his new and close connection with the shogun himself.

The lead-in to this public display of close imperial-bakufu relations in 1863 was an event in 1858, when Tokugawa *roju* Hotta Masayoshi—in favor of opening Japan's ports to Western powers—dispatched scholar-official and chief education expert (*daigaku-no kami*) Hayashi Akira to seek the emperor's approval for the Harris Treaty. Why the *roju* felt it necessary to seek his approval is not entirely clear beyond the fact that the Mito daimyo Tokugawa Nariaki, who at this point held firmly to his position on preserving *sakoku* and expelling Western powers, was in touch with the imperial court in correlation with his pro-imperial *mitogaku* conceptions of Japanese unity and revival and in accordance with the fact that the bakufu's policy of Western appeasement had already gained approval from a variety of key daimyos. The outcome was that even the bakufu, which in the 1840s was critical of Nariaki's seemingly disruptive desire to militarize the daimyos and unify Japan under a powerful anti-Western imperial center, was now in the late 1850s relenting to the growing power of the emperor partly in accordance with the shogunate's weaknesses. The shogun's visit to the emperor in 1863 was essentially unprecedented, given that the shogunate center of Edo (Tokyo) was largely constructed after Kyoto- and Edo-based Ieyasu's reign as the first shogun. When Iemochi died prematurely in 1866, Nariaki's conception of a *mitogaku*-inspired emperor-led imperial-bakufu alliance finally came to virtual fruition. Nariaki came from the Tokugawa family, and the following shogun was his own son.

The rise in 1866 of Tokugawa Yoshinobu, Nariaki's son, could have represented the final chapter of Nariaki's vision back in the 1840s of a bakufu that ruled together with a powerful emperor over a series of militarized daimyo-led domains expelling Western powers. In theory, the friction between the two factions could have been resolved: the rebelling Choshu and Mito domains in favor of *sakoku* and imperial unity, on the one hand, and a shogunate administration now under the pro-*sakoku* former Mito daimyo's son, on the other. In practice, the power of the Tokugawa shogunate over powerful domains like Choshu, an arrangement that dated back more than 250 years, was an increasingly central concern to groups pushing ahead with rebellion. This question pitted Satsuma domain, which itself had an old relationship with Western powers and a long history of Westernizing military reform, against Mito domain. As mentioned, Satsuma defected from an alliance with the shogunate in favor of joining Choshu in rebellion, while the previously rebellious Mito domain's new daimyo in the 1860s was

Nariaki's other influential son, Tokugawa Yoshiatsu, the natural brother of the new shogun Yoshinobu.

In other words, by 1867, the possibilities of a united emperor-shogun-daimyo-led front against Western encroachment on Japanese territory temporarily took a backseat to an unsettled debate about the Tokugawa shogun's power over domain-level daimyos and samurai. This fact is ambiguously articulated in the banner that tied rebel groups together—namely "Revere the Emperor, expel the barbarians" (尊皇攘夷, *sonno joi*).

In a sense, while the first half of the banner's slogan correlated with on-the-ground realities of an anti-shogun rebellion launched under the pretext of supporting the emperor's renewed leadership, the second half contradicted the fact that the armed domains in rebellion had already cultivated close connections with Western powers and, in practice, abandoned *sakoku*'s restrictions on Japanese-Western economic exchange. That the Choshu- and Satsuma-based samurai who took power during the Meiji Restoration continued Tokugawa Yoshinobu's policies of using Japanese-Western diplomatic proximity to arm the Japanese state illustrates the extent that "expel the barbarians" did not actually constitute some rebellious break from the shogun's own policies.

From one perspective, therefore, the slogan appears almost as a thin pretext for a much wider push among rebel domains to restrain the shogun's power over the domains. Indeed, domain authorities in Choshu, Owari, Fukui, Satsuma, and Toku only allowed *sonno* intellectuals and samurai—that is, those in favor of empowering the emperor over the shogun—to be active without restraint when these movements were in alignment with each daimyo's bureaucratic ideals of strengthening the domain's authority at the expense of the shogun.[32] For many of these bureaucratic cliques, however, empowering the emperor in Kyoto over the daimyos was not actually the goal. The daimyos were not interested in replacing one ruling family in Tokyo with an even more powerful imperial family in Kyoto when the more immediate goal was to consolidate independent domain-level authority. Still, for the daimyos, the language of restoring Japan's imperial power in Kyoto at the expense of the shoguns in Tokyo was useful. It drew on Japan's Sino-centric philosophy of emperor-centric politics and, as a result, emboldened local intellectuals and samurai to turn against the shoguns.

From another perspective, while the intellectuals' and samurai's pro-emperor *sonno* slogan cloaked the deeper reality of shogun-daimyo rivalries and the daimyos' push to break down the shogunate, the slogan's widespread appeal illustrated the enduring China-centered dimensions of Japan's political philosophy even as it transformed from a Sinocentric Edo-era shogunate to a Westernized Meiji-era empire. In other words, even as domain-level Japanese administrators began to adopt British political and socioeconomic reforms, concepts from Chinese intellectual history continued to shape Japan's new politically syncretic model of modernization. From this perspective, the remarkable break in political history seen in the fall of the shogunate in 1868 belied the true continuity in Japan's central and domain-level Western-influenced industrialization during the years of its close proximity with Western powers after the Harris Treaty of 1858. Japan would become an industrialized empire evocative of the British Empire in the 1900s, and education at the military and popular levels would closely mirror British education, but the empire would still be Japanese in terms of its Asia-centered conceptions of political history and its enduringly Sinocentric vocabulary of local values and culture. China's cultural currency in Japan would be contested by Western industrialization, but it would never be eclipsed completely.

Tokugawa Yoshinobu stepped down in 1868 during the civil conflict that brought two modern armies together: the bakufu's forces and those of the rebelling domains. The shogun's design to resign rather than quell the rebellion calls to mind the late Qing-era military leader Yuan Shikai's negotiations with Chinese nationalists almost half a century later in 1911. Following a transitional period, the new Japanese imperial government rapidly transformed the country's political and social order along Western lines. The outcome was a transformation not only in Japan, but also in Japan's relationship with its ancient neighbor: China.

MEIJI AFTERMATH: REORIENTING CHINESE INTELLECTUAL CULTURE DURING JAPAN'S WESTERNIZING REFORMS

Euro-American Reform

In November 1867, despite commanding a shogunate that was rapidly modernizing its military institutions in accordance with Japan's close diplomatic relations with Western powers, Nariaki's son Tokugawa Yoshinobu announced his resignation as Japan's last shogun and, thus, accommodated the anti-bakufu rebellion that he likely could have quelled. Emperor Komei, himself critical of the anti-bakufu rebellion, died of illness earlier that year in a development that was convenient for the nominally pro-emperor circles who were critical of the shogunate. Komei's son, the Meiji Emperor, ascended to the throne in February 1867 just months before Tokugawa Yoshinobu's resignation. Interestingly, despite the breakdown of Japanese politics in 1868, late Edo-era trends in Tokyo and across the most powerful domains were turning towards a massive overhaul of Japanese governance based partly on Western models. In this mix of politically reformist trends, however, what distinguished figures involved in the transition from the Edo-era Tokugawa shogunate to the Meiji-era Japanese empire was their interest in the entire edifice of Western governance and social organization. Interestingly, in what points to the extent that Chinese intellectual culture was both enduring and contested during the Meiji era, Chinese intellectual concepts in the Japanese language frequently constituted the idiom of choice for articulating a new Western-influenced Japanese political and social order. What follows is a look at key figures involved in the formation of this new order. Their profiles illustrate just how quickly Edo-era political and military figures propelled Japan's Westernization reforms at the end of the 1800s, almost a century before China's late twentieth-century industrialization.

Sakamoto Ryoma of Tosa domain was one of the early power brokers who negotiated a truce and alliance between Choshu and Satsuma in the final years of the Edo period.[33] Before Choshu and Satsuma domains embarked on their final rebellion against the bakufu, Ryoma himself attempted to accommodate the continued existence of the shogunate by negotiating with the shogun (Yoshinobu) to accept a proposal for transitioning Japan's political system into a British-style bicameral legislature. Ryoma's knowledge of Western politics came from his exposure to Western learning through a Tokugawa bakufu figure named Katsu Kaishu (Katsu Rintaro), who was a key figure in the development of Japan's navy under the last shogun.[34] Ryoma himself was the author of a short treatise called "Eight Proposals Composed Aboard a Ship," which he wrote in dialogue with political reformer and samurai Goto Shojiro while onboard a Tosa ship outside Nagasaki in 1867.[35] Drawing on his interest in British and American governance, Ryoma's proposals included the implementation of a bicameral legislature, the formation of a constitution, and the establishment of a national army and navy. It was in this context that Ryoma proposed a continuing role of Yoshinobu in a bicameral legislature. The irony of Ryoma's proposing this inclusion of the shogun in a new British-style government was that, as mentioned, Ryoma previously negotiated a rapprochement and alliance between the rebellious

Choshu and Satsuma leaders who, upon reconciling, rejected the peace proposal, rebelled against the shogun, and called for the appropriation of all
Tokugawa political power and lands.

What was notable about Ryoma's rejected proposal is the extent that it
foreshadowed the Westernizing political and social reforms that Japanese
ruling circles ended up pursuing under a variety of Meiji-era Choshu- and
Satsuma-born leaders, many of whom shared the profile of Goto Shojiro—
that is, young samurai educated in the Edo era's multifaceted official and
private academies who became political administrators in the late 1860s.

One of these samurai-turned-Meiji politicians was Ito Hirobumi. Hirobumi was a young samurai from Choshu during the late Edo period who was
in favor of anti-bakufu *sonno* imperial reform. In the years leading up to the
Meiji Restoration, he was one of the so-called Choshu Five who traveled to
Europe in 1863 to study at the University of London.[36] In 1870, he traveled
to the United States to study the American currency system, and by 1882
he was in Europe studying European constitutions. In what illustrates the
extent to which Japan was making headway against China's political power
in Northeast Asia, Hirobumi met the previously discussed Chinese reformer
Li Hung-chang in 1885 to negotiate a peace agreement over their respective states' support of rival groups in Korea—namely, the Chinese-backed
Joseon dynasty and a Japanese-backed rebel group. The outcome was the
transformation of Korea from a Chinese protectorate to a co-protectorate of
China and Japan, and the ultimate withdrawal of both Japanese and Chinese
troops. The latter outcome was led by the previously discussed late Qing-era
reformer Yuan Shikai, the figure who negotiated with Sun Yat-Sen over the
fall of the Qing dynasty and the declaration of a republic in 1911.

Kido Takayoshi was another Meiji-era reformer from Choshu. Among
his legacies was his role contributing to the abolition of the Han system,
a process that saw daimyo domains transformed into modern prefectures.
Takayoshi's trip to the United States between 1871 and 1873 to study Western
education and politics was among the principle reasons for his support of
a constitutional government in Japan.[37]

Matsukata Masayoshi, a Meiji politician and founder of the Bank of
Japan, was originally a samurai from Satsuma and one-time student at the
Confucian academy of Zoshikan. When the previously discussed Ito Hirobumi of Choshu was named prime minister in 1885, Masayoshi was named
the first finance minister. Among his most influential reforms was drafting

laws for land tax reform throughout the 1870s, when tax payments changed from rice to monetary payment and when taxes were assessed based on the price of estates as opposed to potential agricultural produce.[38] By the 1880s, as the language of political and economic reform expanded, Japan's Meiji-era political transformation began to translate into a social one as well. Notably, despite the extent that Chinese cultural currency was contested in the Meiji era, the discourse of political and social reform remained intertwined with Japan's Sinocentric intellectual past.

Debating European Reforms in a Chinese Idiom

Many of the social reforms that were conceived during the first two decades of the Meiji era had the effect of bringing to the wider Japanese population the early Meiji-era political ethos that drove these Westernizing reforms in the military, governance, and finance. Mori Arinori, Japan's first envoy to the United States (1871–1873), was a founding member of the Meirokusha Society (明六社). The organization was a kind of intellectual coterie that published a journal called *Meiroku zasshi*, which explored topics including Western ethics and Horace Mann's conception of universal education. One of the first topics discussed was language reform, especially the question of whether Japan's use of three scripts (kanji, hiragana, katakana) needed to be reformed in some manner.

In what illustrates how wide the spectrum of opinions about reform were in the early Meiji period, Arinori offered a perspective on language that attracted criticism even among his American interlocutors: introducing a simplified form of English into Japan in order to advance its access to the world of Western commerce and society.[39] Others called for the removal of Chinese kanji characters from Japanese in favor of more exclusive reliance on the phonetic kana scripts, while still others called for the use of *romaji*—that is, the Roman (Latin) script used in Western European languages. All of these options ran into the challenge of implementation. The second two options in particular were problematic because complex Japanese words of Chinese origin use multiple Chinese characters that help clarify the multicharacter word's full meaning. That is, Chinese characters can offer multiple visual cues of a long Japanese word's meaning. These clues were especially useful for understanding the variety of neologisms of the Meiji era, such as "philosophy" (哲学, *tetsu-gaku*) as a reference specifically to Western philosophy.

Nishi Amane (d. 1897) coined the term *tetsu-gaku*—that is, "wisdom learning" or "the study of wisdom"—as a new Japanese term to mean "Western philosophy." With knowledge of the two Chinese characters, a Japanese reader would know that the individual characters referred to "wisdom" and "learning," respectively, and would understand that the characters together referred to "the study of wisdom." Still, it would not be immediately obvious out of context that Japanese writers like Amane were using this term in reference to the European study of philosophy. Doing away with Chinese characters altogether would potentially make this elusive neologism that referred to Western philosophy even more difficult to decipher.

Critics of the abolishment of Chinese characters argued that the haphazard integration of either Roman or kana-script substitutions for familiar kanji characters would impede learning and communication at a time when Japanese writers were simultaneously coining a variety of new words from old Chinese characters and shifting the semantic range of older character-based words. Examples of written Japanese neologisms that included either new combinations of old Chinese characters or new meanings applied to multicharacter words included subjectivity (*shukan*, 主観), objectivity (*kyakkan*, 客観), phenomenon (*gensho*, 現象), psychology (*shinrigaku*, 心理学), reality (*jitsuzai*, 実在), and understanding (*gosei*, 悟性).[40] Unsurprisingly, the last word already existed prior to the Meiji era, but was previously a more Buddhism-oriented word connected to conceptions of enlightenment. In the long run, the coining of neologisms out of new combinations of known Chinese characters as well as the use of older multicharacter Sino-Japanese words to mean new things became two of the central vehicles for expanding the versatility of the Japanese language to communicate Western thought.

A New Asia

From the comparative perspective of China's and Japan's respective late nineteenth-century intellectual and social reforms, one outcome was both remarkable and unexpected: the cultural transfer of Meiji-era Japanese intellectual reform to late Qing China. By the late 1800s, Chinese writers were studying European concepts through combinations of Chinese characters that Japanese writers had devised and endowed with new European meanings. There were parallels in the way writers of Arabic, Turkish, and Persian in the Ottoman and Qajar Middle East brought modern European political meanings to older words like *dawla* (imperial dynasty, nation-state) that the three languages shared across their Arabic writing system.

The linguistic shifts in Japan and their outcomes in China offer a useful metaphor for the new intellectual relationship that resulted. In a sense, as much as China initiated Japan into a Japanese writing system oriented heavily around Chinese words and concepts, and as much as Chinese cultural currency permeated the political and intellectual culture of Edo-era Japan, it was Japan in the late nineteenth century that shaped China's modernization through the new and modern Japanese cultural currency that the Meiji-era government cultivated through its politically syncretic Westernizing reforms.

What this development potentially points to is something extraordinary. While politicians and intellectuals were willing to implement various Westernizing reforms, neither in the case of Meiji-era Japan nor in Qing China was the European cultural currency that informed these Japanese and Chinese Westernizing reforms self-evident. Simply stated, for many early Meiji-era Japanese reformers, while European military dominance offered an urgent argument for the necessity of Western-style Japanese political and social reforms, it still did not indicate the superiority of European ethics and a European worldview over those of Japan or China. It is for this reason that those Japanese reformers who took the argument for Westernization to its furthest extremes, including calls for changing the multifaceted Japanese writing system to a Romanized one, remained controversial. The enduring Sinocentric dimensions of the Japanese language's accommodation of European political and social norms illustrate this larger paradigm of how Japan's Sinocentric Edo-era past mediated its turn towards European political culture and social reform. The Sino-Japanese Western synthesis that resulted was translatable enough for Chinese reformers to use as a model for Chinese modernization in the final years of the Qing.

By the 1890s, following the demonstration of Japan's surprise military superiority over China during the Sino-Japanese war, it was Japan that was hosting Chinese intellectuals interested in the new Sino-Japanese language of modern politics. Among the most prominent of them was a young Sun Yat-Sen. What Meiji-era Japan offered late Qing-era Chinese reformers was both a living model and linguistic idiom for the articulation of Chinese modernization. From the perspective of the previous millennium of Chinese cultural transfer across Northeast Asia, the novelty of this Meiji-era exchange was staggering. A new global order was emerging in the early twentieth century that saw Qing China and the various European powers in Northeast Asia begin to take a back seat to Japan's rise as a global empire. By the end of the Meiji period in 1912, the Japanese empire represented an unprecedented and syncretic mix of Western industrialization, Japanese nationalism along European and local models, and a reinterpretation of Confucian principles in service of both militarization and a new theory of Japan-led pan-Asianism that looked towards the western reaches of Asia once visited by Ming admiral Zheng He.

The rise of the Japanese Empire and, following it, a postwar American Pacific signaled to the world that the era of China's global cultural transfer initiated during the Great Ming had come to an end. It would take another century before discussions of a rising China would reappear in international political discourse. By then, the geopolitical landscape in Asia would be dominated by the new tiger economies of Hong Kong, Taiwan, Singapore, and South Korea, as well as the neighboring "tiger cubs" of Malaysia, Indonesia, the Philippines, Thailand, and Vietnam. Between the tech innovations of Singapore and Kuala Lumpur, the global soft power of Seoul, the enduring economic growth of Tokyo, and the growing interest of the United States in the Pacific, that rise of a new global China would be contested, but not unprecedented.

A New Turn to the East

In 1979, the award-winning Japanese art director and costume designer Eiko Ishioka created a memorable advertising campaign for the Japanese department store Parco. The advertisement featured an American actress draped in a robe and winged headdress, which was intended to evoke the goddess Kennon. Ishioka wrote of the campaign, "Japan has learned from the West . . . but the situation is now changing. Today's trends show that the West is starting to look East . . . 'Can West wear East?' is being asked by the New Japan, which looks forward to the future."[1] Ishioka's words offered a prescient picture of the decades ahead. The designer behind the clothing in Ishioka's ad campaign was Issey Miyake, who was known for, among other designs, the minimalist black turtleneck worn by Steve Jobs in the latter part of his career.

The European and American fashion world's early interest in Miyake foreshadowed the arrival of fellow designers Rei Kawakubo and Yohji Yamamoto onto the Parisian haute couture fashion scene in the 1980s. For contemporary Western journalists, Kawakubo and Yamamoto's flowing loose-fitting fabrics and extensive use of black represented the new Japanese avant-garde and its abstract conceptions of a postapocalyptic world. For Kawakubo and Yamamoto themselves, the fabrics were not abstract but ready to wear (prêt-à-porter), and black was not morbid but a nod to simpler more minimalist aesthetics than what Western designers offered. For historians of late twentieth-century Japan, the Japanese avant-garde fashion scene helped mark the start of Japanese cultural currency in the West, where "Made in Japan" represented the innovations of Sony, Nintendo, Toyota, and Sanrio. On a more subtle and perhaps more profound level was the transfer westward of Japanese film and anime plots in readapted English translation, *kawaii* tropes, and the conflation of Zen-influenced interior design with conceptions of modern sophistication.

Underneath this narrative of a new Japanese and broader Asian cultural currency, however, lies a paradox identified in this book's narrative: the inability of many Western observers to recognize that modern international consumption of Chinese and Japanese cultural production stretches back not half a century but half a millennium, giving China and Japan a much more global cultural legacy than historians of modern Europe imagine. Chinese and Japanese absorption of wider Asian and European cultural production likewise dates back long before the postwar reconstruction era of the 1950s and 1960s. Throughout the centuries of Japan's and China's semi-protectionist policies that called for restrictions on private trade in favor of state-sponsored commercial exchange, administrators and merchants in both states continuously interacted with and were patrons of a variety of Asian and European actors, from Jesuit astronomers and cartographers to British military experts.

Against this backdrop of multiple centuries of exchange, why do economic historians argue that China and Japan were historically isolated states that lagged behind European innovation since the Age of Exploration, when in fact much of preindustrial global innovation moved from East to West?[2] Why do modern observers of Chinese and Japanese cultural production write similarly that the East "learned from the West . . . but the situation is now changing"? The answer illustrated in this book is twofold: First, historians have overlooked the dynamics of a half millennium of direct exchange between Europe and Asia, which saw Europe on the consuming side of much of Chinese and Japanese cultural and intellectual production. Second, historians have ignored the dynamics of China's and Japan's historical approaches to modernization and their emulation of Western sociopolitical models. Even after Euro-American military might was demonstrated in Northeast Asia during the Opium Wars in China and Commodore Perry's so-called "gunboat diplomacy" in Japan (ca. 1830s–1850s), the argument for the superiority of Western models of political and social organization over local models never entirely took hold. More frequently, Chinese and Japanese officials and intellectuals articulated a call for sociopolitical reform along Western models in the context of, more specifically, the reformation of military and industrial technology and the preservation of local sovereignty over Chinese and Japanese regional ports. Absorbing the cultural underpinnings of Western industrialization was part of this endeavor, but the wholesale replacement of local traditions with Western counterparts never quite occurred. Westernizing social reforms, while welcomed, were always mediated through the lens of local histories, giving late nineteenth-century Tokyo and Shanghai their characteristic social and aesthetic cosmopolitanism that blended East and West.

As social reforms accelerated in the twentieth century, China's and Japan's transformative modernization still saw officials, intellectuals, and artists cultivate an enduring sense of Asian centeredness in the world, where Europe was somehow also center yet still a periphery. From this perspective, designer Ishioka's observation that "Japan has learned from the West . . . but . . . the West is starting to look East" is both new and surprising, but only if history begins with the fall of the shoguns and the start of Japan's industrialization. With a closer look at history's previous half millennium, when European seafaring expeditions studied Chinese and Japanese innovation, what Ishioka describes as a new turn to the East is in fact both familiar and even predictable: from Singapore to Seoul, Asian capitals have again become centers of profound innovation in a world that is today more polycentric and interconnected than ever before.

ACKNOWLEDGMENTS

This book was completed while teaching, conducting research, and giving talks at several institutions, especially Bates College, Harvard University, MIT, Stanford University, Georgetown University, the University of Wisconsin–Madison, Ewha Women's University (Seoul), Yonsei University, the University of Hong Kong, the University of Tokyo, New York University, Columbia University, Monash University, the University of Malaya, and the National University of Singapore. At UW-Madison, where I was Robert M. Kingdon Fellow at the Institute for the Research in the Humanities (IRH), I thank Director Dr. Susan Friedman for her leadership in encouraging fellows to collaborate and build connections across disciplines. I also thank Dr. Elaine Fisher, Dr. André Wink, and Dr. William Noseworthy for fantastic and continuing collaborations at the intersection of the digital humanities and the study of Asia. At NYU, where I conducted research as a Visiting Scholar and am also a doctoral alumnus, I thank the entire faculty of the Departments of East Asian Studies, Economics, Sociology, History, and Middle Eastern and Islamic Studies for making Manhattan a welcome intellectual home once again as I embarked on new projects. At Ewha Women's University in Seoul, I thank Dr. Harris Kim for inviting me to teach my award-winning course on women's movements and industrialization, and for supporting my research on the intersection of economics and sociology. I also thank Dr. Hyunhee Park of the City University of New York for being a great research interlocutor in my commitment to building intellectual communities that connect both sides of the Pacific. At the University of Tokyo, I thank Dr. Eiji Nagasawa and Dr. Goto for welcoming me in Tokyo and being supportive of my interest in rediscovering many of the connections between Asia and the West across history. At the National University of Singapore, I thank Dr. Peter Borschberg for demonstrating how research in global history can offer truly profound and insightful lessons for the modern world. At Cornell University, I thank Dr. Chiara Formichi, Dr. Eric Tagliacozzo, and the entire faculty of the Departments of Asian Studies and History. At Bates, I thank all of the faculty for their research and teaching excellence, and for creating an environment conducive of the kind of interdisciplinary work at the core of this book. I thank especially the faculty and students of the Departments of Asian Studies, Religious Studies, History, Economics, Art and Visual Culture, Classical and Medieval Studies, Sociology, Politics, Africana, Anthropology, French and Francophone Studies, European Studies, American Studies, Anthropology, Philosophy, and Latin American Studies. I'm particularly grateful to the current and former chairs of these departments with whom I've enjoyed many fascinating conversations about global history and contemporary society, including Drs. Marcus Bruce, Cynthia Baker, Thomas Tracy, John Strong, Brian Ruppert, Daniel Riera-Crichton, Lynne Lewis, Paul Shea, Francesco Duina, Karen Melvin, Joe Hall, Alex Dauge-Roth, Kirk Read, Mary Rice-Defosse, Elizabeth Eames, Loring Danforth, Dennis Browne, David George, Claudia Aburto Guzmán, Baltasar Fra-Molinero, Francisca López, Edward Harwood, Trian Nguyen, Rebecca Corrie, Sylvia Federico, Susan Stark, Therí Pickens, Myron Beasley, Charles Nero, Sue Houchins, Senem Aslan, and others among the current and former chairs of the Humanities and Social Sciences Divisions. I also thank the staff of all of the international research and archival libraries and museums that welcomed my project throughout the course of this book's completion. I'm tremendously grateful to Stanford University Press and particularly Senior Editor Marcela Maxfield for taking on this project and offering profound and invaluable insights on its content. I also thank Editorial Assistant Sunna Juhn, Production Editor Gigi Mark, and Copyeditor Catherine Mallon for shepherding it with expertise and care through production.

NOTES

CHAPTER 1: FIVE HUNDRED YEARS ACROSS THE INDIAN OCEAN AND SOUTH CHINA SEA

1. Hyunhee Park, *Mapping the Chinese and Islamic Worlds: Cross-Cultural Exchange in Pre-Modern Asia* (Cambridge: Cambridge University Press, 2012), 43–46; Timothy Brook, *The Troubled Empire: China in the Yuan and Ming Dynasties* (Cambridge, Mass.: Harvard University Press, 2013), 179–80.

2. Rowe has shown how this Western image of a formidable Qing empire changed very late in history, specifically with the modernization of the British military in the 1800s during the lead-up to the Opium Wars. William T. Rowe, *China's Last Empire: The Great Qing* (Cambridge, Mass.: Belknap Press of Harvard University Press, 2009), 167–74; Peter Borschberg, *Journal, Memorials and Letters of Cornelis Matelieff De Jonge: Security, Diplomacy and Commerce in 17th-Century Southeast Asia* (Singapore: National University of Singapore Press, 2015), 6–14.

3. Daniel O. Spence, *A History of the Royal Navy—Empire and Imperialism* (London: I. B. Tauris, 2015), 45–84.

4. Bruno Maçães, *Belt and Road: A Chinese World Order* (Oxford: Oxford University Press, 2019), 9–38.

5. José Luis Gasch-Tomás, *The Atlantic World and the Manila Galleons: Circulation, Market, and Consumption of Asian Goods in the Spanish Empire, 1565–1650* (Leiden: Brill, 2018), 131–139.

6. Stacey Pierson's examination of the Ming-era ceramics manufacturing illustrates that while centers like Jingdezhen saw the mass production of porcelain, the process was not mechanized in the way pseudo-ceramics were produced during the Industrial Revolution. Stacey Pierson, *From Object to Concept: Global Consumption and the Transformation of Ming Porcelain* (Hong Kong: Hong Kong University Press, 2013), 9–14.

7. Borschberg, *Journal, Memorials and Letters of Cornelis Matelieff de Jonge*; Peter Borschberg, *The Memoirs and Memorials of Jacques De Coutre: Security, Trade and Society*

in 16th- and 17-Century Southeast Asia (Singapore: National University of Singapore Press, 2014); Peter Borschberg, *Hugo Grotius, the Portuguese and Free Trade in the East Indies* (Singapore: National University of Singapore Press, 2011).

8. Andre Gunder Frank, *ReORIENT: Global Economy in the Asian Age* (Berkeley: University of California Press, 1998).

9. Janet L. Abu-Lughod, *Before European Hegemony: The World System A.D. 1250–1350* (Oxford: Oxford University Press, 1998).

CHAPTER 2: GLOBAL BEIJING UNDER THE GREAT MING

1. Jonathan D. Spence, *The Search for Modern China* (New York: Norton, 1991), 189.

2. Dru C. Gladney, "Muslim Tombs and Ethnic Folklore: Charters for Hui Identity," *Journal of Asian Studies* 46 (1987): 495–532.

3. John Chaffee, "Muslim Merchants and Quanzhou in the Late Yuan-Early Ming," in *The East Asian Mediterranean: Maritime Crossroads of Culture, Commerce and Human Migration*, ed. Angela Schottenhammer (Wiesbaden, Germany: Harrassowitz, 2008), 117–118.

4. On the Muslim Yunnanese, see David G. Atwill, *The Chinese Sultanate: Islam, Ethnicity, and the Panthay Rebellion in Southwest China, 1856–1873* (Stanford, Calif.: Stanford University Press, 2006), 34–47.

5. Michael C. Brose, "Yunnan's Muslim Heritage," in *China's Encounters on the South and Southwest: Reforging the Fiery Frontier over Two Millennia* (Leiden: Brill, 2015), 135–155.

6. Yokkaichi Yasuhiro, "Chinese and Muslim Diasporas and the Indian Ocean Trade Network under Mongol Hegemony," in *The East Asian Mediterranean: Maritime Crossroads of Culture, Commerce and Human Migration*, ed. Angela Schottenhammer (Wiesbaden, Germany: Harrassowitz, 2008), 73–102.

7. David C. Kang, *East Asia before the West: Five Centuries of Trade and Tribute* (New York: Columbia University Press, 2012), 115–117.

8. Hyunhee Park, *Mapping the Chinese and Islamic Worlds: Cross-cultural Exchange in Pre-Modern Asia* (Cambridge: Cambridge University Press, 2015), 170–172.

9. Wang Gungwu, "Ming Foreign Relations: Southeast Asia," in *The Cambridge History of China: Vol. 8, Part 2*, eds. Denis C. Twitchett and Frederick W. Mote (Cambridge: Cambridge University Press, 2008), 301–332.

10. Chris Baker, "Ayutthaya Rising: From Land or Sea?" *Journal of Southeast Asian Studies* 34 (2003): 41–62.

11. See Chapter Three.

12. See Chapter Three, note 5.

13. The original text is available in "Wang Ch'ung-wu, *Ming pen chi Mao chu*" (Shanghai, 1948; facsimile rpt. Hong Kong, 1967), 107–108.

14. On the opposite end of the spectrum was the Tran state of Da Viet on the Southeast frontier of China, which sent an embassy recognizing the Ming in 1369. Kathlene Baldanza, *Ming China and Vietnam: Negotiating Borders in Early Modern Asia* (Cambridge: Cambridge University Press, 2017), 55–56.

15. John D. Langlois Jr., "The Hung-Wu Reign 1368–1398," in *The Cambridge History of China: Vol. 7, Part 1*, eds. Denis C. Twitchett and Frederick W. Mote (Cambridge: Cambridge University Press, 2008), 165–167.

16. William C. Hannas and John DeFrancis, *Asia's Orthographic Dilemma* (Honolulu: University of Hawai'i Press, 1997), 48–72.

17. J. B. Palais, *Confucian Statecraft and Korean Institutions: Yu Hyŏngwŏn and the late Chosŏn Dynasty* (Seattle: University of Washington Press, 1995), 25–60; Ki-Moon Lee, "The Inventor of the Korean Alphabet," in *The Korean Alphabet: Its History and Structure*, ed. Young-Key Kim-Renaud (Honolulu: University of Hawai'i Press), 11–30.

18. On the case of the fallen Ming minister Hu Wei-Yung (Weiyong) and its effect on Ming-Japanese relations, see Timothy Brook, *The Troubled Empire: China in the Yuan and Ming Dynasties* (Cambridge, Mass.: Belknap Press of Harvard University Press, 2013), 89–91; Feng Zhang, "Regionalization in the Tingxia: Continuity and Change in China's Foreign Policy," in *China and the Global Politics of Regionalization*, ed. Emilian Kavalski (London: Routledge, 2016), 24–26.

19. Wang Yi-t'ung, *Official Relations between China and Japan. 1368–1549* (Cambridge, Mass.: Harvard University Press, 1953), 21–24, 34–53.

20. Zhang, "Regionalization in the Tingxia," 25–27.

21. Edward Y. J. Chung, *The Korean Neo-Confucianism of Yi T'oegye and Yi Yulgok: A Reappraisal of the "Four-Seven Thesis" and Its Practical Implications for Self-Cultivation* (Albany: State University of New York Press, 1995), 10–16.

22. Jeffrey L. Broughton, *Zongmi on Chan*, (New York: Columbia University Press, 2012), 57–59.

23. Mary E. Tucker, *Moral and Spiritual Cultivation in Japanese Neo-Confucianism: The Life and Thought of Kaibara Ekken, 1630–1740* (Albany: State University of New York Press, 1989), 13–30.

CHAPTER 3: PICTURING CHINA IN PERSIAN ALONG THE SILK ROUTES

1. The account of Naqqash was preserved in the writings of Hafiz-i Abru (d. 1430), a Persian chronicler who worked in Shahrukh's court. Abd al-Razzaq al-Samarqandi also included Naqqash's account in his *Maṭla'-i sa'dayn wa majma'-i baḥrayn*. Morris Rossabi has offered a useful historical contextualization of this embassy against the backdrop of embassies in the reverse direction from Ming

China to Central Asia, and specifically the embassies of Isiha (亦失哈) to the Jurched and of Ch'en Ch'eng (陳誠) to Central Asia. Morris Rossabi, "Two Ming Envoys to Inner Asia," *T'oung Pao* 62 (1976): 15–21.

2. The Persian edition used in this section is Abd al-Razzaq's copy that was published in Etienne M. Quatremère, "Notice de l'ouvrage persan qui a pour titre: *Matla-assaadein ou-madjma-albahrein* et qui contient l'histoire des deux sultans Schah-Rokh et Abou-Said," *Notices et extraits des manuscrits de la Bibliothèque du roi et autres bibliothèques* 14 (1843): 308–386. Thackston has collated two manuscripts in his translation: Ghayathuddin Naqqash, "Report to Mirza Baysunghur on the Timurid Legation to the Ming Court at Peking," in *A Century of Princes, Sources on Timurid Art and History*, ed. Wheeler M. Thackston (Cambridge: Aga Khan Program for Islamic Architecture, 1989), 279–297.

3. This chapter relies on the following Persian edition: Ali Akbar Khitayi, *Khitay namah: Sharh-i Mushahidat-i Sayyid Ali Akbar Khata'i, Mu'asir-i Shah Isma'il Safavi Dar Chin*, ed. Iraj Afshar (Tehran: Markaz-i Asnad-i Farhangi-i Asiya, 1993).

4. This text, completed in 1516 and translated from Persian to Ottoman Turkish in 1582, was popularized by Katip Çelebi. Pınar Emiralioğlu, "Relocating the Center of the Universe: China and the Ottoman Imperial Project in the Sixteenth Century," *Osmanlı Araştırmaları/Journal of Ottoman Studies* 39 (2012): 161–187.

5. Rossabi, "Two Ming Envoys to Inner Asia," 109–142

6. E. Bretschneider, *Mediaeval Research from Eastern Asiatic Sources: Fragments towards the Knowledge of the Geography and History of Central and Western Asia from the 13th to the 17th Century* (London: Kegan Paul, Trench, Trübner & Co. Ltd., 1910), 283–285.

7. S. F. Starr, *Lost Enlightenment: Central Asia's Golden Age from the Arab Conquest to Tamerlane* (Princeton, N.J.: Princeton University Press, 2015), 478–514.

8. Sheila Blair and Jonathan M. Bloom, *The Art and Architecture of Islam, 1250–1800* (New Haven, Conn.: Yale University Press, 1996), 59–61.

9. *Matla-Assaadein Ou-Madjma-Albahrein*, 309–311.

10. *Matla-Assaadein Ou-Madjma-Albahrein*, 309–311.

11. *Matla-Assaadein Ou-Madjma-Albahrein*, 323–324.

12. The Persian edition of *Matla Al-Sadayn Wa-Majma Al-Bahrayn* used in this chapter is the copy transmitted by Timurid chronicler Abd al-Razzaq al-Samarqandi (1413–1482), which was published in Etienne M. Quatremère, "Notice de l'ouvrage persan qui a pour titre: Matla-assaadein ou-madjma-albahrein et qui contient l'histoire des deux sultans Schah-Rokh et Abou-Said," *Notices et extraits des manuscrits de la Bibliothèque du roi et autres bibliothèques* 14, no.1 (1843): 308–386.

13. *Matla Al-Sadayn Wa-Majma Al-Bahrayn*, 332.

14. *Matla Al-Sadayn Wa-Majma Al-Bahrayn*, 327.

15. *Matla Al-Sadayn Wa-Majma Al-Bahrayn*, 328.

16. *Matla Al-Sadayn Wa-Majma Al-Bahrayn*, 332.

17. Morris Rossabi, "The Silk Trade in China and Central Asia," in James C. Y. Watt, Anne E. Wardwell, and Morris Rossabi, *When Silk Was Gold: Central Asian and Chinese Textiles* (New York: Metropolitan Museum of Art, 1997), 7–20.

18. Mary M. Dusenbury and Carol Bier, *Flowers, Dragons and Pine Trees: Asian Textiles in the Spencer Museum of Art* (New York: Hudson Hills Press, 2004), 104–105.

19. Trudy Ring, Noelle Watson, and Paul Schellinger, *Asia and Oceania: International Dictionary of Historic Places* (Hoboken, N.J.: Taylor and Francis, 2012), 528–529.

20. 'Ali Akbar Khita'i, *Khitay namah: Sharh-i Mushahidat-i Sayyid Ali Akbar Khata'i, Mu'asir-i Shah Isma'il Safavi Dar Chin*, ed. Iraj Afshar (Tehran: Markaz-i Asnad-i Farhangi-i Asiya, 1993), 39.

21. Khita'i, 40.

22. Khita'i, 41.

23. Khita'i, 144.

24. Khita'i, 147.

25. Khita'i, 114.

26. Khita'i, 119.

27. Khita'i, 120.

28. Jonathan M. Bloom and Sheila S. Blair, eds. *The Grove Encyclopedia of Islamic Art and Architecture* (Oxford: Oxford University Press, 2009), 340–342.

29. Khita'i, *Khitay namah*, 118.

30. Khita'i, 114.

31. Khita'i, 116.

32. Alan Chong, Stephen A. Murphy, Michael Flecker, Regina Krahl, and John Guy, eds. *The Tang Shipwreck: Art and Exchange in the 9th Century* (Singapore: Asian Civilisations Museum, 2017).

33. Denise P. Leidy, Mark Polizzotti, and Barbara Cavaliere, *How to Read Chinese Ceramics* (New York: Metropolitan Museum of Art, 2015), 36.

34. Géza Fehérvári, *Ceramics of the Islamic World: In the Tareq Rajab Museum* (London: I. B. Tauris, 2000), 37.

35. Maris Boyd Gillette, *China's Porcelain Capital: The Rise, Fall and Reinvention of Ceramics in Jingdezhen* (London: Bloomsbury, 2016), 21ff.

CHAPTER 4: TRADING WITH CHINA IN
MALAY ALONG THE SPICE ROUTES

1. The editions used are: A. H. Hill, "Hikayat Raja-Raja Pasai," *Journal of the Malayan Branch of the Royal Asiatic Society* 33 (1960): 1–215; "Hikayat Hang Tuah," in *The Epic of Hang Tuah*, ed. Rosemary Robson, trans. Muhammad Haji Salleh (Kuala Lumpur: Institut Terjemahan Negara Malaysia, 2010); "Sejarah Melayu," in John

Leyden, *Malay Annals* (London: Printed for Longman, Hurst, Rees, Orme, and Brown, 1821).

2. Siti Hawa Haji Salleh, *Malay Literature of the 19th Century* (Kuala Lumpur: Institut Terjemahan Negara Malaysia, 2010).

3. Ma Huan, *Ying-yai Sheng-Lan: The Overall Survey of the Ocean's Shores* [1433], ed. Chengjun Feng, trans. J.V.G. Mills (Bangkok: White Lotus, 1996), 93.

4. David G. Atwill, *The Chinese Sultanate: Islam, Ethnicity, and the Panthay Rebellion in Southwest China, 1856–1873* (Stanford, Calif.: Stanford University Press, 2006), 34–36.

5. On the movement of late Yuan-era and early Ming-era Muslims from China to Southeast Asia beyond Melaka, see Alexander Wain, "China and the Rise of Islam in China," in *Islamisation: Comparative Perspectives from History*, ed. A.C.S. Peacock (Edinburgh: Edinburgh University Press, 2017), 419–443.

6. Kenneth R. Hall, "Upstream and Downstream Unification in Southeast Asia's First Islamic Polity: The Changing Sense of Community in the Fifteenth Century *Hikayat Raja-Raja Pasai* Court Chronicle," *Journal of the Economic and Social History of the Orient* 44 (2001): 198–229; Kenneth R. Hall, "Trade and Statecraft in the Western Archipelago at the Dawn of the European Age," *Journal of the Malaysian Branch of the Royal Asiatic Society* 54 (1981): 21–47.

7. Anthony Reid, *Southeast Asia in the Age of Commerce, 1450–1680, Vol. 1: The Lands below the Winds* (New Haven, Conn.: Yale University Press, 1988), 83–96.

8. Alexander Wain, "Chinese Muslims and the Conversion of Melaka to Islam," *Proceedings of Economics Development and Research: Humanities, Society and Culture II* 51 (2012): 35–40.

9. *Hikayat Raja Raja Pasai,* 145.

10. *Hikayat Raja Raja Pasai,* 136.

11. In the context of the use of music and dance in martial arts, Cheng Yingshi has traced some of the interconnections across East and Southeast Asia in the performance of self-defense disciplines such as *silat.* Cheng Yingshi, "A Report on Chinese Research into the Dunhuang Music Manuscript," in *Musica Asiatica,* ed. Allan Marett (Cambridge: Cambridge University Press 1991), 61–94.

12. *Hikayat Raja Raja Pasai,* 137.

13. For the origin and meaning of terms like *orang besar* and *orang kaya,* see Anthony J. S. Reid, ed. *Southeast Asia in the Early Modern Era: Trade, Power, and Belief* (Ithaca, N.Y.: Cornell University Press, 1993), 273–276.

14. Eredia's description of the *kampong china* that existed prior to the establishment of the sultanate can be compared with later European descriptions of kampong china as one of four districts of the native merchants' section of Melaka, called *bandar Melaka* by the Dutch. J. V. Mills, "Eredia's Description of Melaka,

Meridional India and Cathay," *Journal of the Malayan Branch of the Royal Asiatic Society* 8 (1930): 18–20.

15. Fei Xin, *Hsing-ch'a-sheng-lan: The Overall Survey of the Star Raft*, ed. Roderich Ptak, trans. J.V.G. Mills, (Wiesbaden: Harrassowitz, 1996), 91.

16. Yuka Kado, *Islamic Chinoiserie: The Art of Mongol Iran* (Edinburgh: Edinburgh University Press, 2018), 25–27, 158–160; Sara Kuehn, *The Dragon in Medieval East Christian and Islamic Art* (Leiden: Brill, 2011).

17. In reference to a scholar of Islam, the narrative describes his fame reaching as far as Samarqand: "As for Tun Abu'l-Fazil he was a profound scholar, well read in all branches of knowledge. Many were the learned men from the west who came to put questions to him. But he was never at a loss for an answer, so great was his wisdom. His fame spread as far as the land of Samarkand." *Hikayat Raja Raja Pasai*, 135; For the horse of Persian origin, *Hikayat Raja Raja Pasai*, 140.

18. *Hikayat Hang Tuah*, 380.

19. *Hikayat Hang Tuah*, 380.

20. *Hikayat Hang Tuah*, 381.

21. *Hikayat Hang Tuah*, 384.

22. *Hikayat Hang Tuah*, 384.

23. *Hikayat Hang Tuah*, 385.

24. *Hikayat Hang Tuah*, 386.

25. *Hikayat Hang Tuah*, 399.

26. *Hikayat Hang Tuah*, 400.

27. *Hikayat Hang Tuah*, 400.

28. *Hikayat Hang Tuah*, 401.

29. *Hikayat Hang Tuah*, 401.

30. *Hikayat Hang Tuah*, 402.

31. *Hikayat Hang Tuah*, 403.

32. *Hikayat Hang Tuah*, 403.

33. *Hikayat Hang Tuah*, 403.

34. *Hikayat Hang Tuah*, 403.

35. *Hikayat Hang Tuah*, 404.

36. Markus Stock, *Alexander the Great in the Middle Ages: Transcultural Perspectives* (Toronto: University of Toronto, 2016), 104–122.

37. *Sejarah Melayu*, 30–31.

38. *Sejarah Melayu*, 32.

39. *Sejarah Melayu*, 172.

40. *Sejarah Melayu*, 175.

41. Joseph Needham and Tsuen-Hsuin Tsien, *Science and Civilisation in China: Vol. 5, Pt. 1* (Cambridge: Cambridge University Press, 1993), 48–57.

42. Michael Dillon, *Encyclopedia of Chinese History* (London, New York: Routledge 2017), 283–284.

43. Carlos Rojas, *The Great Wall: A Cultural History* (Cambridge, Mass.: Harvard University Press, 2011), 100–102.

CHAPTER 5: EUROPE'S SEARCH FOR THE SPICE ISLANDS

1. M.D.D. Newitt, *A History of Portuguese Overseas Expansion, 1400–1668* (London: Routledge, 2009), 184–186.

2. J. H. Elliott, "The Spanish Conquest and Settlement of America," in *The Cambridge History of Latin America, Vol. 1.*, ed. Leslie Bethell (Cambridge: Cambridge University Press, 1988), 149–206.

3. Donald D. Brand, "Geographical Exploration by the Spaniards," in *European Entry into the Pacific: Spain and the Acapulco-Manila Galleons*, eds. Dennis O. Flyn, Arturo Giráldez, and James Sobredo (Cambridge: Cambridge University Press, 2017), 1–54.

4. Antonio Pigafetta, *Magellan's Voyage around the World: Vol. 1.*, ed. trans. James A. Robertson, 2 vols. (Cleveland, Ohio: Arthur C. Clark Company, 1906), 91–92.

5. Pigafetta, *Magellan's Voyage around the World*, 1: 103–104.

6. Pigafetta, 1: 178–180.

7. Pigafetta, 2: 28–30.

8. Stacey Pierson, *From Object to Concept: Global Consumption and the Transformation of Ming Porcelain* (Hong Kong: Hong Kong University Press, 2013), 41–43.

9. Pigafetta, *Magellan's Voyage around the World*, 2: 31–32.

10. Pigafetta, 2: 33–34.

11. Pigafetta, 2: 33–34.

12. Anthony Reid, "Flows and Seepages in the Long-Term Chinese Interaction with Southeast Asia," in *Sojourners and Settlers: Histories of Southeast Asia and the Chinese*, eds. Anthony Reid and Kristine Alilunas-Rodgers (Honolulu: University of Hawai'i Press), 15–50.

13. Pigafetta, *Magellan's Voyage around the World*, 2: 201, f421

14. Pigafetta, 2: 40–41.

15. Drawing on the Philippines national archives and specifically the document "Descendientes de Don Carlos Lacandola (1748–1885)," Luciano P. R. Santiago has shown that Raja Ache and Raja Matanda are the same figure.

16. Rodrigo de Aganduru Moriz, *Historia General de las Islas Occidentales a la Asia Adyacentes, Llamadas Philipinas* (Madrid: Impr. de Miguel Ginesta, 1882), v 78–79.

17. An overview of the intertwined alliances between the Philippine islands and Borneo can be found in Graham E. Saunders, *A History of Brunei* (London: Routledge, 2015), 49–61.

18. The custom of marrying within a large family network illustrates how the ruling circles of Brunei, Manila, and Sulu came to be connected. Laura L. Junker, *Raiding, Trading, and Feasting: The Political Economy of Philippine Chiefdoms* (Honolulu: University of Hawaiʻi Press, 1999), 106–107.

19. Nicholas Tarling, *The Cambridge History of Southeast Asia—Volume One, Part Two—From c. 1500 to c. 1800* (Cambridge: Cambridge University Press, 1999), 12–13.

20. Hernando Riquel, "Relation of the Voyage to Luzon (Relacion del Viaje a Luzon)," in *The Philippine Islands, 1493–1803: Explorations by Early Navigators, Descriptions of the Islands and Their Peoples, Their History and Records of the Catholic Missions, As Related in Contemporaneous Books and Manuscripts, Showing the Political, Economic, Commercial and Religious Conditions of Those Islands from Their Earliest Relations with European Nations to the Beginning of the Nineteenth Century*, eds. Emma H. Blair, James A. Robertson, and Edward G. Bourne (Cleveland, Ohio: A. H. Clark Co., 1903), 3: 76.

21. Laura Lee Junker, "The Long-Distance Porcelain Trade," in *Raiding, Trading, and Feasting*, 183–220, 196–197.

22. Riquel, "Relation of the Voyage to Luzon," 76–77.

23. Riquel, 77–78.

24. Linda A. Newson, *Conquest and Pestilence in the Early Spanish Philippines* (Honolulu: University of Hawaiʻi Press, 2016), 53–79.

25. M. N. Pearson, "Spain and Spanish Trade in Southeast Asia," in *European Entry into the Pacific*, eds. Dennis O. Flynn, Arturo Giráldez, and James Sobredo (New York: Routledge, 2017), 117–138.

26. Roderich Ptak, "The Fujianese, Ryukyuans and Portuguese (c. 1511 to 1540s): Allies or Competitors?" *Anais de História de Além-Mar* 3 (2002): 447–467.

27. Roderick Ptak, "Reconsidering Melaka and Central Guangdong: Portugal's and Fujian's Impact on Southeast Asian Trade (Early Sixteenth Century)," in *Iberians in the Singapore-Melaka Area and Adjacent Regions (16th to 18th Century)*, ed. Peter Borschberg (Wiesbaden: Harrassowitz, 2004), 1–22.

28. Kangying Li (李康英), *The Ming Maritime Trade Policy in Transition, 1368 to 1567* (Wiesbaden: Harrassowitz, 2010), 122–124; Peter Borschberg, *Hugo Grotius, the Portuguese and Free Trade in the East Indies* (Singapore: National University Press, 2011), 155–157.

29. J.S.A. Elisonas, "Nagasaki: The Early Years of an Early Modern Japanese City," in *Portuguese Colonial Cities in the Early Modern World*, ed. Liam M. Brockey (London: Routledge, 2016), 63–104.

30. R. Po-Chia Hsia, *Jesuit in the Forbidden City: Matteo Ricci 1552–1610* (Oxford: Oxford University Press, 2010), 202–223.

31. Jean Berenger, *History of the Habsburg Empire 1273–1700* (New York: Routledge, 2016), 210–215.

32. Colin Jack-Hinton, "The Political and Cosmographical Background to the Spanish Incursion into the Pacific in the Sixteenth Century," in *South East Asia Colonial History, Vol. 1 Imperialism Before 1800*, eds. Peter Borschberg and Paul H. Kratoska (London: Routledge, 2001), 9–41.

33. Peter Borschberg, *Journal, Memorials and Letters of Cornelis Matelieff De Jonge: Security, Diplomacy and Commerce in 17th-Century Southeast Asia* (Singapore: Singapore National University Press, 2015), 6–14.

34. M. N. Pearson, "Spain and Spanish Trade in Southeast Asia," 117–138.

35. José L. Gasch-Tomás, *The Atlantic World and Manila Galleons: Circulation, Market, and Consumption of Asian Goods in the Spanish Empire 1565–1650* (Leiden: Brill, 2019), 150–152.

CHAPTER 6: A SINO-JESUIT TRADITION
OF SCIENCE AND MAPMAKING

1. J. F. Moran, *The Japanese and the Jesuits: Alessandro Valignano in Sixteenth Century Japan* (London: Routledge, 2014), 2–5.

2. R. Po-Chia Hsia, *A Jesuit in the Forbidden City: Matteo Ricci 1552–1610* (Oxford: Oxford University Press, 2012), 97–115.

3. Alessandro Valignano: The Jesuits and Culture in the East," in *The Jesuits: Cultures, Sciences, and the Arts, 1540–1773*, eds. John W. O'Malley, Gauvin Alexander Bailey, Steven J. Harris, and T. Frank Kennedy (Toronto: University of Toronto Press, 2009), 336–351.

4. On the Jesuit mission to Japan, see Ikuo Higashibaba, *Christianity in Early Modern Japan: Kirishitan Belief and Practice* (Leiden: Brill, 2001), 2–28.

5. Henry James Coleridge, *The Life and Letters of St. Francis Xavier* (London: Burns and Oates, 1872), 2: 93.

6. Thomas Conland, "The Failed Attempt to Move the Emperor to Yamaguchi and the Fall of the Ōuchi," *Japanese Studies* 2015 (2): 188–189.

7. Eric P. Cunningham, "A Glorious Exile: The Mission of Francis Xavier and Its Consequences on the Chinese Enterprise" in *Voluntary Exile: Chinese Christianity and Cultural Confluence Since 1552*, ed. Anthony E. Clark (Bethlehem, Penn.: Lehigh University Press, 2015), 21–38.

8. Gauvin Alexander Bailey, *Art on the Jesuit Missions in Asia and Latin America, 1542–1773* (Toronto: University of Toronto Press, 1999), 60–71.

9. As Mungello has noted, Franciscan history in Japan did, nonetheless, see examples of theologians experimenting with greater openness to the kind of cultural accommodation adopted by the Jesuits. J. S. Cummins, "Two Missionary Methods in China: Mendicants and Jesuits," *Archivo Ibero-Americano* 38 (1978): 33–108.

10. Jurgis Elisonas, "Christianity and the Daimyo," *The Cambridge History of Japan, Volume 4*, ed. John Whitney Hall (Cambridge: Cambridge University Press, 1988), 301–372, 321–325.

11. Ikuo Higashibaba, *Christianity in Early Modern Japan: Kirishitan Belief and Practice* (Leiden: Brill, 2001), 13–15.

12. An overview of their respective careers can be found in R. Po-Chia Hsia, *Matteo Ricci and the Catholic Mission to China, 1583–1610: A Short History with Documents* (Indianapolis: Hackett, 2016), 21–35.

13. Jorge Flor, *The Mughal Padshah: A Jesuit Treatise on Emperor Jahangir's Court and Household* (Leiden: Brill, 2015), 10–20.

14. Xiaochao Wang, *Christianity and Imperial Culture: Chinese Christian Apologetics in the Seventeenth Century and Their Latin Patristic Equivalent* (Leiden: Brill, 1998), 98–106.

15. An analysis of Ricci's move from a Buddhist-centric adaptation of Christianity to a Confucian-centric one can be found in Qiong Zhang, *Making the New World Their Own: Chinese Encounters with Jesuit Science in the Age of Discovery* (Leiden: Brill, 2015), 77–85.

16. The only surviving copy is found in the Casantense library in Rome and is the basis of the widely consulted 1985 edition published by the Institute of Jesuit Sources. The 2016 revision offers updated translations. Matteo Ricci, *The True Meaning of the Lord of Heaven = Tian Zhu Shi Yi*, eds. Douglas Lancashire, Peter K. Hu, and Thierry Meynard (Chestnut Hill, Mass.: Institute of Jesuit Sources, 2016).

17. Ricci, *True Meaning*, 41–196.

18. Matteo Ricci, *Ten Discourses by a Paradoxical Man* (Yanzhoufu: Catholic Press, 1930).

19. Zurcher argues that China's "marginal religions," including Islam and Christianity, adapted to Chinese sacred discourses on account of a "cultural imperative" allowing the religions' survival in a Chinese context. The Chinese Rites controversy, he explains, can be understood in the context of the Jesuits' having adapted to this pattern of Sinicization that preceded them. E. Zurcher, "Jesuit Accommodation and the Chinese Cultural Imperative," in *The Chinese Rites Controversy: Its History and Meaning*, ed. D. E. Mungello (Nettetal: Steyler Verlag, 1994), 36–41; David E. Mungello, *The Great Encounter of China and the West, 1500–1800* (Lanham, Md.: Rowman & Littlefield, 2013), 96–98.

20. William G. Liu, *Chinese Market Economy, 1000–1500* (Albany: State University of New York Press, 2016), 57–76.

21. Hyunhee Park, *Mapping the Chinese and Islamic Worlds: Cross-Cultural Exchange in Pre-Modern Asia* (Cambridge: Cambridge University Press, 2015), 2–19.

22. D. E. Mungello, *The Forgotten Christians of Hangzhou* (Honolulu: University of Hawai'i Press, 1994), 16–18.

23. Rujivacaharakul Vimalin, "Asia in World Architecture and World Cartography," in *Architecturalized Asia: Mapping a Continent through History*, eds. Vimalin Rujivacaharakul, H. H. Hahn, Ken T. Ōshima, and Peter Christensen (Honolulu: University of Hawai'i Press, 2014), 17–34; Catherine Jami, *The Emperor's New Mathematics: Western Learning and Imperial Authority during the Kangxi Reign (1662–1722)* (Oxford: Oxford University Press, 2012), 28–30.

24. David E. Mungello, *Curious Land: Jesuit Accommodation and the Origins of Sinology* (Honolulu: University of Hawai'i Press), 46–49.

25. Toby E. Huff, *Intellectual Curiosity and the Scientific Revolution: A Global Perspective* (New York: Cambridge University Press, 2011), 72–114.

26. Mungello, *Curious Land*, 107–08.

27. Elizabeth A. Sutton, *Capitalism and Cartography in the Dutch Golden Age* (Chicago: University of Chicago Press, 2015), 21–72.

28. Adam Clulow, *The Company and the Shogun: The Dutch Encounter with Tokugawa Japan* (New York: Columbia University Press, 2016), 25–58.

29. Donald F. Lach and Edwin J. Van Kley, *Asia in the Making of Europe: Volume III, Book One* (Chicago: University of Chicago Press, 1998), 473–92.

30. Norman J. W. Thrower, *Maps and Civilization: Cartography in Culture and Society* (Chicago: University of Chicago Press, 1999), 58–90.

31. Timothy Brook, *The Troubled Empire: China in the Yuan and Ming Dynasties* (Cambridge, Mass.: Belknap Press of Harvard University Press, 2013), 161–185.

32. For an overview of the changing connections between Confucianism and literati education across time, including the relationship between the literati and the monarchy in the context of Confucianism-related political theory practice, see Joseph R. Levenson, "The Suggestiveness of Vestiges: Confucianism and Monarchy at the Last," in *Confucianism and Chinese Civilization*, ed. Arthur F. Wright (Stanford, Calif.: Stanford University Press, 1975), 291–316.

33. Thijs Westeijn, "Encounters between the Middle Kingdom and the Low Countries," in *Reshaping the Boundaries: The Christian Intersection of China and the West in the Modern Era*, ed. Song Gang (Hong Kong: Hong Kong University Press, 2017), 9–34.

34. Thierry Meynard, *The Jesuit Reading of Confucius: The First Complete Translation of the Lunyu (1687) Published in the West* (Leiden: Brill, 2015), 2–18.

35. Thomas Paine, *The Works of Thomas Paine, Secretary for Foreign Affairs to the Congress of the United States, in the Late War. In Two Volumes* (Philadelphia: James Carey, 1797), 8–9.

36. Feng Lan, *Ezra Pound and Confucianism: Remaking Humanism in the Face of Modernity* (Toronto: University of Toronto Press, 2016), 183–199.

37. "François Marie Voltaire," in *The Bloomsbury Dictionary of Eighteenth-Century German Philosophers*, eds. Heiner Klemme and Manfred Kuehn (New York: Bloomsbury, 2016), 817–821.

38. Frederic Wakeman, *Great Enterprise: The Manchu Reconstruction of Imperial Order in Seventeenth-Century China* (Berkeley: University of California Press, 1986), 1: 90–92.

39. Takehiko Okada, "Neo-Confucian Thinkers in Nineteenth-Century Japan," in *Confucianism and Tokugawa Culture*, ed. Peter Nosco (Princeton, N.J.: Princeton Univ. Press, 1989), 215–250.

40. Kai-Wing Chow, *The Rise of Confucian Ritualism in Late Imperial China: Ethics, Classics, and Lineage Discourse* (Stanford, Calif.: Stanford University Press, 1994), 35–37.

41. Lionel M. Jensen, *Manufacturing Confucianism: Chinese Traditions and Universal Civilization* (Durham, N.C.. Duke University Press, 2012), 41–43.

CHAPTER 7: PORCELAIN ACROSS THE DUTCH EMPIRE

1. R. Po-Chia Hsia, *Jesuit in the Forbidden City: Matteo Ricci 1552–1610* (Oxford: Oxford University Press, 2010), 202–223.

2. Jan de Vries and Ad van der Woude, *The First Modern Economy: Success, Failure, and Perseverance of the Dutch Economy, 1500–1815* (Cambridge: Cambridge University Press, 1997), 382–395.

3. Kenchi Ono, "Ethics and Entrepreneurship in Tokugawa Japan: Social Dimensions of the Maritime and the Domestic Merchant," in *Maritime Asia: Profit Maximisation, Ethics, And Trade Structure C. 1300–1800*, eds. Karl Anton Sprengard and Roger Ptak (Wiesbaden: Harrassowitz, 1994), 221–230.

4. Niels Steensgaard, *The Asian Trade Revolution of the Seventeenth Century: The East India Companies and the Decline of the Caravan Trade* (Chicago: University of Chicago Press, 1973), 406–407.

5. Clare le Corbeiller, *China Trade Porcelain: Patterns of Exchange* (New York: Metropolitan Museum of Art, 1974), 4–6.

6. See Chapter Two.

7. Ilda Arez, *Portugal and Porcelain* (Lisbon: Ministerio da Cultura, 1984), 14–16.

8. Jean M. Massing "The Quest for the Exotic: Albrecht Durer in the Netherlands," in *Circa 1492: Art during the Age of Exploration*, ed. Jay A. Levenson (National Gallery of Art: Washington, D.C., 1991), 115–119.

9. Shi-shan Henry Tsai, *Maritime Taiwan: Historical Encounters with the East and the West* (New York: Routledge, 2016), 19–44, 20–22.

10. Wei-chung Cheng, *War, Trade and Piracy in the China Seas: 1622–1683* (Leiden: Brill, 2013), 32–34.

11. John R. Shepherd, *Statecraft and Political Economy on the Taiwan Frontier, 1600–1800* (Stanford, Calif.: Stanford University Press, 1993), 47–90.

12. T. Volker, *Porcelain and the Dutch East India Company as Recorded in the Dagh-Registers of Batavia Castle, Those of Hirado and Deshima and Other Contemporary Papers 1602–1682* (Leiden: Brill, 1971), 25–26.

13. Xing Hang, *Conflict and Commerce in Maritime East Asia: The Zheng Family and the Shaping of the Modern World 1620–1720* (Cambridge: Cambridge University Press, 2016), 40–44.

14. Volker, *Porcelain and the Dutch East India Company*, 117–118.

15. Volker, 113–114.

16. Julie Hoshstrasser, "Remapping Dutch Art in Global Perspective: Other Points of View," in *Cultural Contact and the Making of European Art Since the Age of Exploration*, ed. Mary D. Sheriff (Chapel Hill: University of North Carolina Press, 2012), 43–45.

17. Walter Liedtke, "Genre Painting in Delft after 1650: De Hooch and Vermeer," in *Vermeer and the Delft School: The Metropolitan Museum of Art, New York*, eds. Walter Liedtke and Van D. J. Vermeer (New Haven, Conn.: Yale University Press, 2001), 130–169.

18. Walter Liedtke, "Willem Kalf," in *Dutch Paintings in the Metropolitan Museum of Art* (New York: Metropolitan Museum of Art, 2007), 1: 390.

CHAPTER 8: TEA ACROSS THE BRITISH EMPIRE

1. Christopher M. S. Johns, *China and the Church: Chinoiserie in Global Context* (Berkeley: University of California Press, 2016), 51–82.

2. Stephen D. Ouwyang, "Tea in China: From Its Mythological Origins to the Qing Dynasty," in *Steeped in History: The Art of Tea*, eds. Beatrice and Terese T. Bartholomew (Los Angeles: Fowler Museum at UCLA, 2009), 10–53.

3. Martha Avery, *The Tea Road: China and Russia Meet across the Steppe* (Beijing: China Intercontinental Press, 2004), 12–14.

4. Denis C. Twitchett, *Financial Administration under the T'ang Dynasty* (Cambridge: Cambridge University Press, 1970), 63–65.

5. T. Griffith Foulk, "*Chanyuan qinggui* and Other 'Rules of Purity' in Chinese Buddhism," in *The Zen Canon: Understanding the Classic Texts*, ed. Steven Heine (Oxford: Oxford University Press, 2005), 275–312.

6. Tong Liu, *Chinese Tea* (Cambridge: Cambridge University Press, 2012), 94–96.

7. Eugene N. Anderson and Paul D. Buell, *Soup for the Qan: Chinese Dietary Medicine of the Mongol Era as Seen in Hu Sihui's Yinshan Zhengyao: Introduction, Translation, Commentary, and Chinese Text* (Leiden: Brill, 2010), 11–15.

8. Morris Rossabi, *From Yuan to Modern China and Mongolia: The Writings of Morris Rossabi* (Leiden: Brill, 2014), 61–63.

9. Morris Rossabi, "The Tea and Horse Trade with Inner Asia during the Ming," *Journal of Asian History* 4 (1970): 136–168.

10. One example of this picture of a closed Ming-era China can be found in the influential economic history Daron Acemoglu and James A. Robinson, *Why Nations Fail: The Origins of Power, Prosperity and Poverty* (New York: Random House, 2012), 230–235.

11. John F. Baddeley, *Russia, Mongolia, China* (New York: Burt Franklin, 1919), 118–119.

12. Baddeley, 118.

13. Van Driem provides the original text in George L. Van Driem, *The Tale of Tea: A Comprehensive History of Tea from Prehistoric Times to the Present Day* (Leiden: Brill, 2019), 82–84; Gaspar da Cruz, *Tractado Em Que Se Co[m]tam Muito Por Este[n]so As Cousas Da China* (Impresso Evora: Em casa de Andre de Burgos), 1569–1570.

14. Van Driem, *The Tale of Tea*, 274–276.

15. Jan H. Linschoten and Arthur C. Burnell, *The Voyage of John Huyghen Van Linschoten to the East Indies from the Old English Translation of 1598*, vol. 1 (London: Writing and Co., Sardinia Street, Lincoln's Inn Fields, Council of the Hakluyt Society, 1885), 156–158.

16. Linschoten and Burnell, *The Voyage of John Huyghen Van Linschoten* ,158.

17. Van Driem, *A Tale of Tea*, 317–318.

18. Bennett A. Weinberg and Bonnie K. Bealer, *The World of Caffeine: The Science and Culture of the World's Most Popular Drug* (New York: Routledge, 2001), 66–67.

19. Cemal Kafadar, "A Death in Venice (1575): Anatolian Muslim Merchants Trading in the Serenissima," *Journal of Turkish Studies* 10 (1986): 191–218.

20. Ina B. McCabe, *Orientalism in Early Modern France: Eurasian Trade, Exoticism, and the Ancien Régime* (Oxford: Berg, 2008), 17–19.

21. Niels Steensgaard, "The Growth and Composition of the Long-Distance Trade of England and the Dutch Republic before 1750," in *Rise of Merchant Empires: Long Distance Trade in the Early Modern World, 1350–1750*, ed. James D. Tracy (Cambridge: Cambridge University Press, 2011), 102–152.

22. George Birdwood, *Report on the Old Records of the India Office* (London, Calcutta: W. H. Allen & Co., 1891), 25–27.

23. Peter Mundy and John Keast, *The Travels of Peter Mundy: 1597–1667* (Redruth, UK: Dyllansow Truran, 1984), 42–44.

24. Van Driem, *The Tale of Tea*.

25. Kendall Johnson, *The New Middle Kingdom: China and the Early American Romance of Free Trade* (Baltimore, Md.: Johns Hopkins University Press, 201), 44–46.

26. Erika D. Rappaport, *A Thirst for Empire: How Tea Shaped the Modern World* (Princeton, N.J.: Princeton University Press, 2019), 98–100.

27. Daniel O. Spence, *A History of the Royal Navy—Empire and Imperialism* (London: I. B. Tauris, 2015), 45–84.

28. David Y. H. Wu, "Chinese Cafe in Hong Kong," *Changing Chinese Foodways in Asia*, eds. David Y. H. Wu and Chee B. Tan (Hong Kong: Chinese University Press, 2001), 71–81.

29. Darra Goldstein, *The Oxford Companion to Sugar and Sweets* (Oxford: Oxford University Press, 2015), 243–245.

30. Goldstein, *The Oxford Companion to Sugar and Sweets*, 174–176.

31. Albert M. Wu, *From Christ to Confucius: German Missionaries, Chinese Christians, and the Globalization of Christianity, 1860–1950* (New Haven, Conn.: Yale University Press, 2016), 46–48.

32. Yuanchong Wang, *Remaking the Chinese Empire: Manchu-Korean Relations, 1616–1911* (Ithaca, N.Y.: Cornell University Press, 2018), 113–115.

33. William Theodore De Bary and Richard Lufrano, eds., *Sources of Chinese Tradition: From 1600 through the Twentieth Century* (New York: Columbia University Press), 251–253

34. Wang, *Remaking the Chinese Empire*, 114–116.

35. Kwang-Ching Liu, "The Beginnings of China's Modernization," in *Li Hung-Chang and China's Early Modernization* (Abingdon, Va.: Routledge, 2015), 3–16.

36. Yen-P'ing Hao and Erh-Min Wang, "Changing Views of Western Relations 1840–1895," in *The Cambridge History of China: Vol. 11, Part 2*, eds. John Fairbank and Kwang-Ching Liu (Cambridge: Cambridge University Press, 1980), 190–191.

37. Zhang Huateng, "The Qing's Three Armies after the Wuchang Uprising," in *China: How the Empire Fell*, eds. Joseph W. Esherick and C.X. George Wei (London: Routledge 2015), 214–232.

38. Zhuoyun Xu, *China: A New Cultural History* (New York: Columbia University Press, 2012), 527–528.

39. Dorothy Perkins, *Encyclopedia of China: The Essential Reference to China, Its History and Culture* (London: Routledge, 2013), 93–94.

40. FungYee Wang and Chan-Yeung Mo Wah Moira, *To Serve and to Lead: History of the Diocesan Boys' School in Hong Kong* (Hong Kong: Hong Kong University Press, 2009), 22–24.

CHAPTER 9: CHINA'S ECLIPSE AND JAPAN'S MODERNIZATION

1. The shogun Tokugawa Tsunayashi and the *daimyo* Hotta Masatoshi, like the scholar and bureaucrat Arai Hakuseki, shared an enthusiasm for Confucianism. Tsunayashi's model of political leadership appears to have drawn on the Confucian notion of a sage-king. It was Kinoshita Jun'an, a Neo-Confucian scholar whom Masatoshi recruited as an adviser to the bakufu in 1682, who was the mentor of Arai Hakuseki that furthered his career. James McMullen's analysis of this era highlights the various political dimensions of Confucianism. James

McMullen, *Idealism, Protest, and the Tale of Genji: The Confucianism of Kumazawa Banzan (1619–91)* (Oxford: Clarendon Press, 1999), 411–448.

2. Omar Prakash Chouhan, *The Dutch East India Company and the Economy of Bengal, 1630–1720* (Princeton, N.J.: Princeton University Press, 1985), 118–141.

3. By the 1660s, following declining domestic silver reserves, the Japanese government curbed exports of silver and prohibited the export of silver and copper altogether in 1668. This ban of silver exports was intended as a temporary four-year ban, the lifting of which was requested not by the Dutch but by China, when silver continued to be exported after 1672. The Dutch lack of interest in lifting the silver ban appears connected to their growing role as exporters of gold from Japan, where an earlier ban on gold exports was lifted in 1664. Yasuko Suzuku, *Japan-Netherlands Trade 1600–1800: The Dutch East India Company and Beyond* (Kyoto: Kyoto University Press, 2012), 1–26; William Philippus Coolhaas, *A Critical Survey of Studies on Dutch Colonial History* (The Hague: M. Nijhoff, 1980); Maurius P. H. Roessingh, *Sources of the History of Asia and Oceania in the Netherlands, Part I: Sources up to 1796* (Munich: Saur, 1982).

4. Rudolph P. Matthee, *The Politics of Trade in Safavid Iran: Silk for Silver, 1600–1730* (Cambridge: Cambridge University Press, 1999), 203–230.

5. On these military figures and their clothing, see Toh Sugimura, "Japan xi. Collections of Persian Art in Japan," *Encyclopedia Iranica* 14 (2008): 571–574.

6. Joyce Denney, "Japan and the Textile Trade in Context," in *Interwoven Globe: The Worldwide Textile Trade, 1500–1800*, ed. Amelia Peck (London: Thames & Hudson, 2013), 56–65.

7. Denney, "Japan and the Textile Trade in Context," 59–61.

8. Yumiko Kamada, "The Use of Imported Persian and Indian Textiles in Early Modern Japan," in *Textiles and Politics: Textile Society of America 13th Biennial Symposium Proceedings*, Washington, D.C., September 18–September 22, 2012, 3–10.

9. Kamada, "The Use of Imported Persian and Indian Textiles," 3–10; See also Yumiko Kamada, "The Attribution and Circulation of Flowering Tree and Medallion Design Deccani Embroideries," in *Sultans of the South: Arts of the India's Deccan Courts*, eds. Navina Najat Haidar and Marika Sardar (New York: Metropolitan Museum of Art, 2011), 132–146.

10. Sugimura, 571–74. See also Gloria Gonick, *Matsuri: Japanese Festival Arts* (Los Angeles: UCLA Fowler Museum of Cultural History, 2002), 183–209.

11. On this eclecticism, and specifically the absorption by Persian weavers of Chinese and Southeast Asian designs into Indian textile designs, see John Gillow and Nicholas Bernard, *Traditional Indian Textiles* (London: Thames and Hudson, 1991), 11–13.

12. On the rise of the European maritime companies in this trade of textiles and metals, see Matthee, *The Politics of Trade in Safavid Iran*, 96–118.

13. Grant Goodman contextualizes this work in the context of Japanese intellectual history's encounter with both regional and European modes of learning. Grant K. Goodman, *Japan and the Dutch, 1600–1853* (New York: Routledge, 2000), 43–65.

14. Henk de Groot, "Engelbert Kaempfer, Imamura Gen'emon and Arai Hakuseki: An Early Exchange of Knowledge between Japan and the Netherlands," in *The Dutch Trading Companies as Knowledge Networks*, eds. Siegfried Huigen, Jan L. Jong, and Elmer Kolfin (Leiden: Brill, 2010), 201–210.

15. On the policy changes during the reign of Tokugawa Yoshimune towards the absorption of European works, including the writings of Ricci, see Goodman, *Japan and the Dutch*, 49–65.

16. Grant Goodman, "Dutch Learning" in *Sources of Japanese Tradition: 1600 to 2000*, eds. W. M. Theodore de Bary, Carol Gluck, and Arthur E. Tiedemann (New York: Columbia University Press, 2005), 361–389.

17. Candan Badem, *Ottoman Crimean War, 1853–1856* (Leiden: Brill, 2010), 109–143, 125–127.

18. Thomas Brassey, *The British Navy: Its Strength, Resources and Administration* (Cambridge: Cambridge University Press, 2010), 6–8.

19. Masami Yamazumi, "State Control and the Evolution of Ultranational Textbooks," in *Japanese Schooling: Patterns of Socialization, Equality, and Political Control*, ed. James J. Shields (University Park: Pennsylvania State University Press, 1995), 234–242, 224–226.

20. Margarita Winkel, "Gift Exchange and Reciprocity: Understanding Antiquarian/Ethnographic Communities within and beyond Tokugawa Borders," in *Gifts: Politics and Society in Japan, 1350–1850*, ed. Martha Chaiklin (Leiden: Brill, 2017), 219–246.

21. Tuvia Blumenthal, "The Japanese Shipbuilding Industry," in *Japanese Industrialization and Its Social Consequences*, ed. Hugh Patrick (Berkeley: University of California Press, 1976), 129–160, 133–135.

22. Brian J. McVeigh, *The History of Japanese Psychology: Global Perspectives, 1875–1950* (London: Bloomsbury Academic, 2018), 74–76.

23. Joshua A. Fogel, *Maiden Voyage: The Senzaimaru and the Creation of Modern Sino-Japanese Relations* (Berkeley: University of California Press, 2015), 215 n. 23.

24. Conrad D. Totman, *Early Modern Japan* (Berkeley: University of California Press, 1995), 538–539.

25. Marius B. Jansen, *Making of Modern Japan* (Cambridge, Mass.: Harvard University Press, 2009), 279–285.

26. Kate Wildman Nakai, "Tokugawa Confucian Historiography: The Hayashi, Early Mito School, and Arai Hakuseki," in *Confucianism and Tokugawa Culture*, ed. Peter Nosco (Honolulu: University of Hawai'i Press), 62–91.

27. Mark J. Hudson, "Tales Told in a Dream," in ed. Michael Weiner, *Race, Ethnicity and Migration in Modern Japan: Race, Ethnicity and Culture in Modern Japan* (London: Routledge, 2006), 119–154.

28. W. G. Beasley, "The Foreign Threat and the Opening of the Ports," *The Cambridge History of Japan. Vol. 5: The Nineteenth Century*, ed. Marius B. Jansen (Cambridge: Cambridge University Press, 1989), 259–307, 273–275.

29. Beasley, 275–257.

30. D. C. Jaundrill, *Samurai to Soldier: Remaking Military Service in Nineteenth-Century Japan* (Ithaca, N.Y.: Cornell University Press), 47–72.

31. Marius B. Jansen, "The Meiji Restoration," in *The Emergence of Meiji Japan*, ed. Marius B. Jansen (Cambridge: Cambridge University Press, 1997), 144–202, 167.

32. Albert M. Craig, *Chōshū in the Meiji Restoration* (Cambridge, Mass.: Harvard University Press, 1961), 153–155.

33. L. M. Cullen, *A History of Japan, 1582–1941: Internal and External Worlds* (Cambridge: Cambridge University Press, 2003), 195–197.

34. Marius B. Jensen, *Sakamoto Ryoma and the Meiji Restoration* (New York: Columbia University Press, 1961), 153–159.

35. Donald Keene, *Emperor of Japan: Meiji and His World, 1852–1912* (New York: Columbia University Press, 2002), 113–119.

36. Benjamin C. Duke, *The History of Modern Japanese Education: Constructing the National School System, 1872–1890* (New Brunswick, N.J.: Rutgers University Press, 2014), 28–46.

37. Daikichi Irokawa, *The Culture of the Meiji Period*, trans. Marius B. Jansen (Princeton, N.J.: Princeton University, 1985), 51–76.

38. Kären Wigen, *The Making of a Japanese Periphery, 1750–1920* (Berkeley: University of California Press, 1995), 194–201; Wenkai He, *Paths toward the Modern Fiscal State: England, Japan, and China* (Cambridge, Mass.: Harvard University Press), 120–122.

39. Maki Hirano Hubbard, *The Ideology of Kokugo: Nationalizing Language in Modern Japan*, trans. Lee Yoeon-suk (Honolulu: University of Hawai'i, 2016), 8–14.

40. Thomas R. H. Havens, *Nishi Amane and Modern Japanese Thought* (Princeton, N.J.: Princeton University Press, 1970), 105–157.

EPILOGUE: A NEW TURN TO THE EAST

1. Kathryn B. Hiesinger and Felice Fischer, *Japanese Design: A Survey Since 1950* (Philadelphia: Philadelphia Museum of Art, 1994), 125–126.

2. Daron Acemoglu and James A. Robinson, *Why Nations Fail: The Origins of Power, Prosperity and Poverty* (New York: Random House, 2012), 230–235.

INDEX

CPSIA information can be obtained
at www.ICGtesting.com
Printed in the USA
BVHW071943070722
641575BV00003B/3/J

9 781503 627475